OUR SPIRITUAL DNA

"This book is fabulous, a real fount of knowledge. Through the medium of channeling, it reaches into the depths of history and reveals the links that powerful souls have with each other and their many incarnations on Earth and in other realms. It provides a direct link from the Ascended Masters to early humans and all the way back to God. Its aim is to show you how you may be linked to each other, to them, and, ultimately, to God."

— **Lorraine Flaherty**, hypnotherapist, past life therapist,
and author of *Healing with Past Life Therapy*

"*Our Spiritual DNA* is a veritable Who's Who of the esoteric world, listing the major characters who have defined the caliber of our spiritual lives in the Western world over the past 6,000 years. At the core of the book is a depiction of the Council of White Light and as you leap the divide between history and myth in order to find the face of the Divine, to know the unknowable, you will encounter the great wonder of St. Germain, our contemporary Christos. Little of any substance has been written about this extraordinary Master for some time, and yet now is the time as we center our lives in the nature of the Aquarian Age. This book is particularly welcome and will inform the esoteric student of the Master's lineage and how his odyssey is always present to define the true nature of love. In awe you will find St. Germain with the eleven other Ascended Masters, evoking dreams within you that are way beyond your current imagination!"

— **Stewart Pearce**, master of voice, angelic emissary,
and author of *The Angels of Atlantis*

OUR
SPIRITUAL
DNA

—— TWELVE ——
ASCENDED MASTERS
AND THE EVIDENCE FOR
OUR DIVINE ANCESTRY

CARMEL NILAND

FINDHORN PRESS

Findhorn Press
One Park Street
Rochester, Vermont 05767
www.findhornpress.com

Text stock is SFI certified

Findhorn Press is a division of Inner Traditions International

Disclaimer
The information in this book is given in good faith and intended for information only. Neither author nor publisher can be held liable by any person for any loss or damage whatsoever which may arise directly or indirectly from the use of this book or any of the information therein.

Cataloging-in-Publication data for this title is available from the Library of Congress

ISBN 978-1-64411-263-2 (print)
ISBN 978-1-64411-264-9 (ebook)

Printed and bound in the United States by Lake Book Manufacturing, Inc.®
The text stock is SFI certified. The Sustainable Forestry Initiative program promotes sustainable forest management.

10 9 8 7 6 5 4 3 2 1

Edited by Nicky Leach
Text design and layout by Richard Crookes
This book was typeset in Adobe Garamond Pro

To send correspondence to the author of this book, mail a first-class letter to the author c/o Inner Traditions • Bear & Company, One Park Street, Rochester, VT 05767, USA and we will forward the communication, or contact the author directly at **www.ourspiritualdna.com**.

CONTENTS

INTRODUCTION

Mystery. Magic. Quests. Buried treasure. Do you remember the childhood delight in solving puzzles, asking questions, searching for answers, and gazing with wonder at the night sky?

Today's scientists are beginning to unravel many of the mysteries and codes behind the physical world, making it easier for us to understand. We know, for example, that all humans possess DNA, the genetic code that makes us each an individual. Our spiritual world, on the other hand, remains mostly incomprehensible.

This book asks these questions: Is it possible for our spiritual life to have the certitudes of chemistry and physics? If we have physical DNA, can we also have spiritual DNA? Does God have a genealogy with direct descendants on Earth?

I didn't set out to answer these questions, but they were the constant white noise in my life. As I tried to discover who I was, I became increasingly fascinated with who everyone else was. Before long, I found myself on a quest to discover the true identity of an 18th-century diplomat and magician called Comte de St. Germain, a man who was long hidden in the shadows of the occult tradition and with whom I had become completely captivated. What began as a fascination with this alchemist became a search for buried treasure and an accidental discovery of the genealogy of God.

In other words, I believe I found the line to God.

As I began to learn about St. Germain, I became increasingly interested in what I saw as curious links and connections among significant historical figures. Great circles of illuminated beings began to captivate me, especially when contrasted with the darker circles of light who opposed them—Churchill and Roosevelt, who opposed Stalin and Hitler; Sir Thomas More, who opposed King Henry VIII.

I found myself asking, why do we have golden ages of enlightenment like those during the reign of Queen Elizabeth surrounded by Shakespeare, Marlow, Spenser, Raleigh, Drake, and Bacon? Or Lorenzo De Medici, whose contemporaries were Michelangelo, Raphael, Leonardo da Vinci, Machiavelli, and Botticelli? What created the unfettered imagination of the Romantic era with Wordsworth, Keats, Byron, and Shelley? What mysterious forces were at hand in bringing together the visionary Washington, Adams, Franklin, Paine, Hamilton, and Jefferson to found the United States of America? Or the spiritual awakening in Asia, with the lives of Buddha, Lao Tzu, and Confucius, all of whom were born within 50 years of one another?

Could it be an accident that people of such genius bloomed simultaneously in magnificent bursts of creative energy? Or was it by design, part of a larger plan, a plan with elegance and complexity—a Divine Plan? What was it, and why did evil have to fit into it? Why are people born so different, some with towering intellects and creative gifts while others are born into lives where death extinguishes them almost before they begin?

There was nothing new in any of my questions or my search. The command of the Delphic oracle "Know Thyself" is a universal theme. It is said that characters who act out the human quest for self-knowledge, such as Hamlet or Faust, have sooner or later dealings with angels, demons, and spirits. I was not going to be an exception.

Mysticism intrigued me. As a Catholic, that most supernatural and mystic of faiths, I was well versed in miracles, mysteries, and prophetic teachings as well as the prophets, who were able to have a direct experience of God, and others who were said to communicate with angels like Isaiah or saints like Theresa of Avila. Through their experiences, they provided me with fresh insights into the human dilemma. Why not ask them or other historical characters directly for firsthand accounts of what happened to them? Surely after their deaths, they would have all the answers.

The question was, how?

I first heard of channeling when I read Shirley MacLaine's 1986 book *Dancing in the Light*. It seemed to be a new name for the process by which prophets and saints were given insights and revelations during meditations or through their dreams. It appeared to be a way to stretch through time to gain answers and unlock history's secrets. So I set out to find someone in Sydney, Australia, who could not only channel but channel beings who could answer my questions.

And I found them. In this book, all names of channelers have been changed to protect their privacy.

My First Meeting with St. Germain

On a Sunday night, in a late Sydney summer, when the currawongs whistled to one another well after dark and the cicadas drummed hard, I sat waiting for Peter Abraham,* who I hoped would channel St. Germain. According to history books, Le Comte de St. Germain was a count in revolutionary France who lived from 1691 to 1712. Here was someone with an intriguing resume: adventurer, explorer, philosopher, scientist, alchemist, and magician. He was said to be extraordinarily intelligent, articulate, and widely published. He appeared to live many lives in one lifetime, and I was soon to discover that he had lived many lifetimes on Earth, too. St. Germain should be a man who had answers to my questions if Peter Abraham could channel him.

Of course, I was well prepared should he show up. I brought everything I thought I needed, including a list of questions, a tape recorder, a notebook, pens, and spare batteries.

The birds and the barking dogs settled. Peter, together with friends, led an invocation, followed by a guided meditation and prayers to open a sacred space to allow beings of great power to come through and enter his body.

First, a group of angels cleared the room, then a host of beings entered with both familiar and strange names: Master Kuthumi with Lady Portia, El Morya and Pallas Athene, Master Hilarion with Lady Nada, Djwhal Khul and Lady Leto, and Serapis Bey and Lakshmi. They would speak through Peter or his friend Michaela Clinton and guide others in the room. Their presence and their movement around the room were vividly described by Peter and by others who could "see" their unseen presence. St. Germain, however, was not among them.

Then a being called Lord Sananda entered, unannounced.

Everyone except me seemed to know of Lord Sananda, but when he said, "I speak as Jeshua," I felt the pulse of excitement go through the room. He spoke gently, recounting a parable about patience and mercy using the Middle Eastern imagery of the natural beauty and fruitfulness of the vines, the vibrant color of the flowers, lilies of the field, and his love for his flock, his children. When he left, we remained in contemplation for a while until there was a rustle. The dog started barking loudly, and the cicadas joined him.

Someone new had arrived. St. Germain was here!

Only those who saw him clairvoyantly knew it was St. Germain. I saw nothing.

"What's happening?" I mouthed to my friend. She whispered that a bearded man with glossy black hair and a violet cloak was in the room. He was spinning like a top and sparkled with amethyst and gold.

9

"He's like an electric shock crackling through time," someone else explained. After the calm of Lord Sananda, this was a dramatic entrance.

St. Germain spoke precisely and only through Peter. He offered advice and answered questions about healing, career progression, conflict resolution, dancing, music, and spiritual development. He appeared quirky but charming, compassionate, witty, and wise.

Peter, still channeling St. Germain, rose from his chair, came over to me and said, "Give me your hand."

I was very reluctant to do so because I had been warned never to touch a channel while they were channeling for fear of causing them a shock.

"Give me your hand," he insisted.

I held it out, and he kissed it. I was so surprised I snatched it back.

"Don't you know who I am?" he asked.

"Yes, you are St. Germain, and you are a Master."

"And what is that?" he asked.

Tongue-tied, I could not answer him.

I decided then to find out more about what it meant to be a Master and about St. Germain. That decision would take me to places I never thought I would go and would result in a relationship with St. Germain that would lead to this book and the uncovering of long-held secrets.

I used two different channels, Peter Abraham, and Dr. George Litchfield, to connect with him. Both used prayers to create a sacred space before they opened themselves up to other realms. They called on protective beings to help them, they put aside their egos to allow beings of light, and no others, to speak through them, and they worked privately, discreetly, and with patience. They were men of integrity.

Dr. George Litchfield and The Gatekeeper

Dr. George Litchfield was a medical practitioner and a trance medium who was methodical and precise in his professional life. Before each session, he would ask me to meditate on my questions and request, through prayer, that appropriate guidance would come through him so he could answer them. At the beginning of a session, he would cross himself, lie back on a reclining chair, and appear to go to sleep.

An entity calling himself "The Gatekeeper" would come through, laughing. He was a former Tibetan lama referred to by the honorific Rinpoche, like every other Tibetan lama. After inquiring about my day's topics, he would organize my sessions like an impresario, arranging a line-up of carefully vetted guests who were available to shed light on my questions, or he would answer all my queries himself.

He reminded me of Joseph Campbell's description of a threshold guardian in *The Hero with a Thousand Faces* as being one "who sits at the entrance to the zone of magnified power."

The Gatekeeper would birth, like a "spiritual obstetrician," fully formed adults from the unseen world, while Dr. Litchfield appeared to sleep soundly in his chair.

The Gatekeeper described himself as follows: "I am tall for a Tibetan, with a Mongolian cast of features. I dress in a lama's cinnamon and saffron robes, with my three-pointed hat. I died at 30 years, in 1786. I've lived once since then and returned to learn about 'discarding the world.' I tasted the sweetness of life before surrendering it to die through pneumonia at 18 months of age."

The Gatekeeper's other role was to monitor Dr. Litchfield's heart rate and blood pressure. Litchfield had had a triple bypass, and because he was a trance channel, information was communicated "electrically." (The concept of electricity is the nearest we have to convey the unexplained process by which this form of channeling happens.) He had to ensure that Litchfield had no sudden bolts of energy from discarnate beings that could jar his electrical circuitry during the time they settled into his physical body to use his voice box to express themselves. The Gatekeeper would strictly watch the time. When the critical moment came, he would, if he had to, cut them off mid-sentence, saying to me, "Count him back immediately from 20, if you please." On the count of "one," the Doctor would come groggily awake with no memory of what had occurred in the previous 30–45 minutes. I would then go through the highlights with him from my notes.

Many times, I asked to speak to the Comte de St. Germain, but he was never available. His vibrational force was so strong that Dr. Litchfield could not contain him without risk of a coronary attack. He would, however, occasionally drop in from a distance to say something enigmatic in French to The Gatekeeper, who would then translate it for me. This intermittent reinforcement kept me hoping that one day he would be able to get around these circuitry problems, as I had been reliably informed that one of his most successful lives was as Nikola Tesla, the man who invented alternating currents, so he should be able to fix this.

Early on in the sessions with Dr. Litchfield, I was sceptical. Were these beings conjured from Dr. Litchfield's imagination, his historical knowledge, or from his unconscious? Could they be other aspects of his personality? Had they truly lived when they said they had lived?

For example, when a 17th-century being called Matthew Wren came through, who lectured me on the meaning of truth and called himself the Master of Peterhouse (a college of Cambridge University), I was dubious. Being suspicious of him and his credentials, I said that I had never heard of

Peterhouse. He said I would have to take him on trust and verify his biographical details later.

Determined to check the historical facts, I eventually went to Cambridge and visited Peterhouse, the university's oldest college. My purpose was to discover if my communicant, Matthew Wren, had ever existed. At Porter's House, near the entrance to the college, I asked about past rectors.

"Would there be an honor board of previous Masters of Peterhouse somewhere?"

"Which one are you interested in?"

"A Matthew Wren, a Master from around 1660."

"Our library is called after him. It's upstairs."

So I had found him. A cold shiver went through me.

I always sought verification that this array of characters channeled by Litchfield spoke the truth. I quizzed them about the historical detail of their lives. Sometimes, if they were historically significant, I could easily verify them, but other times, their lives were so obscure that they did not leave the slightest trace. They would offer some insight into St. Germain who, I was beginning to learn, had lived many lives besides that of Nikola Tesla.

Someone once said, "Dead men tell no tales."

I can assure them that they do.

The Ascended Masters

In my first meeting with St. Germain, I experienced the Ascended Masters but realized little about who they were and why Peter Abraham channeled them. In that session, St. Germain directed me to learn more, and what I since discovered was captivating.

The Ascended Masters are 12 energetic beings that have been star-seeded to Earth and whose spiritual DNA is spread into every human being here. Below are their names and a thumbnail biography for each one that includes some of their incarnations. Those listed are just a small sample of their worldwide contributions over millennia and are biased towards the West, simply because of my limited historical knowledge; however, the incarnations of the Ascended Masters are many, and they are rich with detail, purpose, and intrigue, much of which you will learn about in this book, just as I once did.

Lord Sananda is the spiritual leader of this group. He seldom incarnates, but when he does, it is usually apparent. This book captures three meaningful lives of his as Lord Vishnu, Buddha, and Jeshua ben Joseph. Of course, there were many others, not as notable; for example, he returned in one lifetime as an insignificant rabbi to die with members of his Jewish temple in the Holocaust.

Mother Mary incarnated as Maya, the mother of Buddha; Sarah, the mother of Isaac; and Mary, the mother of Jesus. She was also Kwan Yin, Nefertiti, Isis, Cleopatra, Mary the Magdalene, Mary the High Priestess, Philip the Apostle, King James I, Jane Austen, Emily Dickinson, Titian, Admiral Nelson, Claude Monet, Nelson Mandela, and Madonna. I will be focusing a great deal on her in this book.

St. Germain lived as Noah, Samuel, Jacob, Homer, Lao Tzu, Plato, Julius Caesar, Cicero, St. Joseph, Merlin, Dante Alighieri, Raphael, Christopher Columbus, Francis Drake, Edward de Vere, Miguel de Cervantes, Christopher Wren, Benjamin Franklin, and Nikola Tesla. He is the other Ascended Master that I will be focusing on in *Our Spiritual DNA*.

The Twelve Masters are headed on Earth by El Morya and Pallas Athene.

Some aspects of **El Morya** are like his founding energy, Abraham: they are our seers, mystics, shamans, priests, and sometimes warlocks (two prominent warlocks were Adolf Hitler and Joseph Stalin); they also include the greatest principled warriors, men like Mark Antony, King Arthur, Duke of Wellington, Napoleon, and Ataturk. While some of El Morya's warrior aspects are notorious for their hidden cunning and guile, many more of his aspects are honorable, courageous, heroic, honest, straight forward and extraordinarily gifted and include men like US Presidents Abraham Lincoln and John Adams, the pharaoh Akhenaton, and St. Peter, head of the Apostles, and St. Mark, the Evangelist. You will also see aspects of El Morya incarnated as brilliant writers and scientists, including Nicolai Tolstoy, Charles Darwin, Sigmund Freud, and Charles Dickens.

Pallas Athene embodied the lives of some of the greatest women who ever lived, beginning with the Greek goddess Athena, renowned for her wisdom, courage, strategy, and dedication to law and justice. Name a great warrior woman like Boudica or Joan of Arc, and you will instantly recognize Pallas Athene. Her aspects include remarkable monarchs like Queen Elizabeth I, Queen Catherine the Great, and Queen Victoria. She is also found in tough, powerful, intelligent, charismatic, female leaders, such as St. Catherine of Sienna, Margaret Thatcher, Oprah Winfrey, Nancy Pelosi and Christine Lagarde.

Kuthumi is the world's teacher, psychologist, philosopher, mathematician, astronomer, musician and consummate persuader. He is the man who, when people are drawing up a list of the greatest people to have lived, they frequently nominate one of the lives of Kuthumi. Aspects of Kuthumi are not afraid to pursue an agenda. They are farsighted and weavers of words and ideas. They often have searing intelligence, such as the geniuses Socrates and Leonardo da Vinci, or superb virtuosos, such as Bach or Mozart. Kuthumi also experiences the gentle lives of Francis of Assisi and John the Beloved Apostle and the toughest and cleverest warriors, such as King David or the man of twists and turns, Ulysses, who invented the Trojan Horse. His lives include the mathematical genius Pythagoras and Galileo, father of astronomy. He also lived as the leading psychologists William James and Carl Jung.

He was my favorite Beatle, John Lennon, and my favorite tenor, Luciano Pavarotti. Kuthumi has also served with moral authority as US Presidents Dwight Eisenhower and Franklin D. Roosevelt during tough times. There is only one Master I know of who created a poem in marble for his other half. Shah Jahan, an aspect of Kuthumi, built the Taj Mahal as a monument to his love for Lady Portia.

Lady Portia incarnates as wise and beautiful women in leadership positions. Many of us first encountered her as Portia, the heroine in Shakespeare's *The Merchant of Venice*, where she is quick-witted, resourceful, intelligent, and beautiful. Perhaps Shakespeare knew an aspect of Lady Portia in real life because he deftly captures her passion for justice. Often, Lady Portia chooses lives of religious service in which she can focus on divine mercy, justice, and peace. As St. Clare, she incarnated as the founder of an order that came to be known as the Poor Clares in Assisi, at the same time as Kuthumi incarnated as Francis, the founder of the Franciscans. Both orders lead lives of austere poverty, but Poor Clares insist on one of seclusion as well. As the influential St. Catherine of Sienna, Lady Portia was a mystic, wrote extensively, and became the patron saint of Italy. As St. Therese of Lisieux, she was known as "the Little Flower," and devoted her life to prayer, dying of tuberculosis at 24. In two further influential lives, as Grace Kelly and Jacqueline Kennedy, she took the form of two great beauties with lives of exquisite sophistication and taste and private devotion to God.

Hilarion is the joyous, handsome, tall, musical Ascended Master who leads battles, founds nations, and codifies religious principles. He loves to sing and plays a vast array of instruments. He dictates his exploits to either his brother or his lover, as he is a man of action, not of writing. As Moses, for example, he dictated the Ten Commandments to his brother, Aaron, and as St. Paul, his letters were written by Titus and Thecla (silent partnerships that allow Mary the High Priestess to be either a man [Titus] or a woman [Thecla] to ensure whatever he accomplished would be universally known).

In the second century BC, Hilarion dictated the story of his conquests as Alexander the Great to his lover, Hephaestion, then in the fifth century AD, as Sunzi (also called Sun Tzu, "Master Sun"), he dictated in practical, pithy prose, the leading Chinese military text known as *The Art of War*. As Uther Pendragon, the father of King Arthur, he used St. Germain as Merlin and as King Henry VIII, he had a whole court at his disposal. Hilarion shone as

George Washington and Alexander Hamilton, in the founding of the United States. He was assassinated as Gandhi, John F. Kennedy, and Martin Luther King. Hilarion has lived as not one, but two, of the Beatles: the late George Harrison and the still-living Paul McCartney.

His feminine aspect is **Lady Nada** who, although she seldom incarnates, has currently two prominent public lives as Hillary Clinton and Yoko Ono.

The final four Masters are Djwhal Khul and Lady Fortunata and Serapis Bey and Lady Leto.

While **Djwhal Khul** (often shortened to DK) incarnates less frequently, he seems to like being king or president, and when he incarnates in this way, he does it differently from anyone else confounding preconceptions. With him, things are never what they seem; what may appear bad can turn out to be good. For example, Djwhal Khul lived as King George VI, father to the present Queen Elizabeth II, who became king when his brother, the Duke of Windsor, abdicated. George VI (known as Bertie) was dubbed the "reluctant king" and is often underestimated. His shortcomings, highlighted as chain-smoking and stuttering (which we saw in the biopic *The King's Speech*), were considered weaknesses, but he proved his strength and determination when he successfully led Great Britain through its darkest hour in World War II.

Djwhal Khul's purpose in his earthly lifetimes is to drive through significant changes in society. He has done this in lives as disparate as that of President Ronald Reagan, where you barely knew that he was doing anything special, and Martin Luther, where he broke the power of the Catholic Church in Germany. Conversely, his role is also to "fester the rot" of corruption and malfeasance until everyone can see it, or more particularly, smell it and be inspired to change it, such as in his role as former US President Donald Trump. He was also the writer Edgar Allen Poe, the seer and astrologer Nostradamus, and the painter Vincent van Gogh.

His female aspect **Lady Fortunata** is the razzle-dazzle queen of mistresses. She is known for her beauty and her glitz. She is a wily manipulator who, behind the scenes, influences history and charts a different course. Think Marilyn Monroe, Christine Keeler, Heddy Lamar, Lola Montez, and Monica Lewinsky! She also incarnates as males and her current prominent life is as the dictatorial Vladimir Putin.

Serapis Bey comes to Earth rarely compared with someone like St. Germain, but when he does, you know a polymath is here and wonder at his accomplishments, including his recent Nobel Prizes. Serapis drives change with his outstanding intellect, his commitment to justice, and his kindness and integrity—he also seems to love the name Thomas. His lives include Osiris, the partner of Isis in Ancient Egypt, who, whenever possible, quietly incarnate and work together—Isis as Elizabeth, the British Queen Mother, for example, with Osiris incarnating as British Prime Minister Winston Churchill in the 20th century. Other lives include philosophers Confucius and Aristotle and St. Thomas the Apostle, who was known as "Doubting Thomas" for his habit of questioning everything; St. Ignatius Loyola, who co-founded the Jesuits; and philosopher and theologian St. Thomas Aquinas. He also incarnated as mathematician, astronomer, and theologian Isaac Newton; Thomas Cromwell, Henry VIII's secretary of state; and American president and founding father Thomas Jefferson. In the 20th century, he was Albert Einstein, the physicist who received the Nobel Prize for his theory of relativity; Thomas Stearns Eliot, the American-born poet and Nobel Prize winner; and as noted above, British Prime Minister Winston Churchill, who in addition to his leading role in World War II was a writer, artist, and winner of two Nobel Prizes.

His female aspect is **Lady Leto**, who seldom incarnates but when she does, tends to touch on magic such as in the form of Madam Blavatsky or Miriam Zimmer Bradley. Mary, the mother of Jeshua, chose her as her mother, St. Anne, so she became Jeshua's grandmother.

⁂ Commissioner Kuthumi ⁂

I consider this book to be a commissioned work. Once I had spent a few years diligently tracing St. Germain, Kuthumi, the world's teacher, spoke to me unexpectedly through Peter Litchfield. He told me to focus only on the lives of St. Germain and Mary, saying: "It is a powerful document you seek to undertake. Some will view it as heretical, some as a flight of fancy, and others with disbelief. However, we the Ascended Masters know and understand what it is. *Our Spiritual DNA* reveals the pathway back to God; it is a map that lives in your genetic code."

When I agreed to explore more fully the lives of St. Germain and Mary, I assumed some being would dictate every word in the manner of Jane Roberts's experience with the discarnate being Seth or Neale Donald Walsh, when writing *Conversations with God*, typing questions into his computer and instantly receiving the replies. For me, however, relevant information came as a fragment here or a morsel there. I was teased with truth to keep pursuing my goal. The revelations that I received through Dr. Litchfield are the basis for *Our Spiritual DNA*.

As noted earlier, this book documents the lives of two Ascended Masters, St. Germain and Mother Mary, while sketching fragments of the lives of other beings along the way, particularly those of Lord Sananda, who is recognized in many faiths as the Son of God. The purpose of *Our Spiritual DNA* can be found in the power of the stories of the lives of St. Germain and Mary.

It opens the gates to dark houses filled with secrets and expounds a different view of the complexities and elegance of the spiritual universe.

Our leading guide, The Gatekeeper, an irreverent Tibetan lama channeled by Dr. Litchfield, leaps the divide between history and myth and reveals the lessons learned in each lifetime, their spiritual and earthly purpose, and whether they achieved that purpose or not. We learn of their frailties and humanness as they reach for the Divine. We see the physical and spiritual difficulties they encountered in the limitations of the lives of flesh and blood.

In the beginning, my quest was to find and understand St. Germain and his mysterious line of descent as he experienced his lives on Earth and in his role as an Ascended Master, to explore his connection to God. My spiritual hunt, however, led to buried treasure in the discovery of his feminine counterpart, Mary. I also learned of the myriad lives of all the Ascended Masters and discovered a direct link from you and me to God through each Ascended Master. I found that each person on Earth, no matter how ordinary or extraordinary, is an aspect of one of these Masters and that the Platonic ideal of a quest for some perfect other half had a simple explanation. It's one step from you to your higher self, which must be an aspect of one of 12 original Ascended Masters, and then it's another step to God. But which Master are you? This book will help you determine your spiritual roots.

The ultimate purpose of *Our Spiritual DNA* is to know the unknowable, to know God, and to understand our spiritual and genetic connection to God and everyone else. It will help you discover your spiritual DNA and your lineage and unlock where you may fit into the universal pattern.

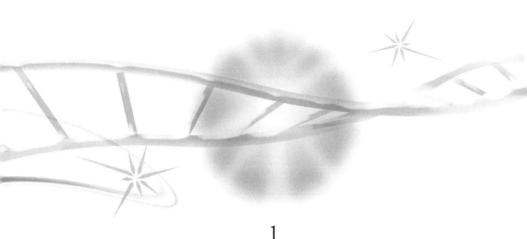

1

Take a Bow, St. Germain — You Are On!

So, who is the mysterious St. Germain, and what is an Ascended Master?

When King Louis XV of France gave a short, intense man the title of Claude-Louis, Comte de Saint-Germain, he already had many names.

His story could have begun in 1707 with the birth of the third son of Francis II Rakoczi, the deposed Prince of Transylvania, or it could have started with the birth of an unknown Portuguese Jew. Saint-Germain's origin and birth are obscure, and during his lifetime, he never, I believe, clarified who he was. But 35 years later, when he blazed across the European sky in pre-revolutionary France, he had become a French count who was a linguist, violinist, raconteur, philosopher, mystic, and an alchemist, a man of indeterminate age who dazzled his admirers with his huge glittering jewels and mesmerizing stories of exotic travels and exploits in past eras. At the same time, as the count's star ascended, he was passionately denounced by prominent men as a charlatan, a trickster, and a spy. Voltaire described him sarcastically as the man who never dies and knows everything ("C'est un homme qui ne meurt jamais et qui sait tout").

Saint-Germain's first properly documented appearance was not in France but in London, in 1743, when he met Jean-Jacques Rousseau (1712–1778). Two years later, he was in Edinburgh, where he was arrested as a Jacobite spy. When released, he returned to London, where his fame spread as a violinist. Horace Walpole (1717–1797), the English man of letters, observed to a friend, "He sings, plays the violin wonderfully, composes, is mad and not very sensible."

Described as of medium build and height, with dark hair and a pleasant countenance, our one painting of the count has him adorned in a white wig, clean-shaven with the shadow of a beard, a large nose, and direct, full, dark eyes. While he wore large diamonds on his shoes and every finger of each hand, otherwise he dressed plainly.

Besides his title, Louis XV gave the count a suite of rooms in the Chateau de Chambord adjoining Versailles. There, he was to remove any flaws from the king's diamonds, turn base metals into gold, and prepare the elixir of youth for the king's mistress, Madame de Pompadour. With that job description, it's no wonder he was called a charlatan!

Nevertheless, the king appeared to be satisfied and expanded his duties. He sent Saint-Germain without the agreement of his Foreign Affairs minister, the Duke of Choiseul, on a secret diplomatic mission to promote a United States of Europe, an early version of the European Union. Choiseul tried to have him arrested in Holland, after he had interfered, at the king's behest, in a dispute between Austria and France using Holland as an intermediary. Saint-Germain fled to his haven in England in 1760. By 1762, he was back in play, this time in St. Petersburg, where he was supposed to have assumed an essential role in the conspiracy that deposed Tsar Peter III and placed Catherine the Great on the Russian throne.

As the count moved around Europe, he used a variety of names: Surmount in 1763, Count Tsaroqy in 1774, Chevalier Welldone in 1776, and Francis Rakoczi II in 1784. During this time, according to Count di Cagliostro, he founded European freemasonry by establishing lodges throughout Holland, Belgium, Denmark, Germany, Russia, Austria, Poland, and France. Fortunately, his knowledge of languages was extensive, and he spoke English, Spanish, Italian, German, and French fluently with a Piedmontese accent. He is also said to have mastered Greek, Latin, Chinese, Arabic, and Sanskrit.

Contemporaries quote Saint-Germain as saying he lived when Jesus Christ lived, again at the time of a Roman Emperor, and then in medieval France. This claim implies that he had lived 700 years continuously since being born in medieval France and had never died. He is supposed to have eventually died of pneumonia at the Court of Prince Karl of Hesse in Schleswig on 27 February 1784. Still, his tombstone reads:

> "HE WHO CALLED HIMSELF COMTE DE ST. GERMAIN
> AND WELLDONE, OF WHOM THERE IS NO
> OTHER INFORMATION,
> HAS BEEN BURIED IN THIS CHURCH."

Saint- Germain left behind a manuscript called "The Most Holy Trinosophia," a work of Hermetic, Kabalistic, and Masonic mystery, an indifferent poem, and an opera. There is also a book on palmistry attributed to him.

Once the count was allegedly dead, his life became much more interesting, because people kept bumping into him in the most amazing places. The Comte de Saint-Germain now merged with Ascended Master St. Germain to inspire the works of Madame Blavatsky, the founder of theosophy and acquired magical powers, whereby he could influence people, including her, telepathically, walking through walls and teleporting vast distances. He based his activities, she said, in Tibet. Please note: In this book, I have used two different spellings of his surname to clearly distinguish between these two identities—Count (Saint-Germain) and Ascended Master (St. Germain).

As portrayed in his biographies, St. Germain has become the "Wonder Man of Europe," skilled in the use of medicinal herbs, anti-aging potions, and able to extract flaws from diamonds. Not only is he an accomplished alchemist, but he can also meditate in the lotus position, calm distraught animals, then disappear into thin air. Occasionally, he retreats from public life and experiments with chemicals and technology. He laid out the groundwork, as he told a contemporary, for the invention of the steam engine a hundred years later, manufacturing paint, leather treatments, and even created hair dye. He bases his activities; it is claimed, in Transylvania.

St. Germain taught Mesmer how to mesmerize, and while he spent time with Casanova, the commentaries are silent on what exactly he taught him, although he did manage to turn his copper penny into a gold coin.

One biographer claimed St. Germain tried unsuccessfully to warn Queen Marie Antoinette of the impending bloodbath of the French Revolution and her inevitable death.

In yet another account, St. Germain worked behind the scenes to help found the United States of America and, using Masonic imagery, designed the Great Seal of the United States. For these interventions, and more, he based his activities in Mount Shasta.

There is nothing, it seems, he cannot do, and nowhere he has not been! Is this what it means to be a Master? To be an enigmatic, talented polymath who can hypnotize and do tricks and live a complicated life, work with secret societies that specialize in ceremonial magic, moonlight as a diplomat spy in a shadowy world of ambiguity, and after disputed accomplishments, ascend and inspire the 20th century? Who is this man really?

What Is a Master?

Madame Helena Blavatsky, founder of the 19th-century movement of Theosophy, claimed she had the answers to everything. Three men guided her, she said, and dictated to her the philosophical concepts for her (almost unreadable) books. These men were called *Mahatmas*, a Sanskrit word meaning "Masters." They communicated with her in person, by letter, through visions, and in dreams. She claimed they were "mysterious sages from Tibet" with extraordinary powers, who were named El Morya, Koot Hoomi Lal Singh (today referred to as Kuthumi), and Djwhal Khul. Later, she was influenced by a fourth Master whom she knew either by his French title of Comte de Saint-Germain or by his birth name of Count Rakoczi.

Blavatsky posed alone for a photograph, and, when developed, three of her Masters stood around her: Kuthumi, El Morya, and St. Germain, dressed in 18th-century French court regalia. (Some argue the photograph is a fake.)

Besides introducing four Masters by name, the Theosophists provided insight into what a Master did. Masters claimed Annie Besant, a co-founder of the Theosophical Society, were great spirits who ascended after many Earth lives, having passed all of their tests. It was then that they decided to return and teach others on Earth. Such beings are described by Mahayana Buddhists as *bodhisattvas*. The Theosophists believed these beings had shed the limitations and weaknesses of their ordinary lives and, through pain and suffering, achieved adeptship, ascending from Earth to a higher plane. From there, the Masters aided the progress of humanity, inspired every religion, and transmitted advanced scientific thought to humans of genius to develop and disseminate. Meanwhile, they watched events, correcting, and neutralizing negative currents, while strengthening the good and weakening the evil. Besant argued that their very existence implied that we are not alone; there is help, a purpose to our lives, and divine inspiration for a grand scheme that stretches throughout cultures and nations. They have a plan, and we are part of it.

The I AM Collection

In America, in the late 1920s through the '30s, groups of spiritually aware people gathered around gifted channels (or "messengers," as they called them) to learn from a larger group of disincarnate teachers. Led by St. Germain, this group was described as the Great Cosmic Beings, and they taught followers about their "I AM" presence or their divine connection to God. One entity called Hilarion, for example, revealed he was St. Paul, the missionary of early Christianity. The feminine energies were deferentially titled as "Lady" and called Nada, Kwan Yin, Leto, Portia, Mother Mary, and the Goddess of Liberty. They joined the masculine energies of Maitreya, Lanto, Sanat Kumara, Jesus, and Serapis Bey.

They discoursed on the meaning and purpose of love, harmony, joy, peace, truth and freedom, and the evils of gossip and the self-destruction of hatred. These beings encouraged Americans to activate their connection to their "I AM" presence, their God within, to allow the Masters to radiate enormous pulses of energy or white light to protect America in the lead up to World War II.

There was, even in these teachings, an ambiguity about whether these Masters were living or dead, incarnate, or disincarnate. It was also unclear whether aspects of these Masters were simultaneously exploring contemporary lives as a highly regarded metaphysical writer, Alice Bailey, suggested. There was little or no explanation of who they were, how many of them there were, why these beings were teaching and not others, or whether some had greater power or knowledge than others. Nor was it explained whether the Masters ever had special relationships with one another or why the being they called "Beloved St. Germain" was leading the teachings. What they did demonstrate, however, was profound love and admiration for St. Germain.

Intriguingly, included in this group of beings were two Christian figures, Mary and Jesus, and two Buddhist entities, Maitreya and Kwan Yin, as active participants in these discourses. Their inclusion was the first time in the esoteric literature that prominent religious leaders were included with other Masters. Mary, who is identified with Catholic religious devotion and celebrated in exquisite paintings and cathedrals as Our Lady, the Mother of God, is not usually associated with such occult activity; the same is true of Kwan Yin, the Chinese goddess of Compassion and Mercy. She is one of the 12 bodhisattvas of Buddhism and one of the most universally loved of that tradition. Kwan Yin is also known as Avalokiteshvara in India, Quan Am in Vietnam, Kannon in Japan, and Kanin in Bali, and her qualities have a powerful resonance with Mary and with the Tibetan goddess Tara.

In the 1970s and '80s, there was an explosion of activity and interest in the Masters. Koot Hoomi Singh Lal reappeared in a shortened version of his name as Kuthumi. He was channeled in many countries as White Feather, as the Gentle Brother Bartholomew, Socrates, Wotan, Zoroaster, and Francis of Assisi. Serapis Bey, on the other hand, limited his appearances and lectured exclusively through JZ Knight as Ramtha. Meanwhile, Lord Sananda, as Jesus, dictated *The Course in Miracles*, an inspiring life-changing teaching tool popularized in the United States by author Marianne Williamson.

While the Theosophists quarantined the physical presence of the Masters to the rarified energies of the Himalayas, Alice Bailey (in *Initiations Human and Solar*) claimed they were alive and living in the most unlikely places, participating in various roles, influencing religions, sciences, and philosophies.

A picture of who makes up this circle of beings, what they do, why they do it, and how they are related began to emerge as a result of 35 years of teachings by Mark and Elizabeth Clare Prophet, founders of the Summit Lighthouse in Montana, close to Yellowstone National Park. The couple specialized in the teachings of the Ascended Masters under the direction of St. Germain.

In 1962, Elizabeth Clare Prophet channeled and published a book dictated by St. Germain on the subject of alchemy. In later editions, she included an excellent index, which identified three Masters: El Morya, Kuthumi, and St. Germain, providing a thumbnail sketch of a few of their lives. St. Germain had the most extensive entry. Eleven of his lives were identified, including the Hebrew prophet Samuel; Joseph, the father of Jesus; St. Alban, the first English martyr; Merlin, the enchanter of Arthur's court; Christopher Columbus, the Italian rediscoverer of America; and Le Comte de Saint-Germain.

I found it an intoxicating mix, and well worth exploring further. But while the lives attributed to St. Germain over the last 2,000 years show a diversity of purpose, superficially, they did not fit my idea of a person working toward adeptship or spiritual advancement, moving in a progression toward enlightenment. Instead, I saw him, as a Catholic would: peaking as St. Joseph and sliding downhill ever since.

So, what is a Master? The sources agree that Masters are beings who have become perfect; they have ascended to a higher realm, where they continue to work as divine teachers, inspiring others to believe that similar perfection is within their reach. They take on students to coach, motivate, energize, guide, and teach. Many of them have spiritual retreats, akin to monasteries or ashrams, in different dimensions from ours, where followers can study or learn from them while they are sleeping or between their lives.

Together, the Masters form a group called the Great White Brotherhood. It is a title far more appropriate to another age, and one I find personally distasteful. It has an ominous resonance of Big Brother and overtones of both racism and sexism. In fact, the title refers to the white robes worn by those who can see clairvoyantly, who emit white light and form a circle, and describes their close relationship as a fraternity, brotherhood, or lodge. The Egyptians had an alternative title for them, "The White Order," which I prefer and will use.

Elizabeth Clare Prophet, in her treatise on the White Brotherhood (Prophet: 176) defined them as: "A spiritual order of hierarchy, an organization of Ascended Masters unified for the highest purpose of God . . . . The word 'white' refers not to race, but to the white light of the Christ that surrounds the saints and sages of all ages . . . ."

Once, through a channel, I asked the question "What is a Master?" and received a concise response: "A cosmic executive." I followed it up with a second question to Paolo, a merchant from 16th-century Sienna, asking him what the White Order is. This was his reply:

It is like the governing body of a large university, where each soul group has levels of initiation, as in the Masonic Lodges. There are three levels: Initiate, Adept, and Master. These are like three levels that students pass through: Bachelor, Master, and Doctor. There are no steps, but there are levels. There are nine levels from each point of initiation. Having achieved a Master in one college, you can be invited to join another. The Masters, male and female, about whom you speak, are all members of the White Order. One transfers from level to level once you are offered this chance by a circle of grand Masters.

You rise a level once you fulfill all that is necessary for that level. You rise like a cork in water, sometimes experiencing bodily discomfort like an illness or even a mild heart attack, when it happens. There is no degree of superiority with a level; it does not confer seniority. It is an acquired power that is earned through relinquishing it.

Two other similar colleges are the Sisterhood of the White Flame, convened by Asteroth, whom you would call Our Lady, and the Order of the Rosy Croix, organized by Lord Sananda, who lived as Joseph, the son of Jacob, and as Jesus and Buddha.

The overseeing point of light of the White Brotherhood is Malachi, the holder of the blue sapphire of Solomon, previously the fearsome warrior Judeus Maccabeus, a zealot of Zionism, who led an unsuccessful revolt against Rome. You know him as El Morya or Peter, the leader of the apostles. He is also the Angel of Death.

St. Germain is an officer of the White Order. In a few years of your time, when you explore the building of Solomon's Temple and Roslyn Chapel, The Gatekeeper will explain further.

In the meantime, Paolo referred me to the Pistis Sophia, a collection of teachings in the Gnostic gospels that were rediscovered by two peasants at Nag Hammadi in Egypt in 1949, two years before the discovery of the Dead Sea Scrolls. In this dissertation, the newly arisen Jesus gives intensive teaching to his 12 apostles, Mary Magdalene, and his mother, Mary. During it, he refers to a heavenly "treasury," in which a group of "12 saviors" reside. I would eventually come to recognize the 12 saviors as a circle of 12 Masters, most of whom were sitting around him.

My Assumptions about Masters

Based on what I had read about Masters and my ideas about reincarnation, I concluded that:

- Masters experienced occasional lives on Earth.

- Masters were geniuses, who led highly ethical, principled, saintly lives.

- Their lives were rare, occurring, say, once every 200–400 years.

- Before one aspect of a Master could be born, another aspect of that Master had to die.

- A Master never met himself or herself.

- Masters believed in God.

- Masters were always leaders in their field.

- Masters' lives progressed one after the other toward further enlightenment.

But how did these assumptions mesh with the record of the life of Le Comte de Saint-Germain? Over 15 years, every one of my assumptions was proved wrong, sometimes in an unexpected and challenging way that stopped me in my tracks.

Take, for example, when I started delving into St. Germain's lives to discover who he was and found that after an incarnation as the greatest saint, he could be, in his next life, the greatest sinner! I discovered that one existence of inspiring virtue and leadership could be simultaneously experienced with another of carnage and debauchery. I learned that light and dark co-existed, not only in separate beings but together within the one; that the hero was a tyrant and the goddess was a whore.

When I was doing an inventory of St. Germain's lives with The Gatekeeper, he mentioned St. Germain's life as St. Augustine of Hippo. He was a great doctor of the Christian Church, who he claimed reincarnated nearly 2,000 years later as Joseph Goebbels, Hitler's minister for propaganda, one of the most influential men in Nazi Germany. But that was not all. Each member of the inner circle around Hitler, or the ring around George Washington, King Arthur, and Jesus bore a Master's name! And even around the Apostles, there would be female energies having male lives. For example, St. Phillip and St. Simon the Canaanite were both females: Mary the High Priestess and Lady Portia.

The Role of Evil in Masters' Lives

Confronted by the central role of Masters in the Third Reich, I stopped all work on this project. I had intended to write songs of praise for illustrious beings that battled and conquered the forces of Darkness—think: Boudica, Joan of Arc, Winston Churchill, or Gandhi. I had intended a limited exploration of the Dark forces' role as a counterpoint to the exploits of the Master. Evil, I believed, existed outside of good, not inside of it. My part was to describe evil from a safe distance and show how an incarnated Master conquered it and saved us all.

If, on the other hand, an Ascended Master pursues a life of pure evil, I would have to explore with distaste historical events that I had placed, squeamishly in the shadows, like the horrors of the Third Reich, the Gulags of Stalin, the excesses of Nero. All I wanted to do was leave the question of evil as a rhetorical one and tiptoe away.

Nevertheless, I sought advice from Kuthumi through a channel, and he was, for Kuthumi, unusually succinct:

> Suspend your judgment, my dear one, and persevere. Do you merely want to continue this cult of heroes?

Later The Gatekeeper added, crossly:

> Only Hollywood and philosophers would seek to present life as one-dimensional, a simple duel between good and evil. This earth is a proving ground; it is very complicated, and the analysis of the lives of the Great Ones would engage us for one or several lifetimes.
>
> Evil men and women want to understand divinity in the muddiest of waters, to experience God in more uncomfortable areas. They are the same as the seers in caves who seek that understanding in solitude, leading their sad, uncomfortable, and lonely lives. They want to know what God is not. The fullness of creation is both light and dark. There is only a thin line that separates them. Understand that the light of day could not be known if we did not have the dark of night. Do not despair about your book. You must complete your task. The road is stony and tiring, and the closer you come to the top of the mountain, the stonier it will become.

How's that for encouragement! The Gatekeeper suggested that if I explored the seven Hermetic Principles of Hermes Trismegistus and studied the fourth principle, in particular, on polarity, it would assist in moving me forward.

Hermes Trismegistus, an Egyptian priest who was a contemporary of Moses, enunciated seven principles, or laws, to summarize the wisdom of God, whom he called "The All." The fourth principle reads:

> Everything is dual; everything has its pair of opposites. Like and unlike are the same; opposites are identical in nature, but different in degree; extremes meet; all truths are but half-truths; all paradoxes may be reconciled.

While I found it difficult to accept that evil and goodness were the same, when I returned to my task, The Gatekeeper laughed and, speaking with the wisdom of a Tibetan sage, asked:

> Now you are starting to learn about the contradictory being who is
> St. Germain. Have you not learned that the lotus has its roots in
> mud so that perfection can flower from the filth?

It had been a struggle. While I could not comfortably reconcile good and evil
and transcend this pair of opposites, I prepared to persevere. So, it was back
to the main game.

Understanding St. Germain

A few months later, I had a new question for The Gatekeeper. "I want
to understand St. Germain, but I still find him difficult to describe and
summarize. Although he is called saint, he does not appear to be very
'saintly.' How would you describe him, Gatekeeper?"

> He is a being of contradictions, the bits of which do not add up.
> He is capable of a life of exceptional charm and exceptional
> cruelty. He has mastered magic. He has achievements in both
> arts and science that give him left- and right-sided balance. He's
> always in more than one place at the same time. He shows a
> curious conservatism, a sparkling sense of human wit with a
> capacity for verbal cruelty, and great sensitivity with a capacity
> to destroy opinion in situations that displease him. He has divine
> purity and rutting sexuality. He is a perfect reflection of the eternal
> contradictions of the human race. Start with the Greek gods—so
> human and so unlike the Judeo-Christian god. They were
> super-humans, the Captain Americas of their day. The same
> cast of characters, of course, are the Masters. They are super-
> powerful, bringing together seemingly irreconcilable differences
> that are warp and weft, together making a good strong cloth, a
> cloth that creates the mirage of the seeming contradictions of their
> characters. To understand St. Germain, you will have to study
> hundreds of his lives to even glimpse his complexity.

"Would the Comte de Saint-Germain agree with what you've said,
Gatekeeper?"

> [I'll ask him. He's answering in French. Oh, dear, he is so effete.
> I will translate]:

> St. Germain is not a "who" but a "what." What is St. Germain?
> St. Germain is a multiplicity of qualities. Each of my qualities

has intelligence and consciousness and can take many forms. Within these qualities, there is a seed of desire. This desire creates the passion for being born, for exploring, discovering, and experiencing the expression of itself. St. Germain, when planted in a human womb, is like a seed and in favorable conditions, will bring forth a certain fruit.

St. Germain was referring to himself as a genus, or clan in which a multiplicity of qualities could form a life.

⁂ The Feminine Aspect of St. Germain ⁂

Another of the Hermetic principles states that gender is in everything. Masculine and feminine are present in all things on all planes. If St. Germain was the masculine principle, was Mary indeed his feminine principle? Mary seemed a most unlikely pairing with St. Germain. Why was this pairing kept secret for so long? The Gatekeeper explained it like this:

It was Mary's choice; she was known as Ashtoreth, Demeter, Artemis, Isis, and Diana around the Mediterranean. She decided to phase them out as objects of veneration and focus instead on Mary throughout the Piscean Age, as a complement to her son, Jeshua. In the Aquarian Age, she is perceived differently again. Her former role in the Piscean age was Mary, the Immaculate Conception, the Mother of God, and the Queen of Heaven.

Her role was, and is, complementary to St. Germain; to understand St. Germain, you must understand her: St. Germain is the doer; she is the placater. What St. Germain mucks up; she puts it right. She is a fixer, a born organizer, with unbounded compassion that allows love to flow. St. Germain's focus is over there; hers is down here at those around her feet. St. Germain looks 50 years into the future; she works in the present. What a comfort to St. Germain she is, because he knows when he stuffs up, she will be there moving him onto the straight and narrow and fixing things up.

They are complementary; they are partners. He is purple; she is green. Mary's color green allows her to tell the purpose of wheat. The purple of St. Germain means he can calculate how it may be improved. Sometimes they are in opposition, but always in balance. If he is competitive, she is collaborative, and so on.

Think of them as the Magician and the High Priestess. Watch how they explore this as Joseph and Mary, as Merlin and Morgana, as Dante and Beatrice, or as Chopin and George Sand, Nureyev and Fonteyn.

As the High Priestess, Mary is the bearer of wisdom, the oracle, the seer, and the being who is in the know, who writes everything down, and who is consciously connected to the higher realms. To be so connected to the Divine can be seen to be magical. The Magician does not share his knowledge; he creates it. The High Priestess makes herself available to share her knowledge and her wisdom; she teaches, guides, and advises, allowing the development of new systems and insights.

The Magician is the doer, while the High Priestess is the sharer. Her part in this new age will be expanded; you will recognize that as a priest, as well as a mother and god bearer. It is now time to emphasize her complementarily with St. Germain, and for you to recognize if you want to know him, you must understand her. But she is not an afterthought. She is just reticent.

Mary will help. She will slowly reveal the full extent of her participation in world affairs, allowing you to discover the multiplicity of her roles from leading nations to leading as a medical scientist, geneticist, theologian, children's advocate, poet, king, novelist, conservationist, social reformer, impressionist painter, playwright, military hero, feminist, queen, ruler, president, conqueror, educator, saint, evangelist of a gospel, and philosopher.

To enable me to understand how St. Germain and Mary live through "the multiplicity of their qualities," The Gatekeeper would take me on a journey back to 6,000 BC, into legends and myths of great heroes and heroines, to find the answers.

What This Book Is Also About

Our Spiritual DNA is about those 12 saviors, 12 Apostles, and 12 Masters, along with a few more. They are Mary and St. Germain, Lady Portia and Kuthumi, Lady Nada and Hilarion, Pallas Athene and El Morya, Lady Leto and Serapis Bey, and Lady Fortunata and Djwhal Khul. Hermes is so well developed from Hilarion that he is mentioned separately. Both he and Lord Sananda have no specific feminine counterpart because they have evolved to be the perfect balance of male and female qualities. This book traces the lives of Mary and St. Germain in both their masculine and feminine forms. It explores the thinking behind their incarnations, the qualities of the Master they bring to each life, and the purpose of the life they pursue. The book will assess whether they achieved their intent. Hundreds of lives will be examined, always under the instruction of the spirit who lived that life. The wisdom and insights of the Tibetan sage, The Gatekeeper, weigh their spiritual and intellectual achievements.

The Gatekeeper, like all historians, will change our understanding of the past as he reveals its secrets. Through his blend of romance, debate, storytelling, and skepticism, The Gatekeeper leads us through 8,000 years. He teases us with yet-to-be-discovered archaeological treasures, until we eventually arrive at a reimagining of who each Master is, why they were here, and how they live in all of us.

"This book," The Gatekeeper says, "is an attempt to provide a missing piece in the jigsaw of human existence." It reveals God's plan.

Our Spiritual DNA is about their service to us, as well as our spiritual line back to God. It's about their ideas, failures, and triumphs, their heroic battles with the Dark, and love affairs with one another. It stretches across millennia and tells of their dreams of Utopia and efforts to bring them into reality. Mostly, it is about their role in God's covenant with the people on Earth. All 12 aspects of God participated in human existence, but some incarnated more frequently than others. For example, Hilarion was in charge of driving the Renaissance in Italy, and he did that spectacularly as Pope Julian II. Others, Lady Nada and Lady Portia, were put in charge of cleaning up the horrors of world wars, leading inquiries, for example, into the Holocaust, where they took male lives because cultural beliefs at that time demanded it.

And you will find *yourself* in this book, and the history of *your* spiritual DNA. The book contains comprehensive charts that identify the roles played by all the Masters to help you understand the diversity of their lives along with their challenges and successes. The lives of Mary and St. Germain are the main focus.

Below are two charts and each one is created to help you identify with the energies of well-known or famous historical beings.

The first chart identifies the spiritual energy of each apostle and known relative of Jeshua ben Joseph. Why did I select them and not the leaders and prominent followers of other religions? There were three reasons. There exists a vast literature written on every person associated with the birth and spread of early Christianity. This provides you with sound biographical material for your search to find your mastery. While I have detailed parallel information on Islam, it's not included here, unfortunately. It was deemed unsafe to print it. Thirdly, other religions, such as Hinduism and Buddhism, are touched on briefly, and I may release additional material about them later.

In chart 1, the first column gives you the name of the largely masculine energies of Ascended Masters who incarnated as relatives and apostles of Jeshua ben Joseph. There are two female Masters in the list of male apostles: Mary the High Priestess, who appears twice, and Pallas Athene, who appears once. In the second column are the saintly lives they took on Earth to support the mission of Jeshua and God's plan.

Notice, for example, that St. Germain incarnated four times. Why is that so? What led to his incarnations?

He was the first pick of the energies that Jesus wanted around him. If you spend time researching the biographical literature that exists about each of these Apostles, you will get the first clues to the kinds of personalities they were, and perhaps that may resonate with you and indicate which energy exists in you. When female energies come in as males, as in the case of Mary the High Priestess as St. Phillip and Pallas Athene as St. James the Less, this is not an accident. This is a deliberate choice to include female energy at a patriarchal time, when the inclusion of a woman like Mary Magdalene could lead to their demonization. And why Mary the High Priestess twice? Because she is the official recorder: in his case, St. Luke who recorded Mary the Mother's recollections, or Katija, the first wife of Muhammad, carefully recording the dictations of his divine experiences.

Each Master experiences millions of lives across all nations and cultures on the Earth. While they were created either male or female, a female Master will explore male lives and a male Master will explore female lives, and they will birth in every race and ethnicity, with every ability or disability. They will also explore a range of occupations. Over time, they will develop strengths in specific areas. When Jeshua selected his Apostles, he would select so that there was not only diversity of talents but balance. One of the ways he achieved that was to select one person of the 12 from every star sign.

Take the time to look at the qualities of the Apostles and Disciples in the second column of the table on the following page and notice with whom you resonate. Your spiritual energy in this life is likely the one carried by the Master you see in the first column, associated with this apostle or disciple.

Who Do You Identify With?

Chart 1 – Apostles and Disciples

Spiritual Energy Masters	Apostles and Disciples
Hermes, who seldom incarnates	John the Baptist, Jeshua's cousin
St. Germain	Joseph, father of Jeshua
	Bartholomew, Apostle
	James the Great, Apostle
	Judas, Disciple and Jeshua's best friend
Mary the Mother	Mary, Mother of Jeshua
Mary the Magdalene	Mary the Magdalene, Disciple
Mary the High Priestess	Luke the Evangelist
	Phillip, Apostle
El Morya	Peter, head of the Apostles
	Mark, Disciple and Evangelist
	Simon the Canaanite, Apostle
Pallas Athene	James the Less, Apostle
Hilarion	Andrew, Peter's fraternal twin, Apostle
	Paul, a convert, and author of Epistles
	Pontius Pilate, Roman ruler
Kuthumi	John the Evangelist, Apostle
	Jude, Apostle
Sanat Kumara, Archangel	Mathias or Matthew, Apostle
Serapis Bey	Thomas, Apostle
Lady Leto	Anne, mother of Mary
Lord Sananda	Jesus, Jeshua ben Joseph

Note: The Masters Djwhal Khul, Lady Fortunata, Lady Portia, and Lady Nada did not have prominent roles around the life of Jeshua ben Joseph

The following chart on the next page selects a summary of well-known people from a Western perspective and identifies their Spiritual DNA or their line to God through the Masters associated with their names.

Chart 2 – Well-Known Personalities

Spiritual Energy Masters	Well-Known Personalities
Hilarion	Ganesh; Adonis, Dan (Son of Jacob); Moses; Daniel; Emperor Hadrian; Emperor Augustus; St. Andrew; Alexander the Great; Constantine the Great; St. Paul; Pope Julian II; Uther Pendragon; Prince Albert; George Washington; Alexander Fleming; Botticelli; Goering; Gandhi; Henry VIII; John F. Kennedy; Martin Luther King, Jr.; Andrew Lloyd Webber; Andy Warhol; Marcus Aurelius; Padraic Pearce.
Lady Nada	Pharaoh Hatshepsut; Rebecca, wife of Isaac; Bathsheba, wife of David and mother of Solomon; St. Martha; Empress Julia of Rome; Queen Zoe of the Medes; Harriet Tubman; Lucy Wilmot Smith; Queen Anne; Harriet Beecher Stowe; Madame Bovary; George Eliot; Barbara McClintock, Nobel Prize 1983; Barbara Streisand; Hillary Clinton.
Kuthumi	Ulysses; Achilles; Hesiod; Leander; Zoroaster; Thutmoses III; Hasdrubal; Darius II; King David; Melchizedek; Pythagoras; Socrates; St. John the Evangelist; Galileo; St. Francis of Assisi; Leonardo da Vinci; John Dee; Vermeer; Fra Angelico; Shah Jahan; Erasmus; King Ferdinand of Aragon; Bach; Mozart; Carl Jung; William Blake; Oscar Wilde; J.R.R. Tolkien; John Wayne; Franklin D. Roosevelt; Dwight Eisenhower; Dag Hammarskjold; D.H. Lawrence, George Bernard Shaw, John Millington Synge; Alfred, Lord Tennyson; James Joyce; John Lennon.
Lady Portia	Ma'at; Lakshmi; Zilpah, wife of Jacob; St. Clare; Princess Grace of Monaco; Marie Antoinette; Clementine Churchill; Queen Elizabeth II; Jacqueline Kennedy; Princess Diana; Elizabeth Taylor; Heddy Lamar; George Eliot; Elizabeth Barrett Browning; Sojourner Truth.

Spiritual Energy Masters	Well-Known Personalities
El Morya	Saturn; Akhenaton; Abraham; Mark Antony; Mohammad; King Arthur; Sophocles; Suetonius; Tacitus; St. Peter; St. Mark; Demosthenes; Pope Gregory; Francis Bacon; Nero; Akbar, Mogul emperor; Robert the Bruce; Thomas Cranmer; Emperor Maximillian; John Adams; John Q. Adams; Abraham Lincoln; Robert E. Lee; John Milton; Napoleon; Sean O'Casey; Michael Faraday; Karl Marx; Sigmund Freud; Charles Dickens; Adolf Hitler; Pablo Picasso; Gregory Peck; Robert Kennedy; John Steinbeck.
Pallas Athene	Goddess Athena; Aphrodite; Venus; Helen of Troy; St. James the Less; Boudica; Joan of Arc; Queen Elizabeth I; Queen Victoria; Emily Pankhurst; Bette Davis; Sophia Loren; Joan Crawford; Margaret Thatcher.
Serapis Bey	Rama; Osiris; Amenhotep III; Naphtali, Son of Jacob; King Leonidas; King Midas; Phidias, architect of the Parthenon; Euripides; St. Thomas Apostle; St. Thomas Aquinas; Thomas Cromwell; Isaac Newton; St. Thomas More; Saint Thomas Becket; Thomas Jefferson; William Gladstone; Adam Smith; Albert Einstein; Albert Camus; Albert Schweitzer; Jules Verne; Winston Churchill; H.G. Wells; T.S. Eliot; Benedict Chifley, prime minister of Australia.
Lady Leto	Sappho; Leto, mother of Apollo and Artemis; St. Anne, mother of Mary; Elizabeth, mother of John the Baptist; St. Teresa of Avila; Marie Curie, Nobel Prize, 1903; Madame Blavatsky; Marion Zimmer Bradley (Leto seldom incarnates).
Djwhal Khul	Lord Varuna; Poseidon, Lord of all Oceans; Gilgamesh; Shiva; Thor; Neptune; Clytemnestra; Simeon, son of Jacob; Martin Luther; Nostradamus; Edgar Allen Poe; Vincent Van Gogh; Clem Atlee; Gough Whitlam; Gerry Adams; Ronald Reagan; Donald Trump.

Spiritual Energy Masters	Well-Known Personalities
Lady Fortunata	Latona; Hestia; Vesta; Nell Gwyn; Madame du Barry; Madame de Pompadour; Marilyn Monroe; Lola Montez; Gina Lollobrigida; Frida Kahlo; Monica Lewinsky; Vladimir Putin.
Lord Sananda	Vishnu; Adam; Buddha; Orpheus; Joseph, son of Jacob; Jeshua ben Joseph (Jesus).

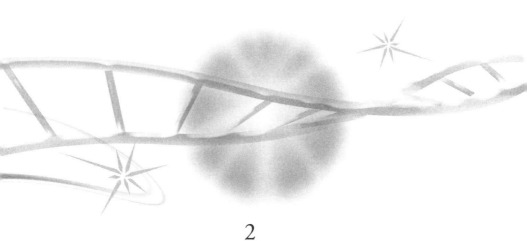

2

St. Germain and Mary as Gods and Goddesses

After five years of asking questions about St. Germain and Mary, I uncovered about 500 lives associated with him and about 250 lives that were associated with her. Most of their existences I discovered were in India, the Middle East, and Europe. It is not that these Masters only incarnated there; instead, it is due to the limitations of our historical records and my Judeo-Christian education.

To find out the commonalities in all of St. Germain's lives and map out his spiritual DNA, I was directed back into the mists of myths and legends. It seems that the intrinsic qualities associated with St. Germain were spread across many lifetimes, in the present and immediate past, when he embodied successful presidents, poets, and painters. His characteristics became clearer, when viewed as being similar to those found among mythic or legendary heroes.

This works well because our hyper-realistic or purely scientific stories do not explain how we come to be, who we are, and why we feel the way we do. Myths help us understand truths, which we cannot always grasp rationally. Legends are not supposed to be history or science; they are not supposed to be factual. Instead, they show us archetypes of men and women, and through them, can teach us truths about being human.

But who are these heroes and heroines? Where do they come from, and what was their purpose? Are legends just silly stories that our ancestors told one another, or could their stories be encoded with truth and still be the source of historical and scientific data?

The Gatekeeper made it clear that to understand a Master, you first had to understand the characteristics of individual legendary beings. He advised:

To understand St. Germain, put your pragmatic, rational mind in a small chest, lock it, and hand it to me. Explore, instead, your collective unconscious and the mythology of Europe, then you will be able to understand that Master energy. Three archetypes will help us understand St. Germain: Pan, Loki, and Eros. St. Germain is benign mischief, luck, and lust. These are the clues to him. Once you have understood them, I will give you more about him before we explore Mary's three archetypes.

The characteristics attributed to these legendary beings, according to The Gatekeeper, bore a symbolic relationship to the actual attributes St. Germain demonstrated in his earthly lives; therefore, the pursuit of the three legendary beings of Pan, Loki, and Eros would lead me to understand him—first, as a hero, then once his consistent personality traits and aptitudes emerged, I could recognize him in public life, movies, and biographies. While I did not realize it at the time, this approach would become essential. By slowly piecing together the complete picture of St. Germain's and Mary's contributions to humanity, the qualities and characteristics they show in each of their lives become consistent.

I began by delving into the netherworld of legends, where Pan, Loki, and Eros would emerge as flawed characters. They do not, however, offer a complete picture of St. Germain, so it would still be necessary to search further.

Pan is first, and he is multidimensional. There are three kinds of Pan: the Greek pastoral god, the lord of nature, and the personification of evil. Pan's persona will shift from good to bad in a similar way to the changes in Loki and Eros. Pan, the son of Hermes, was the Greek pastoral god of fertility and forests, and is often depicted as a leering, ugly man with horns, beard, and goat's ears and feet. Most stories about him deal with his romantic affairs, where he is vigorous and lustful and inhabits lonely country places in order to play his pipe. Pan can make humans stampede in panic or terror. Like a shepherd, he sleeps at noon and dislikes being disturbed. He embodies the forces of Mother Earth. His sensual nature and earthy qualities derive from his earlier form as Dionysus, the god that gave humans both the vine and its wine. The Dionysian rituals will give birth eventually to performing arts in the dramas of tragedy and comedy, which St. Germain will oversee. The Gatekeeper explained:

There is a part of Pan that is typical of St. Germain. He is the dancer, the Boudican image of Pan, playing pipes and dancing on his little goat feet. He has the rutting sexuality of a male goat. Look for those lives of his where those characteristics are preeminent.

I could see him as legendary dancers, as Anna Pavlova, Rudolph Nureyev, and as Hollywood stars Fred Astaire and Gene Kelly, or in other lives, as the legendary seducers Casanova, Julius Caesar, and Errol Flynn, or Krishna with his 14,000 wives.

The second dimension of Pan is as the god of nature spirits. Sometimes, those who are clairvoyant and work in gardens close to nature have seen this Pan—people like Edinburgh-born R. Ogilvie Crombie (ROC) who has been associated with the Findhorn Foundation in Scotland. They describe him as exceptionally tall, over 25 feet, with shaggy legs, cloven hooves, and holding panpipes. According to The Gatekeeper, Pan directs all of the angels, devas, and earth spirits in their work of building and protecting animals, plants, and minerals. He ensures that the blueprint of God's design for creation is followed precisely. It may only be modified, in an evolutionary sense, in order to ensure the survival of some species.

Pan is present in most cultures as a rural entity, joyful and playful, helping harvests to be bountiful and Nature to renew herself. St. Germain expressed those aspects of himself in his lives as the Biblical hero Noah, the American Johnny Appleseed, the British folk hero Robin Hood, and the Celtic spirit of the forest, the Green Man. In his life as Noah, he will save seeds as well as animals in order to repopulate the drowned world after the flood. Then later, as Jethro Tull, he will invent a plow to increase the bounty of the harvest. St. Germain consistently chooses lives that have to do with seeds and grains, such as Luther Burbank, the Californian horticulturalist who improved many varieties of food crops, and William Farrer, the Australian who improved the quality of wheat. He loves wine. As Noah, he was the first drunk recorded in our history. Later, he owned a large proportion of Italy's vineyards as Seneca, the Roman philosopher, while as the French monk, Dom Perignon, he invented Champagne.

The horned and cloven-hoofed joyful god took on another form: as the personification of evil, a form of Satan. This third dimension of Pan is the dark side, expressed in the excesses of wantonness, alcohol, sex, and drugs that almost extinguish his vast creative form. He thus incarnated as King Charles II, Rudolf Nureyev, and Lord Byron—all lives lived in excess.

Pan shares some characteristics with another Greek god: Apollo, who inspired prophetesses; however, in many ways, Pan was his antithesis as he is farmyard crude, rough as guts, compared with Apollo's urbane culture and sophistication. Pan lived as the plain-speaking, homespun President Harry Truman, the antithesis of his diplomatic and sophisticated secretary of state, Dean Acheson—yet both of them were aspects of St. Germain.

St. Germain is the trickster, the liar, the wizard of guileful words. These characteristics exist in his many lives as the trickster magicians Aaron and

Merlin, the cunning of Dante and Cicero, and malevolent Josef Goebbels. He is also the liberator of fettered creatures, as the anti-slavery campaigner William Wilberforce and the American abolitionist William Floyd Harrison and the African American escaped slave and later statesman Frederick Douglass.

Loki is always trouble as he is the mischief maker of the Norse gods. He is the outsider, the father of strife, the trickster who is crafty, fickle, and false but ultimately heroic. He causes the death of Baldur, the just son of Odin and when he is punished, bound like Prometheus to a rock, a snake dropping venom on his face, he writhes in torment, earthquakes shaking the land. There he stays until all the World's slaves are freed.

Eros is the third legendary figure to be reflected in St. Germain. According to Plato, Eros was the first of the Greek gods, a divinity of love that was both male and female. He was physically small, with wings, and carried a bow and arrow. Over the years, he shrank to almost child-like proportions, so that by the time of the Romans, he had become the tiny cherub Cupid.

As Eros, he played at the feet of Aphrodite, goddess of love, and mischievously helped her seduce men and women into embarrassing affairs. One of his most sensational exploits was the seduction of Helen, queen of Sparta and wife of King Menelaus, on behalf of Paris, prince of Troy, a venture that led to the long and destructive Trojan War. St. Germain is often of dubious sexuality and frequently bisexual. As noted above, Byron, Degas, and Nureyev were examples of these characteristics. As a promiscuous seducer, he is without equal; think of Casanova, Vivaldi, Walter Raleigh, and Errol Flynn.

It is easy to see the deceiver, magician, and trickster in some of St. Germain's lives and to acknowledge him as the greatest seducer in history. There is far more to him than caprice, though. More importantly, he enjoyed lives as great medical scientists, diplomats, saints, prophets, chemists, architects, composers, travelers, navigators, philosophers, lawyers, politicians, and poets. Then there are his lives as the adventurers and men who sailed off the edge of maps to explore new worlds. The Gatekeeper said:

> St. Germain is a complex being. By understanding Loki, Eros, Apollo, and Archangel Raphael together, you will gain insight into his greatness and his complexity. George Stephenson (1781–1848) is the perfect case study because as well as being an aspect of St. Germain, as the inventor of the first railway locomotive, he also combined those other qualities of St. Germain: the archetypal energies of Pan, Loki, Eros, and Apollo. George Stephenson had a passion for playing chamber music, and he was renowned as an inventor. Here, we have the characteristics

of Apollo. He was a great practical joker, into whoopee cushions, so here we have the trickster, Loki. But Stephenson also loved the erotic, with a succession of mistresses, so here we have Eros. He combined the characteristics shown in Apollo, Loki, and Eros. But there is more still to St. Germain.

Paraphrasing, The Gatekeeper added that St. Germain was also Brendan the Navigator, Marco Polo, Zeng He, and Captain James Cook. All were outstanding travelers, men who crossed boundaries and oceans, where no-one they knew had ever been before. St. Germain was also a master alchemist, with a detailed knowledge of chemistry, a characteristic that suggests attributes attributable to Raphael the Archangel. Raphael is connected with the symbol of healing, the serpent. He acts as a guide and companion on a journey, making him the angel of travel and safety, a guide to the underworld. The Gatekeeper said:

St. Germain is St. Christopher, the patron saint of travel. He carried the Christ Child on his back and shoulders. He did this as Joseph ben Mathias, when he carried Jeshua, his son. And he repeats this as Christopher Columbus, taking the Christ Child on his ship to the New World.

St. Germain cannot be Raphael completely, but they are related, in that they share the same spiritual DNA. Trapped in a world of words, our degree of description is limited. Archangels can only incarnate under exceptional circumstances; otherwise, we would have them interfering all the time. St. Germain incarnates as a human, but Raphael does not incarnate.

Archangels are a separate species. They take human form temporarily to communicate something significant—as Raphael did in the Tobias story or as Gabriel did at the Annunciation—but this is unusual, because a lesser species of angels usually carries messages. Some of the archangels have a special relationship with humans, but Raphael is the only one I know who has dominion over different universes other than this one; therefore, like St. Germain, he has changeability; like St. Germain, he is a protector against the Dark and the thought-forms it creates. Watch for the role he'll play at the birth of Jeshua. And he shares with Apollo a connection to music. So, you can see, they are similar, but not identical. A being of such diversity as St. Germain is like a three-person god: Pan, Loki, and Apollo with other minor strains as Eros, Dionysus, and Asclepius, the god of healing.

I understood that each of the Masters is identified with one of the archangels and shares their qualities. El Morya and Pallas Athene are associated with Archangel Michael; Kuthumi and Portia with Archangel Uriel; Hilarion and Nada with Archangel Gabriel; Djwhal Khul and Fortunata with Archangel Zadkiel; Serapis Bey and Leto with Archangel Sandalphon; and St. Germain and Mary with Archangel Raphael.

In many of Mary's lives, Archangel Raphael's DNA also emerged, as she explored lives as a healer and physician, traveler, mediator, and musician. For example, in her lifetime as Soranus, a first-century Greek from Ephesus, she concentrated on healing diseases of the eye, as Archangel Raphael does in the Tobias story. As Luke, the evangelist and physician, she popularized iodine as a treatment for wounds. Mary the High Priestess shared Archangel Raphael's ability to move between worlds and across dimensions and to return safely from where she had come. Because of this ability, as Isis, she was able to rescue her husband's body from death.

If St. Germain represents the mythic Apollo, then Mary, St. Germain's feminine counterpart, is Artemis, his twin sister. After many years of study and questioning, I confirmed with The Gatekeeper that St. Germain's lives fulfill the promise of Apollo's birth: to bring light to the world. His existence as Thomas Edison and Nicola Tesla illuminated the world with electricity. He also brought the enlightenment of education to many societies. Five lives, in particular, stand out: as Homer and Plato, he formulated the curriculum of Greek learning. As Lao Tzu, he created the curriculum for Chinese education. In a different culture, and at another time, he embodied St. Patrick, the saint who brought knowledge to the illiterate Irish. Finally, as Columba, he founded the monasteries that kept learning and civilization alive during the Dark Ages of Europe.

What of Mary? How does her energy complement or serve as the antithesis of that of St. Germain?

In Greek legend, Artemis roamed the woodlands like Pan. As the goddess of the wild, she was the virgin hunter with a silver bow, her dogs at her feet. She became the protector of all that is wild and free. She was the goddess of hunters, women, and childbirth, and protector of children. Artemis informs Mary's lives, and she is known as the patron of childbirth just as the Christian Mary is today. The mythic Artemis demonstrated courage, stamina, strength, and resourcefulness when she helped her mother reach the floating island of Delos. At the entrance to Artemis's temple in Ephesus, there was a towering statue of her, showing many tiers of plump breasts, as if she could suckle all the children of the world.

In her life as the mother of Jeshua, Mary used Ephesus as her sanctuary when she fled Jerusalem and dictated her life story to Luke there. She died in the mountains above the temple, and her death signified the change from one incarnation of the goddess to another.

In storytelling, it is Apollo who takes center stage, while Artemis, the bit player, is almost elbowed aside. It's a theme across many of their lives in the line to God: St. Germain gets star billing, while the reticent Mary works hard without recognition, insisting that is how she likes it.

The qualities of Artemis (Diana in Roman mythology) exist throughout Mary's line, in both her male and female forms. The Gatekeeper tells me to look for four clear characteristics.

First, author Jane Austen exemplified her grace and style, as did ballerina Margot Fonteyn, designer Coco Chanel, and Empress Josephine. Look for the huntress, as a second characteristic, always questing, restless, and looking beyond the stars, insistent on the beauty of the human soul with a lack of care of others' opinions. It was evident in Robin Hood heroine Maid Marian, poet Emily Dickinson, and novelists Virginia Woolf and George Sand, philosopher Simone de Beauvoir, and Egyptian Queen Cleopatra. The scandalous love affairs of Sand, de Beauvoir, and Cleopatra showed a disregard for the social norms of their time. In male form, those qualities existed in Admiral Horatio Nelson, hero of the Battle of Trafalgar.

What we also see in some of these lives is the guardianship of nature and creation. In American marine biologist Rachel Carson, author of *Silent Spring*, the energy of Mary spearheaded the environmental movement in the 1960s. The same was evident in Gertrude Jekyll, one of England's most celebrated garden designers, and authors Lady Murasaki from Japan, Emily Dickinson from the USA, and Vita Sackville-West from England, all of whom had much-admired flower gardens. However, it is moral and physical courage that makes Mary's energy remarkable. You can see that shining through in St. Brigid of Ireland, Queen Isabella of Spain, and Queen Katherine Parr of England.

The energies of Isis and Artemis are clear in Mary. Throughout her many existences, Mary is mostly awake to St. Germain. She doesn't expect too much from him. He is a lovable rogue, and women love the rough, the larrikin, the razzle dazzle in him. Only when she is with Lord Sananda or Serapis Bey is there an actual meeting of the minds, a balance. She shares with Morpheus and Jesus Christ the ability, as Mary the High Priestess, to descend into hell or the lower worlds and rescue lost souls. The Gatekeeper reveals more:

Isis was the model mother, and her first duty is often correction: setting others right. You see that in her lives as reformers Elizabeth Fry, Mary Wollstonecraft, Margaret Sanger, and Marie Stopes. Another characteristic of Isis is the enchantress. Her ability to be an enchantress leads to her soul's destruction as Morgana. It can also lead to her increased spiritual understanding. This is evident in Annie Besant, who wrote as a Theosophist. Mary does work magic and can materialize supernatural powers to change things. Remember how Mary made the sun dance when she appeared in Portugal, at Fatima, or how she created the flowering of the rose bush in winter in Guadeloupe, Mexico? Because she can move between planes and time warps, like an advanced saint or a spiritual Master, Mary has an authority to correct certain matters. Her focus in the 20th century was lifting Russia and its republics from darkness to freedom and light. Mary uses the energy from the chi, or the grace generated from the supplication of the massed prayers of people reciting her rosary. She was able to achieve Russia's partial liberation from Communism, but she still awaits its enlightenment.

As I already outlined, most Marian characters are reticent and keep a low profile. Think of Greta Garbo, Emily Dickinson, and Jane Austen. They are not as insistently dramatic as St. Germain's lives, although there are some outstanding exceptions. Take, for example, her experiences as Queen Isabella of Spain, King James I of Britain, Horatio Nelson, Sarah Bernhardt, Cleopatra, or her assassinations as Benazir Bhutto and Indira Gandhi. Her lives, being principally lived as yin energies, are, therefore, more complex than St. Germain's. The DNA, which comes from the vast entity called Mary, has three main strains. She has agreed they are to be named Mary the Mother, Mary the Magdalene, which ties in with Artemis/Diana and Mary the High Priestess, which ties in with Demeter/Persephone and Isis. These are all facets of one being. The only time I know when they unite is in her life as Nefertiti.

Two questions remained. First, I wanted to know if St. Germain and Mary were opposites who faced off, like light and dark, or complementary, like Apollo and Artemis, in the way sunlight and moonlight complement each other. The Gatekeeper was clear:

St. Germain and Mary are complementary, rather than opposites. They translate as gold and silver.

Could they blend into one entity?

There is partial and observable blending. Compare St. Germain's Katherine Hepburn with Mary's Katherine Parr—both of them tall, strong, handsome, outspoken, articulate, and compassionate. But

St. Germain and Mary are like oil and water: swirl them together, and they don't mix. Yin and yang do not mix to make a compound, but they coexist, side by side, in happiness, so that neither loses its identity. In that, ascended souls join the chorus of the Creator to add to the Light while retaining their identity. They make excellent partners.

My second question was about their role as deities in other cultures. Where was St. Germain in Hinduism, Buddhism, and Egyptian religions? Where was Mary? Do their characteristics remain consistent?

The Gatekeeper explained:

St. Germain is present in the Hindu pantheon as Krishna, a life he shared with Hilarion, and as Hanuman, in Buddhism. His trickiness is displayed again, the impertinent Monkey King, who is asked by the Buddha to help a young boy journey from China to India to retrieve Holy Scriptures. As one of the heroes of Wu Cheng's 14th-century novel A Journey to the West, he outwits demons, robbers, and greedy monks. While he is not present in the Egyptian pantheon, he is as Loo Bei, the founder of Daoism, and Lao Tzu prominent in Chinese Daoist beliefs.

Mary, on the other hand, plays a dynamic role in Buddhism and Hinduism. Mary is Tara in Tibetan, and she is Maya and Kwan Yin in Buddhism. Mary is also among consorts as Sita and Parvati in Hinduism. Mary comes from the Judeo tradition of a stern and jealous father, a single dominant god who brooked no others. Just as Parvati and Maya gave birth to gods, so does Mary; she is the bearer of God, the Theotakos.

I started with two simple questions: Who is St. Germain, and who is Mary? The answers took me across history, cultures, fables, fairy stories, saints and sinners, leaders, and also-rans. Where am I and where are you? The strong message of this chapter is that to find yourself in the history of this world, you may have to look in fables, fairy tales, poetry, and plays and find yourself where you least expect it, then, as I did, follow the breadcrumbs.

My friend The Gatekeeper objected to this approach: "This is the cult of heroes," he said. "If I was anywhere there, I must be having down-time."

"Don't be put off," I assured him. "After two world wars when mainly men served, yesterday's heroes are all having a well-earned rest and focusing on the messy bits they couldn't manage in war time!"

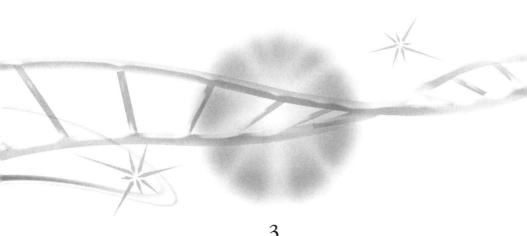

3

God's Covenant with the People of Earth

When I began conversing with The Gatekeeper to explore the lives of St. Germain and Mary, we agreed to discuss them chronologically, examining their purpose, significant achievements, spiritual growth, and any linkages among their former and future lives. For those lives for which we had little or no biographical details, The Gatekeeper agreed to reveal it. Where their lives were more recent, he would look into their dark corners and reveal their hidden secrets, their thinking, mysteries, purpose, and the terrors of their childhood.

At times during our sessions, The Gatekeeper encouraged the subject to offer comments, and we learned how their lives contributed to the Divine Plan for the development of Earth, illuminated philosophical or moral questions and challenges and whether their lives worked with the Light to reach ascension or the Dark and annihilation.

Mary and St. Germain selected lives that were extreme, exciting, critical to world events, or just entertaining examples of their lines to God. They experienced prominent Chinese, Asian, African, and South American lives, but I am unable to deal with those in this volume. Writers and channels from those cultures will examine those lives; I cannot.

Our journey takes us back to 7000 BC to Noah, the first life within our historical or legendary record attributable to St. Germain. The Gatekeeper, however, revealed that God disclosed his laws to humankind over a period of 20,000 years. He began with the most significant early life of St. Germain—Krishna, one of the luminous figures of the Hindu religion, and Mary's role as that of God bearer, mother, or colleague of every significant spiritual leader born to humankind.

Krishna (2595–2554 BC), Avatar

Why would The Gatekeeper insist that the line to God begin with Krishna? According to Hindu belief, Krishna was an avatar, one of the many lives of Vishnu, the God of love. He was Vishnu's greatest incarnation and one of his most joyful expressions, synonymous with pleasure and light-hearted eroticism.

Krishna was born in prison on the vernal equinox, as the eighth son of the king's sister, Devaki, in a town somewhere between Delhi and Agra in northern India. The evil king, Kasma, had imprisoned his sister and her husband because he believed one of their sons would kill him. Consequently, he murdered his first six nephews at birth. The seventh son, Balarama, escaped his wrath. When the eighth son was born, Vishnu himself appeared to help the father smuggle out his newborn baby, Krishna, and exchange him for the daughter of a cowherd. Krishna was brought up by these cowherds, Yashoda and Nanda, and only much later did King Kasma discover that his nephew had survived.

Krishna grew into a naughty child, a trickster, laughing at his foster parents, stealing sweets and whenever he could, helping other gods. As a young man, Krishna hid the clothes of the female cowherds when they bathed. Concealed in a tree, he watched the women splashing in the water before they searched, naked, for their clothes. Krishna would enchant them by playing his flute and dancing in the moonlight. Each woman would believe that he loved only her. According to legend, he multiplied himself so that he could dance with each of the girls before slipping silently into the night. With milkmaid Radha he fell passionately in love. Today you can watch the blue-skinned Krishna dancing with his love Radha and bewitching her with the irresistible call to love of his flute in festivals all over India.

When it was time for Krishna to carry out his mission of removing evil from India and Sri Lanka, he put his love aside. He planned to kill his uncle, the evil king, and rid his country of oppressive rulers.

The Mahabharata, an epic poem, celebrates Krishna's exploits. It contains a narrative of a great battle between two families: the Kavaravas and the Pandavas. Krishna was related to both. He gave his army to one family while joining the opposing force and fighting as the charioteer for his protégé Arjuna, an archer and a Pandu prince. Arjuna was reluctant to fight against his relatives. Krishna, in a Christ-like transfiguration, showed the troubled Arjuna the supreme form of God. Arjuna was terrified and had to be reassured by Krishna as he returned to his earthly shape. Krishna's oration on who or what is God, what is a human being, what is the purpose of life and one's duty persuaded Arjuna that it was right to fight against his kin.

Legend gives Krishna two different deaths. In one, he survived the slaughter of the battle, only to be shot in the heel by a hunter, whom he forgave before he died; in the other, he died by crucifixion like Jesus Christ. After his death, he descended into hell before ascending into heaven, and, on the last day, he returned to India as Vishnu, on a white horse, similar to the image of Christ returning on a white horse in Revelations.

According to The Gatekeeper, Krishna was a unique incarnation, in which two Ascended Masters, St. Germain and Hilarion, combined their energies to exist together in one life. Vishnu, who was an incarnation of Lord Sananda and who would later live as both the Buddha and Jeshua ben Joseph the Christ, also experienced a variety of lives. Krishna's life was one of the most meaningful lives of anyone, anywhere, at any time. St. Germain was the dominant energy, crafting a life full of dash and dazzle, sparkling with the joy as he played his Pan-like flute.

☀ Conversation with The Gatekeeper ☀

Seven significant events occurred in the last 10,000 years, and they created communication between heaven and earth or between the physical universe and spirit. Each event and the major actors changed the destiny of humankind. Chronologically, they are:

1. When Vishnu saved the worlds' seas from being poisoned and received the poison mark around his neck, as recorded in the Hindu faith.

2. When Krishna fought the final battle against the King of Evil in Sri Lanka (where the Flame of the Holy Spirit was anchored), as recorded in the Hindu faith.

3. When Abraham reached a covenant with God, as recorded in the Jewish faith.

4. When Moses "received" the Ten Commandments, as recorded in the Jewish faith.

5. When Buddha gave his instructions on righteous living, as recorded in the Buddhist faith.

6. When Lao Tzu codified The Way, as recorded in Daoism.

7. When Mohammed received Islamic Law and the 1,000 names of God, as recorded in Islamic faith.

These events are the history of the giving of the law, and Krishna played an essential role. Our purpose is to discuss the revelations of the law.

Who decided to reveal God's law to humans in seven stages?

It was a consultative decision among the circle of Masters, led by Lord Sananda, the Son of God. It includes St. Germain, Mary, El Morya, and Hilarion. They determine all purposes for Earth. Sanat Kumara is the guardian angel of the Earth's neutrality and is the entity in charge of this planet. It is a special place: a proving ground, a school, a retraining establishment, a second chance, where a being gets an opportunity to progress based on their success. He shares with Mary, the embodiment of Arjuna, Krishna's companion warrior.

Revelation of God's law was over seven stages. Does that mean that we have to study the revelations step by step?

One would have to be highly developed to bear the burden of such a revelation. All stages are not equal. It is easy for a child to understand Mosaic Law. The Ten Commandments are simple, and you can count them on two hands. It is difficult, however, with Vishnu's and Mohammad's teachings, to see what is true and what the passage of time has tarnished.

Of the circle of Masters, Lord Sananda is involved in the revelatory process three times; El Morya twice as Abraham and Mohammad; Hilarion twice as Moses and Krishna, and Mary the High Priestess twice as a transcriber.

Why is St. Germain also included twice in the revelatory process?

The energy of St. Germain, wherever it incarnates, is the prime establisher of innovation in language, poetry, art, science, dance, music, entertainment, philosophy, engineering, navigation, exploration, and medicine—meet the world's start-up merchant. And secondly, apart from Hermes, St. Germain is the world's best communicator. He disseminates knowledge, spreads understanding, and is our sublime teacher.

Where are the lives of Mary in the giving of the law?

Mary is the co-founder, partner, and colleague in the founding of all spiritual movements. Mary the High Priestess is Arjuna, the scribe and companion warrior to Krishna. She is Abraham's wife, Sarah; Vishnu's mother, Sara; the Buddha's mother, Maya; Jeshua's mother, Mary; and Mohammad's first wife, Khadija. These are the roles the times allowed women. However, she also assumes male lives as the patient and accurate recorder of the law. The scribe Luke, the evangelist, is one example.

Birthing a spiritual movement requires a female identity to establish an idea and grow it as a faith. Mary is fit for that purpose. She has the magisterial authority of motherhood and the ability to move between worlds, always in a ministering or servant role, even when she is a king or a queen. Mary plays a role in the birthing of all spiritual movements. She is Nefertiti to Akhenaton; she is Sarah to Abraham; Maya, the mother of Buddha; and Isis, the wife of the savior Osiris and mother of Horus.

Why is the event with Krishna so significant that it's acknowledged as part of the giving of the law?

His concerns were typical of St. Germain's concerns. He focused on the highways and ports of India, ensuring that they were safe for communication, commerce, and travel. Krishna is a nation builder, developing a system of fiefdoms in order to form a government. Each chief was sworn to him and ruled with local forces. He was good at organizing and deputizing. Even beyond his government areas, rulers were appointed, but only after his approval.

Was that Arjuna's purpose—to keep Krishna grounded?

His purpose was to be Krishna's physical and spiritual bodyguard, the straight man for Krishna's philosophizing. In that way, he made important contributions to the philosophical aspect of Hinduism – this philosopher is not the king; he is the warrior and the recorder of what Krishna pronounced. His spiritual purpose was to help the intellectualizing of Hinduism.

He'd have to be very smart!

Arjuna had Mary's high intelligence, her interest in theology, her gentleness; he was very gentle for a warrior: never a bully, never forceful. For him, violence was the last resort. He was very agile, with a well-developed sense of humor, an excellent archer, and his strong fingers and vice-like grip delivered a superb javelin throw. He's quite short—five foot six inches—broad-shouldered, thickset, muscled forearms, quite light-skinned, and a neatly clipped black beard.

Krishna in *Bhagavad-Gita* shows Arjuna the supreme form of God before they go into battle. Did they share a transcendent experience?

Yes. Krishna took him to a mountaintop, where he revealed himself in all his glory. Krishna gave Arjuna akashic sight, allowing him to see his soul's aura, the shapes of its leaping flames. Arjuna was able to see Krishna speaking to God in the figure of Vishnu, whom you would know as Lord Sananda. Vishnu is the Hindu savior, with a bluish-green throat. Arjuna was in awe—what he saw was miraculous.

Did Krishna write any of the Bhagavad-Gita?

Krishna did not write; he pronounced. He was a teacher, and his words recorded by his scribes.

But was he the actual source of this sacred text?

The majority of it is Krishna. Remember, though: there are embroideries and fanciful additions.

What is the essence of Krishna's teachings?

Krishna posed three main questions about life: What is God? What is a human? Why are we here?

He then set about answering those questions with a focus on two concepts: honor and decency. He described honest and decent behavior and inspired others to follow it. (However, his sexual mores would shock a Victorian, because he was prolific and generous with his sexual favors.) He treated women with honor and respect, ensuring he had hundreds of descendants, and his fecundity was part of his purpose. His genes had to flow into the Chosen People. He didn't influence his offspring significantly

51

because he didn't have the lifestyle to care for them. He also taught that the death portal was not disastrous. Human life could be taken up and laid down easily.

Are there parallels between Krishna's and Christ's lives?

Krishna made no claim to be the Son of God, only God's messenger. The similarities are seized on by those claiming Krishna was a former life of Christ. Most world teachers have parallels in their lives, except Buddha and Mohammad, who are different. Krishna died by impalement, not crucifixion. A minor Mnong chieftain in Burma captured him, and he died an excruciating, agonizing, and slow death, impaled on a sharpened stick driven up his anus. It took three days to die.

Did he, like Christ, forgive his murderers?

Krishna sang his death song, traditional among warriors; it was a self-eulogy. Yes, Krishna forgave his killers, asking God that his death would not be a burden on their karma. It is doubtful that they knew or understood his song, but it was witnessed by his companions who listened, hidden, in the surrounding jungle, and by others who were captured and then escaped. He died surrendering to the Divine, and his spirit ascended.

Did Krishna, like Christ, harrow hell after his death?

Krishna descended into a limbo, as we all do, and went to the Halls of Judgment before he could be reborn. Most souls have to go through these halls and examine themselves, experience nothingness, and contemplate their mistakes, as part of the building for the next life. Although Krishna may have experienced 1,000 years of expiation, he would return a day or two later to the earth!

What was Krishna's life purpose?

His main purpose was to create India as an entity, giving it an identity common to all Indians and reinforced by Hinduism. He gave India a national self-belief so strong that it survived Islam. Another purpose was to create balance in Asia; otherwise, the slumbering giant of China would have been all-pervasive. Krishna also created a musical liturgy for Hinduism and the genetic material for the important migration from the Indus Valley. There are several Indian and Pakistani leaders yet to emerge who are descended directly from him. But Jawaharlal Nehru was his descendant, and his daughter Indira Gandhi.

What did St. Germain learn from this life?

St. Germain used his intelligence and his charm to create a great and memorable life. He learned to be more balanced and responsible but continued to search for inner balance in his lives as Rudolph Nureyev and Julius Caesar, where although they had Krishna's gift of superb physical balance, they did not have the matching spiritual balance. He laid the foundations for Indian sacred music that resonates around the world in Persia, Hebrew psalms, and Broadway musicals. His spiritual challenge was to accept his death with equanimity.

What was his most endearing quality?

He has not one but two qualities: first, his charm, and second, he was highly, highly intelligent.

Maya (c. 540–525 BC), Mother of the Buddha

Tradition tells us that the Buddha and Lao Tzu lived as contemporaries; together, they made an outstanding contribution to the world, Asia in particular. The lives of the Buddha's mother, Maya, and his father were aspects of Mary and St. Germain, and the life of the gentle philosopher Lao Tzu was one of St. Germain's outstanding incarnations.

According to legend, Maya, the mother of Gautama Buddha, died of joy after giving birth to him in 563 BC. It was a time of the showering of stars, of massive bursts of enlightenment when great prophets and sages were born. Mahavira and Buddha, the founders of Jainism and Buddhism, were born in India; Lao Tzu and Confucius, the founders of Daoism and Confucianism, were born in China. The prophets of Judaism, Jeremiah and Zachariah, were born in the Middle East. All these prophets were born within 50 years of each other. While in Greece, Socrates and Plato, the fathers of Western philosophy, were also born (525 BC).

There are legends that bring some of these great ones together. Confucius's meeting with Lao Tzu is quite well detailed, while Lao Tzu's meeting with the

Buddha is commemorated in drawings and paintings that are ethereal and ultimately more divine. These lives have true mythic proportions, significant in the founding of two great religions and complex systems of thought. Maya (an aspect of Mary) will birth the Buddha, while St. Germain will gently birth philosophy.

According to tradition, Maya, or Queen Mahamaya, was the perfect woman to conceive the Buddha; she was devout, calm not passionate, and did not drink alcohol. Shuddhodana, his father, was the king of a province called Kapilavstu at the foot of the Himalayas. Legend says that Shuddhodana was a man of the world and a member of the proud Shakya or Lion tribe. We can assume he was everything Maya was not. The stories around their son's birth, the Buddha, are fantastical, but they contain two familiar events from other famous births: a great light appears in the sky, and foreign kings travel to adore the child.

Maya dreamed that her soon-to-be-born child appeared to her as a white elephant carrying a white lotus in his trunk. Both these symbols signified to her that he would be an enlightened one. In her dream, the white elephant approaches her, touches her right side with his trunk, and in this way, the Buddha entered her to be born from her right side.

Maya carried the Buddha during a 10-month pregnancy, and sensing his imminent birth, traveled to her mother's place to give birth there. She was passing through a beautiful grove of flowers and fruit trees when birth pangs started. She grasped one of the branches of a flowering tree and delivered her son, whom she named Siddhartha, meaning from "her side where he had entered her."

Maya gave birth with no pain. After delivery, her son immediately stood up and took seven steps. Present during his birth were the Hindu gods Indra and Brahma. Seven days later, tradition says, his mother died, leaving her sister to raise her son while she joined the gods.

This legend of Maya, according to The Gatekeeper, couldn't be farther from the truth.

Maya was a small woman, only four feet ten inches, but perfectly formed. She had the round face and skull of a Nepalese with slight almond-shaped eyes, a little nose, and a rosebud mouth. Maya moved like a cat, silently and with fluidity, and her voice was so soft you had to strain to hear her. She was independent, dignified, pious, meticulous, and made her views known within the bounds of royal protocol. Maya came from a long line of Brahmin tribes who practiced a form of animalistic Hinduism. Her Nepalese Gurkha ancestors imbued her with their bravery and impish humor.

✳ Conversation with The Gatekeeper ✳

As a mother, how did she influence her son?

Maya never lost her temper with him. She was calm, measured, and controlled her emotions. Like Mary, she was not submissive to the Buddha's father. As the dominant parent, she did not die at his birth, as legends describe. It was the Buddha's father's senior wife who died. The same astrological portents present at the Buddha's birth were present at Jesus's birth: the same massing of the three planets occurred over his birthplace. Astrologers journeyed to witness his birth from Babylon, China, and Sri Lanka, following a particular constellation in the night sky. And, as in the delivery of Jesus, they took gifts.

Why did Mary incarnate as Maya?

She had to pass through the first gateway of spiritual development to total unconditional love, and Mary had found it hard to do. Her son was respectful, but she found him disobedient and difficult to handle, and she was to love a husband who was violent, unfaithful, and neglectful. Five hundred years later, in her life as Jeshua's mother, she will lose him again, give him up to death. In Maya's life, she will lose him through her death to her husband. Maya was the silent witness to her Masterdom and to that of her son's.

What was her life purpose?

To go through that primary gateway and forget about justice and her rights.

What qualities of Mary did she bring into this incarnation?

Mary's endurance, intelligence, passive strength, beauty, and her love of flowers. Her garden was a paradise.

What caused her death?

Maya died of tuberculosis, but her broken heart contributed greatly to her death. She was sterile after the Buddha's difficult birth, and everyone knew that she was, and this increased her sidelining. When Maya died, it was the passing of a sad life.

How did her son remember her?

The Buddha venerated her memory, which became enshrined in the imperfect memory of a young child. He had weightier matters on his mind, and to his regret Maya faded, but he retained a reverence for what she had taught him.

Lao Tzu (c. 570 BC), Old Master of Taoism

The Old Master, or the Old Sage, are two of the translations of Lao Tzu, a respectful title given to a man who lived around the sixth century BC. Born Li Erh, some scholars believe he was a little older than his fellow philosopher Confucius (Kung-Fu Tzu). He is said to have been born in K7 Prefecture (today's Henan province) of the State of Chu, in China, and to have held an office at court.

One legend places Lao Tzu as the senior archivist at the Emperor's court. By then, as an old man about to retire, he wanted to leave the palace in order to find a peaceful retreat. A gatekeeper stops him and encourages him to record his wisdom. Another legend says his major work, the *Tao*, was simply a collection of sayings written by several Taoists using the pen name "Lao Tzu."

Mainstream tradition holds that Lao Tzu himself recorded the work of the *Tao-Di-Jhing* (pron. Dow-Tee-Ching), which means "The Way of Life and Its Power." It's a collection of 81 sayings, of which 59 are considered the most important, and they are organized in rhyme for emphasis and ease of remembering.

Hundreds of years after his death, Lao Tzu's treatise was divided into two parts. Verses 1–37 were called Tao (pron. Dow), because they all begin with that word; verses 38–81 were called Di because they began with that word. Jing, or Ching, means "Classic or Ancient text." Its 5,250 words are some of the most important ever written. It is the most translated classic after the Bible, with about 700 translations extant. It's the oldest scripture of the religion of Taoism. It gently advocates nonviolence over violence and is the forerunner of Christ's and Gandhi's philosophy. Lao Tzu's principle mode of thinking is through paradox and poetry.

What is the Tao?

The Tao is the mysterious unity underlying and sparking in all things.
There is a thing, formless yet complete
Before Heaven and Earth, it existed.

We do not know its name, but we call it Tao.
It is the mystery of mysteries, incomprehensible.
Look, it cannot be seen – it is beyond form.
Listen, it cannot be heard—it is beyond sound.
Grasp, it cannot be held—it is intangible.
These three are indefinable, they are one.
From above it is not bright.
From below it is not dark:
Unbroken thread beyond description.
It returns to nothingness.
Form of the formless,
Image of the imageless,
It is called indefinable and beyond imagination.
Stand before it—there is no beginning.
Follow it, and there is no end.
Stay with the Tao, move with the present.
Knowing the ancient beginning is the essence of Tao.

In this translation of the opening verses, the Tao is a path that allows us to live in harmony with the universe. There is a mysterious unseen unity that underlies everything, even that which is apparently in conflict. While Lao Tzu never calls the Tao "God," and he does not see it as personal or relating to humans, its presence, like God, sustains everything and, like God, deserves awe and respect.

Taoism is a mystical philosophy influenced by nature, with a slight scepticism permeating it. Lao Tzu believed that a person's life should be governed by instinct and conscience and unconditional acceptance of the laws of the universe. He emphasized spontaneity and harmony with nature, together with complete relaxation and sitting with a blank mind. There was but one virtue in life, and that was to be in harmony with the Tao. Living 600 years before Jesus, he advised repaying evil with good. He saw opposites not as polarities of one another but existing within one another and dissolving into the Tao.

As noted above, one legend has the Buddha and Lao Tzu, the two great philosophers, meeting with one another; another legend has Lao Tzu meeting with Confucius. The story of Lao Tzu's life raises the perennial questions of legendary beings. Did he exist? Where did he come from? What did he have to learn in this life? Where did he work? If he met Confucius and the Buddha, what were their meetings like? What did Lao Tzu take away from them? Why is some of the Tao so similar to the sayings of Jesus Christ about The Way?

✳ Conversation with The Gatekeeper ✳

Did Lao Tzu live, and did he influence other great philosophers like Kung-Fu- Tzu, Buddha, and Jeshua ben Joseph?

His dynastic family name was Li. His parents heard his wisdom and knew he'd been born many times before. He had one life in Siberia, and another in Egypt as Imhotep's tutor, Dhrahippi, but all his other incarnations were in China. He was born where the border of the northern province of China joins Manchuria to a Manchurian father who was an educated man. His mother came from a noble Chinese family that disapproved of her love-match marriage. Lao Tzu was an archivist, a historian, and librarian who kept the scrolls in good condition and cataloged them. He wrote treatises on philosophy and history. Lao Tzu was also a gifted teacher to privileged young boys of the nobility. And yes, he influenced Jeshua, who in his time in Tibet, studied his work.

What was there in Lao Tzu's life experiences that led him to his philosophical position that there is a way of thinking or refusing to think and seeking a modest life of quiet contemplation?

Lao Tzu was different, a genius who was privileged to bring in some knowledge from his previous incarnations. We all bring abilities from our different Master lineages with our spiritual DNA, but with no memory of our lives or the time between them. He brought special abilities and knowledge but no memory. As a philosopher he was able to take what he knew and justify what he knew without knowing where it came from. Any insight he had would, for example, be tried or tested to see if the knot of knowledge held fast under scrutiny. If it did not, he took the knot and painstakingly picked it apart and then he rebuilt the whole hypothesis until it held fast. The difference between him and other philosophers was his flying start. Having been given the prior knowledge he had only to find a structure to justify it.

Why was Lao Tzu given this knowledge?

Humankind in China needed to leap forward. Leonardo da Vinci, an aspect of Kuthumi, is another example of a genius who came in with prior knowledge to bring about a generational shift. Lao Tzu, as a philosopher sitting and teaching in a library, had little opportunity to learn from the experience of exciting challenges.

He had several incarnations as a leader of soldiers, several as a man with a genius intellect in the body of a peasant condemned to do back-breaking work, and two embodiments as a local ruler to experience the wielding of power. He brought all his learning and knowledge of those lives forward into his life as Lao Tzu.

Who made the decision to allow him that access?

The energetic need of Earth in China demanded, like a vacuum, to be filled. The need unfolds like a flower unfolding: it only unfolds when it is ready. Lao Tzu indeed met Kung-Fu (an aspect of Serapis Bey) in today's Shanghai, and they didn't like one another one little bit. Kung-Fu was tall, with piercing black eyes, a large nose, and black hair. He had a thin and rangy build, a typical Northerner. He wore silk, a Mandarin hat covered in gold and silver embroidery, and red frogging on his jacket.

Lao Tzu received him. By contrast, he was small, bird-like with transparent parchment skin, eyes heavily lidded. He was bald, except for a fringe of long white wispy hair, a goatee beard, and long moustache. Lao Tzu was frail, tiny, delicate even, and on this day, he dressed carelessly, like a Franciscan. Lao Tzu thought Kung-Fu precocious, a young man who took intellectual leaps without being able to justify them. Observing his finery, he thought Kung-Fu was too concerned with material matters. On the other hand, Kung-Fu thought that Lao Tzu was in his dotage, completely overestimated and too concerned with "old fashioned" things.

Why did St. Germain choose to incarnate as Lao Tzu?

His energy and gifts were needed to start The Way [Tao], the basis of all Chinese philosophy. Lao Tzu was also the founding father of classical education in China. He was responsible for history, calligraphy, mathematics, poetry, music, astronomy, and law, and welding them into one. He taught the interrelationship of poetry, music, and mathematics. Lao Tzu was a teacher of the cultured and civilized. His teaching resounded through the generations of the Middle Kingdom, and scholars came to study there with him because he was so famous. Before Lao Tzu, the East did not have a systematic philosophy. It had been part of the nature of Athenians to think systematically, but not for those in the Middle Kingdom. Lao Tzu's insistence that philosophy, healing, dance, and rhetoric be taught together in a systematic formula influenced the education of China, India, and Indochina, more than 40 percent of the world's population at that time. However, it was his role in the revelation of the law that was his most outstanding spiritual and intellectual achievement. His teaching style was more comparable to Aristotle (also Serapis Bey) than to Socrates (Kuthumi). Lao Tzu, like Aristotle, didn't like being challenged, while Socrates encouraged it. His followers would, therefore, retain a degree of inflexibility.

There is a tradition that Lao Tzu met the Buddha, an aspect of Lord Sananda. If that is so, could you describe the meeting?

Lao Tzu's followers were keen that their Master should meet the Buddha, who was only 29 at the time. They had been told stories by an Indian emissary to the court, of a remarkable divine person living in India who traveled widely. Lao Tzu expressed interest. They met in Xinjiang province near the Tibetan border.

When Lao Tzu arrived, after many months of travel, the Buddha, an aspect of Lord Sananda, was teaching. Lao Tzu sat humbly in the outer circle, but as soon as the Buddha saw him, he stopped teaching and motioned to Lao Tzu to join him. Immediately, they meditated and enjoyed a telepathic conversation, which took, in observed time, no more than half an hour. However, where the two of them went was timelessness, and took an indeterminate amount of time. They got along well, asking questions of one another. Lao Tzu asked about the ordered structure of Chinese society, with peasants oppressed and abused under the layers of privilege on top. "Is this the way of the celestial kingdom?" he asked the Buddha, who replied, "Each person is on Earth for a temporary period in this kingdom of chaos. When souls return to the garden of the spirit, they can see the orders reversed, whereby the peasant is blessed, and the Mandarin is poor. Each one comes again and again to this kingdom of chaos until achieving nirvana, in other words, union with their Creator."

The Buddha learned from Lao Tzu about formalized and structured philosophy and rhetoric. After their meeting, the Buddha presented his ideas with more significant logic and forcefulness, so they gave each other increased understanding. The 63-year-old Lao Tzu would wander back to Harbin, taking a year to arrive home. The Buddha continued on his journey to Nepal, the home of his mother's ancestors, and then went down through India to Sri Lanka, traveling by sea.

Before their meeting, Lao Tzu did not understand about peace—personal inner peace. Until then, he was a man driven to accumulate wisdom, obsessed with rules and words, with doggedly gathering a band of dedicated men around him so that his ideas would be perceived. But when he met the Buddha, he began to understand personal peace. He also increased his understanding of all creatures. Back then, the Chinese did not respect animals; they were a beast of burden or a food source. Lao Tzu also gained a new technique of teaching, learning to ask questions so that his scholars could work it out for themselves. He no longer laid down the law but caused the law to be understood.

What qualities of St. Germain did Lao Tzu bring into this incarnation?

The inspired teacher, the traveler, the organizer with his start-up energy. He exhibited a refusal, bordering on arrogance, to be discouraged. He shared St. Germain's practical qualities to express ideas clearly and briefly, his gift for aphorism, his charisma, his mischievousness, and his ability to puncture egos.

What was his life purpose?

His life purpose was to give to the Chinese, an essentially pragmatic people, a spiritual life.

Did he achieve his purpose?

Eventually, but not within his lifetime. Progressively, it was achieved; maybe 1,000 years later.

How did Lao Tzu die?

He died of simple heart failure, at 92, and ascended at the moment of his death. He had no later incarnations. It's his love of his fellow man. It is a golden thread that weaves through his whole life: his love and respect for humankind.

Why did Lao Tzu incarnate?

To draw together the strings of disparate wisdom. Taoism already existed; he codified it and gathered together the roads of enlightenment so that it could be taught to us as the Tao, The Way, to prepare a later teacher, who would learn to say: "I am the way, the truth, and the life."

Thinking about These Lives

This chapter embraces two different, almost contradictory lives of St. Germain: Krishna, who lived only in war, and Lao Tzu, who contemplated only peace. Krishna was the performing artist who danced, sang, and seduced maidens as he conquered vast territory. Lao Tzu was an abstract teacher, whose story is taught through gentle contemplation of nature. Both traveled immense distances: Lao Tzu in meditation and as an itinerant teacher; Krishna in battle and as an entertainer.

The chapter also presents two lives of Mary. First, in the section on Krishna, we meet her as Arjuna, the warrior who revels in war, then as Maya, a woman of peace, the mother of the Buddha. Assuming the role of the teacher, The Gatekeeper explains the stages of the revelation of God's laws. We learn of Lord Sananda's role as both the Son, as Buddha, and the Daughter of God and the part played by the Circle of Masters, all of which builds to Lord Sananda's life as Jeshua ben Joseph.

Of all the 12 energies that carry the spiritual DNA of God, only Mary had the right and the spiritual capability to carry Lord Sananda (Jesus Christ) when he was born as a spiritual leader. Only Mary had the spiritual wisdom to instruct him as her child. Her preparation, over many different lives, for her central role, as Jeshua's (Jesus's) mother, was to test her devotion to God. In her incarnation as the Buddha's mother, she lost her son just after he was weaned only to lose him again in her death. She needed to meet every challenge to be prepared for being the God-bearer.

Finally, Lao Tzu, speaking through The Gatekeeper, introduces a reoccurring theme in Our Spiritual DNA. When you progress spiritually, you go through a gateway. At this point, you are absolutely alone—as alone as Krishna in death or Jeshua dying on the cross. He felt abandoned by his Mother/Father, because in everything he did on Earth he had to follow the same rules set down for everyone else: he had to be born, die and pass through a gateway, and go alone. Lao Tzu was saying that human spiritual progress is solitary—so solitary that it creates a feeling of desperation and abandonment. It is at that point that despair leaves you frozen, and anger draws you back and forth. Only your faith or trust in God can pull you through.

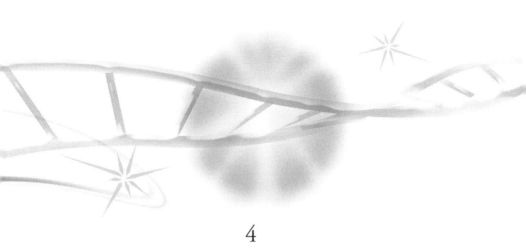

4

ANCIENT EGYPT

The two lines of Mary and St. Germain described in this chapter are linked in a contradictory embrace providing us with insights into their life stories.

Egypt is the land of Isis, one of the earliest forms of the Mary cult. Of the four important women known to us from the Pharaonic period—Nefertiti, Hatshepsut, Nefertari, and Cleopatra—three existed as meaningful lives of Mary. Does Mary, therefore, have any unique influence in Egypt?

And what of St. Germain? Egypt has not been a place where his energy has flourished to greatness. There was one exception: his life as Imhotep, the diminutive prime minister of Egypt during the reign of Pharaoh Djoser, a genius who excelled as a physician and surgeon, architect, and administrator.

Imhotep (2686–2613 BC), Architect, Physician, and Statesman

Occasionally, the world experiences a leader who accelerates change and challenges those around them with their achievements. Egyptian Pharaoh Ramses II, an aspect of Hilarion, was such a leader. Queen Elizabeth I of Great Britain (an aspect of Pallas Athene) was another example. So, too, was Pharaoh Djoser (pron. Zoser), an aspect of Kuthumi, who reigned at the beginning of the Third Dynasty (c. 2635–2610 BC).

Djoser expanded the boundaries of Egypt to the first cataract of the Nile, pushed mineral exploration into Sinai, subdued the Bedouin, and opened up Egyptian deserts to trade, mining, and exploration. He oversaw the building of the first pyramid. He was assisted by the brilliant Imhotep, whose name means "he who comes in peace." He was chief vizier to the Pharaoh. Imhotep was also a high priest at Heliopolis, renowned as a sage, astrologer, and architect, but most of all he was a physician. Imhotep's capacities were so exceptional that Djoser allowed his servant to be immortalized. Djoser permitted Imhotep's titles to be written on his statue at Saqqara, a funeral complex Imhotep had built.

The famous statue of Imhotep in the Louvre in Paris is of a slight man, modestly dressed, seated with an open scroll on his lap. He looks like a humble scribe, a public servant. Ironically, Imhotep is more famous today than the pharaoh he worked for, and not only for his leading role in the *Mummy* movies. He designed and built the first pyramid—the six-step pyramid at Saqqara in Memphis, the oldest known stone monument, which stands 200 feet high.

Little is known of his life other than his parents' names; however, we suspect he was both a great physician and a pharmacist because his "sayings" were recorded and preserved in Egyptian libraries, including an Egyptian medical scroll, which details 90 anatomical terms and describes 48 case studies. It uses the word "brain," the first time it occurs in any literature. It is believed Imhotep wrote it and possibly founded a school of medicine. The inscriptions on his statue imply Imhotep was a universal genius with an extensive range of talents. After his death, Imhotep was partly deified, so devotees could pray in his temples for miraculous cures for their illnesses. His temples became both clinics for healing and teaching centers. We do not know how he died. Looking across the expanse of St. Germain's lives, it is clear that when the world needs someone to do a tough job with modesty, we see an aspect of Imhotep doing it; e.g. Harry Truman, president of the United States.

⁕ Conversation with The Gatekeeper ⁕

How did Imhotep's life begin, Gatekeeper?

> Imhotep was a commoner born on an estate on the outskirts of Thebes. His father was a man of substance, an architect and builder, within the circle of wider royal patronage. His boyhood was happy. His mother was a joyous, happy woman, who was also firm with him. She placed him in the care of a trusted artisan, a brickmaker, who worked for them. Imhotep's father had recognized the brickmaker's brilliance, and we will pursue him centuries later as Lao Tzu. He had this brickmaker schooled to serve his household as a lawyer, teacher, and administrator. He became Imhotep's tutor, along with a slave from Babylonia who tutored mathematics, physics, and engineering. The integration of the mathematical and astronomical is seen in the alignment of the pyramids.

Imhotep learned charioteering and horsemanship, became an accomplished artist, and played the lyre beautifully. In everything he did, he showed exceptional genius. He had the characteristics of Apollo together with his great personal charm.

Let me give you a boyhood story. At the charioteering school, there was an enclosure for fierce, wild animals. Imhotep loved hunting and one day went missing.

"Where is Imhotep?" his teacher shouted.

"He's gone to play with the cheetahs," his friends replied.

"But they are wild and untamed," yelled his teacher, frantically racing to the enclosure. There, Imhotep sat, with a cheetah's head on his lap, while another licked his face.

His great facility with strange animals made him quietly famous and held in awe in the school. Imhotep remained eight years at this prestigious school and became initiated in the membership of The White Brotherhood. He had to pass rigorous exams in meditation, ethos, and religion, and learn to recite the scrolls of the Brotherhood about equity, one god, and reincarnation.

Did he look like his statue in the Louvre, where he looks petite and neat?

It is a good likeness. Actually, now that I look at it closely, it's very accurate. He's only five foot two, and not excessive in his personal appearance. He rarely drank wine, dressed plainly, and ate little— maybe a handful of dates, some nuts, and a little meat. He liked game, duck or quail and loved venison. His fresh fish came from the Nile. He drank some beer, but he mainly drank water.

Imhotep is described as the world's first doctor and as a priest, sage, poet, astrologer, and prime minister or chancellor to Pharaoh Djoser. Are these titles an accurate description of his role?

He was a natural authority on everything. His genius created the first think-tanks, bringing together the best from everywhere, including China. He led these brain trusts in the arts, urban renewal, and canal building. Pharaoh Djoser, an aspect of Kuthumi, and Imhotep had a symbiotic relationship, one which we will see throughout the critical times of history. Kuthumi sets St. Germain up to succeed, and often gets the credit for Germain's achievements.

Is there a modern equivalent to Imhotep?

Some Nobel Prize winners maybe, but in government at the moment, the nearest would be Dr. Anthony Fauci, advisor to former US President Trump.

Was Imhotep responsible for the creation of the step pyramid at Saqqara?

It was designed by a committee, a team, led by Imhotep. Egyptians imported engineers and artisans from unbelievable distances. The step pyramid is unfinished. Large triangular blocks of white marble are needed to finish it. Underneath that pyramid is a crypt used for White Brotherhood meetings and initiations. The Brotherhood designed a crypt system under all the pyramids.

Was Imhotep the author of the famous Edwin Smith papyrus?

Imhotep was the first to catalogue much in medicine. He studied drugs and pharmacy and was intensely interested in cataloging. Born a Virgo, he encouraged order in everything, searching after truth, investigating with intense curiosity anything that puzzled him. He founded a school of medicine at Thebes, and the Edwin Smith papyrus was his teaching scroll.

What was his greatest accomplishment?

A hard question! He established the parameters for temple architecture; his medical codices assisted humanity and made possible the contributions of Hippocrates and Galen; he encouraged improvement in government systems, its ethics, and its ability to deliver infrastructure on time and budget; and he sponsored and encouraged creativity in science and the arts.

Enough for five lifetimes! In addition to all this, dare I ask if he made any medical breakthroughs?

There was one branch of medicine he especially developed: advanced eye surgery. Physicians from everywhere came to study eye surgery with him. He did cataracts, removal of growths. Opium was used as anaesthetic and clamps used to peel back the eyelids. He could take out an eyeball and replace it after he had removed small tumors or the barbs of arrows. He was accomplished in trepanning, where he would remove part of the skull, drain a hematoma, and put in a plate of metal called electrum. He ensured cleanliness before operations by washing his hands then dipping them in lime, and helped design fine cutting tools of iron, drills, and bone saws. Oh, by the way, he discovered the circulation of the blood!

Why did Imhotep have to incarnate?

If he hadn't incarnated at that stage, Egyptian civilization, which was stalled in decay, would have imploded, leaving a vacuum in the known world. Chaos would have resulted. Chaos plays the same role in history as rot does in physical matter: it prepares a social system for destruction, giving a triumph to the Dark and of ignorance over knowledge. Time demanded a life of a genius.

Is that why St. Germain chose this life?

Imhotep was allowed the gift of genius, and St. Germain knows he'll deliver. He will be the seed to produce the tree to allow the intellectual desert of Egypt to flower again. Nobody else could do it as well as St. Germain. Imhotep's life is symbolic of all that is noble in the human spirit. He reached for the stars. Without that nobility, humanity would become enslaved.

What qualities of St. Germain did he bring into this life?

His vast capacity for organization, innovation, deep thought, and genius. He could conceptualize enormous projects. He had St. Germain's skills as a physician, his engineering capacity, his mathematical qualities, as well as his ability as a surgeon, and as an administrator.

What was his spiritual challenge?

I will answer that question with the following proviso. Imhotep saw his spiritual challenge as in continual warfare against his vanity. He defeated it temporarily in that life, but he would struggle with it again as Plato, as Robespierre, and as Jean-Paul Sartre. In my view, his hint of arrogance was merely a realistic assessment of his ability.

Imhotep's name has not been forgotten in over 4,000 years. What kind of a man was he?

> An immensely modest man, despite what he says, with no instinct for self-aggrandizement; he was pleasant, polite, and courteous always. In meetings, he almost always waited until everyone else had spoken, then he either cut through their blather or tied the argument neatly together. He was a kind man with a great natural authority.

Nefertiti and Nefertari

Nefertiti and Nefertari were two remarkable queens of Ancient Egypt whose husbands, Akhenaton and Ramses, left undeniable marks on Egyptian life. Living well over 3,000 years ago, they enjoyed their full status as queens, reflecting the relatively higher status of women in Egyptian society. Egypt had two pharaohs who were women, and both of them, Hatshepsut and Cleopatra, ruled like kings. Egypt passed family inheritances down the matrilineal line, and perhaps emboldened these women to take the initiative in courtship and often to propose marriage. Scholars suspect that both Nefertiti and Nefertari had higher status than their husbands because there is evidence of co-rulership in both reigns.

Nefertiti (c. 1370–1336 BC), Great Royal Wife of Akhenaton

Mary continued her historical association with Egypt as the wife of a pharaoh after her life as Isis. Swan-necked and stunningly beautiful, the sculptured head of Queen Nefertiti is one of the famous icons of Ancient Egypt. The 3,300-year-old bust of the queen from the 14th century BC is the most celebrated exhibit in Berlin's Egyptian Museum.

Nefertiti, meaning "the beautiful one has arrived," was the elegant wife of Pharaoh Amenhotep IV of the 18th dynasty. Nefertiti was by his side when he renamed himself Akhenaton (1379–1362 BC) and declared that there was to be only one god in Egypt, the sun disk Aten. Aten was a different god: unique, indestructible, and all-powerful.

Akhenaton's abandonment of the traditional gods, including Amun, Isis, and Osiris, ushered in a period of intense religious controversy and political instability, when he wrested power from his polytheistic priesthood, closed the temples, and took over their revenue. He built a new capital in the middle of nowhere, called El Amarna, and he deserted the religious capital, Thebes.

He devoted his energies not to foreign policy and territorial acquisition but to religious pursuits. He neglected the administration of both his kingdom and his empire.

Nefertiti, the mother of his six daughters, shared her husband with two other royal wives as well as a "greatly beloved wife," a concubine, Kia. Nefertiti came from a long line of high priestesses of the god Amun and was a descendant of the first queen of the 18th dynasty, Ahmose-Nefertari. They appeared to have a happy marriage, because the surviving stone reliefs show them as a loving couple and family. Nefertiti, who was officially the "great royal wife," played an active role as a priest in the new religion, and she was a devoted worshipper of the new god.

Something strange happened in the 14th year of Akhenaton's reign. Over the course of that year, three of his daughters died, followed by the death of his mother. Then Kia disappeared. The causes are unknown. Was it a plague or a purge? And what were the political implications of such sudden losses within the royal household? Later that same year, Nefertiti also disappeared from official records, virtually vanished. Her tomb was never found. How important was she? Did she die at 30, or was she banished?

⁕ Conversation with The Gatekeeper ⁕

Nefertiti is larger than life to us because of her beautiful sculpture. Did she have time in her life to accomplish something other than mothering six daughters?

> Nefertiti was a fighter for women's rights, winning the admission of women to the school for scribes and allowing them to become lawyers and economists. The head priest had been adamant: no women. Nefertiti devised a method to go around him. If women would apply to the high priestess of Bast to become one of her priestesses, then the head priest could not refuse to admit them to the school. This breakthrough was an enormous step forward for women. She devised the strategy, and her husband gave his passive support. Her victory was one of the reasons Nefertiti was perceived as so dangerous.

But why was Nefertiti, in the first five years of his reign, shown almost twice as often in the reliefs as her husband?

> Nefertiti had a better claim to the throne from both sides of her family. Her mother and father were both from the direct royal line, while Akhenaton was only from the royal line on his father's side;

therefore, she is in more pictures than him. Scholars erroneously believe she was not of royal blood, but she was truly a queen known as "The Heiress."

One relief depicts her racing her husband in a chariot which is kingly behavior and unusual for a woman. Did she do that?

Nefertiti was a tomboy indulged by her father. She was imperious and the dominant one in the relationship. She bet Akhenaton she would beat him, and she did but pulled back at the last minute. He loved her. She didn't love him as he loved her because, unfortunately, she was used to adoration.

Where did the idea of one god come from? Was the idea of religious reform supported by Nefertiti as well as by her husband?

Nefertiti was the originator of the idea. She will be the only life you will come across where all three aspects of Mary the Mother, the Magdalene, and the High Priestess are combined in the one being. She believed in one god. As we discussed with Imhotep, there had always been a small sect in Egypt who held monotheistic beliefs; [they were] known as The White Brotherhood because they only wore white garments. The pharaoh and his queen were members.

Why was Nefertiti made a member?

She was the first female member in hundreds of years. The Brotherhood had lost a great deal in being male only. She was invited because of her goodwill, intelligence, gift for governance, and purity of intention. Additionally, her yin energy and her feminine logic provided a different perspective to the order.

I've heard of a body called The Brotherhood of Light and sometimes The White Brotherhood. Is there any connection?

As above, so below. In the heavens, it's The Brotherhood of Light; on Earth, The White Brotherhood. Nefertiti was initiated into both.

Did her husband's court know that Nefertiti originated the idea to move to one god?

Certain members of the court knew it. The court generally was puzzled by the move to one god because Akhenaton, up to that point, had never had an original thought in his whole head!

Why did they embark on a religious reform to introduce monotheism?

To make Egypt flower. Like Imperial Japan, it was stultified in a love affair with tradition and hide-bound with rules. This rigidity prevented the expansion of ideas and the flourishing of its talent. Nefertiti and Akhenaton were kicking out the windows and letting the air rush in; however, she had real power, and her power, her influence, and her beauty made her dangerous.

But don't we get any whispers of her as a religious innovator or a powerful queen through history?

I'll answer that in two ways. The victors will always decide what you need to know. Nefertiti was clever enough in her handling of Akhenaton to convince him that it was his idea anyway.

And her spiritual challenge?

Nefertiti's spiritual challenge was dealing patiently with people of lesser intellect than her triple-charged intelligence, particularly men who thought they owned all intellectual discourse. She was sweet and kind and used implacable logic; however, Nefertiti committed the unforgivable sin of showing how intelligent she was. From that moment, her life was in danger.

It seems that monotheism was her life purpose. In your view, did she achieve it?

She wanted to make monotheism possible and broaden the scope of women as powerful figures. In the latter, she had success. She was, however, unaffected by the power she wielded.

What happened to her? Did she die at 30, or was she banished?

Nefertiti came from an influential royal family. Around the 14th year of her husband's reign in 1336 BC, she was poisoned by maidservants in the pay of the chief priestess, who was her cousin. She believed Nefertiti was too influential, too smart, and too supportive of her husband Akhenaton's religious obsession. Nefertiti was a political embarrassment because she was supposed to have supported the god Amun, not Aten.

Her husband genuinely adored Nefertiti. When he lost his beloved wife, he also lost the support of her family. Nefertiti's embalmed body and funeral objects were stolen, put on a caravan, and the conspirators buried the body in the Sinai Desert, disposing of it off the beaten track. Akhenaton was beside himself with grief, and because of growing opposition, he was forced to take a co-regent, Nefertiti's uncle.

Just before her death, her mother-in-law and her three daughters all died around the same time. Was there a plague of some kind?

There was foul play; they were poisoned by the high priestess of Bast, under the direction of the chief of army. He intended to marry the surviving daughter and claim the throne for himself!

Surely, the death of half the royal household should have alerted the pharaoh and court to protect Nefertiti?

Akhenaton was so egotistical he didn't think anyone would have the nerve to harm his queen. Akhenaton believed if he snapped his fingers, it was already done. He was not very bright and had an obsessive nature.

Was Akhenaton physically disabled?

The practice of incestuous relationships and multiple wives increased the deterioration of their lineage, as it did in the House of Herod. Akhenaton's body was elongated and twisted with spina bifida from the inbreeding of his ancestors. Incest was an acceptable practice.

Why did Nefertiti incarnate?

She incarnated to experience being a powerful governmental figure in Egypt and the first woman to achieve such power. All aspects of Mary needed to learn how to wield power without intoxication.

Can you give me any future lives of Akhenaton and Nefertiti?

If you look at Akhenaton's most recent life, it is as the musician and Beatle John Lennon. Far more intelligent and an aspect of Kuthumi, you'll see him again kicking out the windows to let the air in, and Akhenaton was as musical as Lennon. Nefertiti's most prominent next life was as the tough Jewish warrior Deborah, one of the judges and leaders of Israel. She is from the Mary Magdalene side of Mary.

Nefertari (1292–1225 BC),
Queen and Wife of Ramses the Great

Nefertari was one of Ramses II's (1303–c.1213 BC) seven wives, and she was his favorite. He celebrated his love for her by inscribing a poem on the wall of her painted tomb:

> My love is unique.
> No one can rival her!
> She is the most beautiful woman alive.
> Just by passing
> She stole away my heart.

Nefertari and Ramses may have been married before he became pharaoh in his early twenties. Together, they had at least five children—three boys and two girls; none of them, however, would inherit the throne. For the first 30 years of Ramses' 67-year reign, Nefertari was seen either standing beside him or shown as part of his entourage, until she, like Nefertiti, suddenly disappeared.

While Nefertari lived, Ramses carved her a small temple from living rock, just north of his great temple at Abu Simbel. In there, her statues were carved equally in size and magnificence to his own statues. One figure showed her together with the goddess Hathor, which implied equality with a goddess.

In 1904, the tomb of Nefertari was discovered in the Valley of the Queens at Thebes. Her red granite sarcophagus was empty, her mummy and her tomb treasures long gone, but the walls remained covered with exquisite paintings of her life and journey into the afterlife.

Her life poses many questions. Why was she given such important titles, which were seldom endowed on other queens? Was she of royal blood? How did she influence Ramses? Was this a love match? Why did her power appear to dissipate when her offspring did not assume the throne? And what really happened to her? Did she die, or was she pushed aside?

✳ Conversation with The Gatekeeper ✳

Was Nefertari from a royal family?

She was more royal than Ramses, from her mother's side. She is directly descended from the last of the old pharaohs, Horembeb.

Her tomb drawings show her as a beautiful woman. Are they accurate?

Nefertari was breathtakingly beautiful, stunning, with almond eyes and blue-black hair around her alabaster skin and face. She used her attractiveness and sexual allure effectively. She was fairly tall, slim, small-breasted, with a neat figure. She looked like Benazir Bhutto. Nefertari played the lute, the flute, and danced, showing musical talent and above-average skill.

Did they marry young?

They married months after he became pharaoh. She was 14; he was 19. She was dark; he was fair—a redhead, in fact, and a typical Hilarion. It was a love match, but she had to share him with other wives, which she didn't like. In the beginning, it was wonderfully passionate, and they were completely in love. Towards the end, it tended to sour. He had hurt her too much with his sexual activities.

What was Ramses like?

He was an autocratic Hilarion: arrogant, physically imposing, athletic, handsome, and a warrior. He was a bad delegator, who kept interfering in everything. He was passionate and terrible in rage. As a bisexual, he was very insecure and completely out of balance.

Was Nefertari able to influence him?

Ramses asked her advice on many cultural matters because of her obvious talents, but he consulted her most of all on statecraft. She was intelligent and shrewder than him. He tended to be trusting and not politically astute like his wife.

You have said that Ramses II was the Pharaoh in the time of Homer. Did Nefertari ever meet him?

This is an important question. Nefertari and Homer experience so many lives together, and their first meeting took place in her beautiful garden at a state banquet for the chief minister. Homer was drunk and completely incomprehensible, yet she persevered, sitting near him and commanding her servants to water his wine. They talked about singing and music. He promised to write a poem for her; he never did in that life. When they met again, he was ill, and she sent for her physician to treat him. He had renal failure, cirrhosis of the liver, bad arthritis, and gout.

What else should I know about Mary's life as Nefertari?

Gardens and pets are consistently important parts of Mary's lives. Nefertari had a pet monkey she kept in a brass tree and a tame cheetah trained not to regard her monkey as a snack. She had two pairs of pharaonic hounds or hunting dogs—their descendants survive in Sardinia. She loved birds and kept an African grey parrot and a red-tailed kite. Animals swarmed around her, and flowers grew abundantly in her beautiful gardens. At the beginning of the 20th century, she will incarnate as the great garden designer Gertrude Jekyll.

Was Nefertari religious like Nefertiti?

She was invited to be a member of the White Order because the priests recognized her purity of intention; therefore, she believed in one god, but she was spiritual rather than religious in her outlook.

Why did Nefertari incarnate?

Like Nefertiti, her purpose was to experience the wielding of power as a woman. There are three divisions of Mary: those who are Mary herself, those who are descended from Artemis and Diana and identified as the Magdalene energy, and those who reflect the energy of Demeter and Persephone and Isis, referred to as the High Priestess energy. Nefertari was the latter, a natural queen. As Ramses' wife, she provided plenty of bright ideas, and theirs was a dual reign. Nefertari had to learn the lesson that trust is rarely repaid with trust; however, her primary purpose was to break or severely fracture the mold that enclosed Egyptian women. She was partly successful in reinstating women as scribes, something won by Nefertiti then lost after her murder, and recognizing women in the official ranking for priestess almost equal to priests, particularly for the priestess of Bast. She pushed also for massive entry of women into the field of medicine. Nefertari brought enormous loyalty and unswerving focused devotion to her husband's people. She possessed a keen practical mind better for civil government than that of Ramses.

What qualities of Mary did she bring?

High intelligence, linguistic ability, compassion, feminism. Nefertari was instinctively regal, and this was a core issue in their marriage. She often had to hold back the answers to questions or problems and feed them to her husband at the right time. There was one other ability that Nefertari possessed: Mary's love of archery.

Haven't we seen that already in the life of Arjuna?

Nefertari was of the High Priestess line, the same as Arjuna!

What was her spiritual challenge?

Dealing with jealousy. The man she adored did not regard faithfulness as a requirement for the role of husband. Nefertari had to live with other wives and concubines, and Ramses would, across his lifetime, have more than 150 children. She would have to deal with her jealousy and grief. Nefertari was proud, and his neglect poisoned her love for him, until it turned to dislike. She had to explore loyalty and faithfulness and learn not to expect her moral standards from anyone else, however much she loved them.

Why does Nefertari disappear from royal life?

Kephor kidnapped and murdered her. They wanted to oust Ramses, who favored the advice of educated commoners over his nobles. Kephor hoped to persuade Ramses to listen to the nobles, and they held Nefertari as ransom. Unfortunately, Ramses lopped off the heads of the nobles in a rage, provoking the kidnappers further. For 15 days, she was held. It was a terrifying experience, and Ramses was almost driven insane. When he wouldn't give in, Nefertari was strangled by her kidnappers, her body discovered eight hours later, dumped in a poor and blameless man's house in Memphis. Ramses ordered that his whole Academy of Artists was to do nothing but furnishings for her tomb.

Everybody knew the chamberlain was both the co-conspirator and the mastermind of the kidnapping, but there was no public trial, no execution. Ramses had the kidnappers bricked alive into the bottom of a pyramid. Publicly, he said the queen had been poisoned. He could not admit the truth, since it would undermine his royal authority. Ramses speedily took himself off to war. Later Nefertari's beautiful tomb would be broken into by robbers and her mummy stolen, abandoned, and now irretrievably lost.

Ultimately, Nefertari accomplished the subtle management of royal policy and was a tremendous influence on Ramses. His statecraft deteriorated after her death.

Thinking about These Lives

Imhotep, the quiet achiever, gives his name to one of the most remarkable lives of St. Germain. In contrast to St. Germain's usual persona of front-line, larger-than-life characters, Imhotep, and those who share the energy of the Imhotep line, are no-frills, nose-to-the-grindstone, dependable men like Captain James Cook or US President Harry Truman. Explorers, navigators, scientists, architects, doctors, politicians, lawyers, physicians, presidents, philosophers, and warriors—they are always meticulous, exact, and hardworking. They will deliver, like Imhotep himself, on the toughest missions, and his mission was to accelerate Egyptian civilization.

The **Imhotep** line is one of the lines of the vast energy called St. Germain. When all lines are taken together, they give us a picture of the embrace of contradictions within him. Let's divide his millions of lives into lines.

The first line of St. Germain is that of the *Comte de Saint-Germain*, the international diplomat—urbane, suave, charming, super intelligent, multilingual, the founder of nations. It has another dimension of this first line as well. I call it the Boaz line of upright, saintly, courageous men who also exercise power, but their incorruptibility can absolutely be relied on. They fight for reform, liberate the oppressed, and are some of the best orators ever created. Joseph of Arimathea, St. Patrick, and St. Columba are examples.

The second of his lines is the **Jacob the Trickster** line. Once again, it is a line of leadership but full of tricky charm, so if you invite him to your home for dinner, you had better count the silver before he leaves. This line not only invented the detective novel but also mastered the spy novel, creating both Sherlock Holmes and James Bond.

The **Dante** line captures St. Germain as this creature of romance. Here are his lives as poets, dramatists, writers, dreamers, diplomats, artists, actors, musicians, and dancers. Dante, formerly Homer, wrote a long love letter to his beloved Beatrix, formerly Nefertari, and as he did, he created the Italian language. Edward de Vere wrote a play about his love for Cleopatra.

The fifth line, the **Caesar** line, is called after the authoritarian Julius Caesar. Charming, graceful, courageous, very intelligent, and a manipulative, honey-tongued persuader, this line founds nations and empires, runs countries, and exercises extreme power by which these lives can become corrupted.

The sixth line is the **Musicians** line, made up solely of musicians. Music permeates St. Germain's creativity. I am often asked about the energies of the four Beatles. Two were Hilarion, one was a Kuthumi, and one was St. Germain. He was Krishna. He invented orchestral music. He created opera, and there is nothing he loves more than a Broadway musical. Have you enjoyed *Hamilton* yet?

Are there more? Possibly. St. Germain sometimes created a hybrid by combining two of his lines for a special impact and purpose. He did this to create the genius Benjamin Franklin, combining the talents of the Imhotep line, shown in his inventions, with the clever wit, wisdom, and trickery of the Jacob line.

The powerful Egyptian queens of this chapter, Nefertiti and Nefertari, are from different lines of Mary. There are only three lines of Mary energy, not five like St. Germain. They are the **Mary the Mother**, **Mary the Magdalene**, and **Mary the High Priestess** lines.

Nefertiti was the only being I ever studied in whom all three aspects of Mary were integrated into one person. Why only three? The Gatekeeper claims Mary is better organized and integrated than St. Germain. Those who share her spiritual DNA tend to be reticent, nurturing, feminist, and intelligent. They are brilliant doctors, writers, and poets.

St. Germain seldom incarnates as a woman, but when he does, he creates those who make your blood race: they are courtesans, actresses, promoters, dancers, and film stars like Katherine Hepburn or Lady Hamilton. Mary frequently incarnates as a man so that she can experience the creative surge and dynamism of the male yang energy. We saw this in Arjuna. Later, she will create an existence as the Romantic poet Percy Shelley, because at that time, as a woman, she could not explore all her capabilities and be taken seriously by St. Germain, who was enjoying life as the incarnation Lord Byron.

Nefertiti and Nefertari shared beauty, dignity, and intelligence. They married strong and unusual men, and both shared the same fate: assassination. History is silent regarding their deaths. Their mummified bodies were never recovered, and their deaths hidden with the agreement of their grieving husbands. In both these lives, Mary only partly achieved her purpose. Nefertiti and her husband failed to establish monotheism as the state religion in Egypt, while Nefertari did not create the opportunities for women as she had hoped. Neither of them experienced marital fidelity. Homer's promise of writing a poetic song for Nefertari would take 3,000 years to be delivered as *The Divine Comedy*, but his promise would be kept.

Also, in this chapter, we stumble across the shadowy White Order. All three of the characters were members. Understanding The White Brotherhood will be a critical objective in *Our Spiritual DNA*. It holds the key to the foundation of Judaism, Christianity, and the Knights Templar, and hides many secrets.

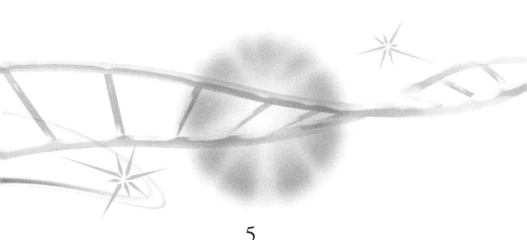

5

THE FOUNDING OF THE BELIEF IN GOD

The Gatekeeper shares the amazing story of humankind.

Humankind is God's big gamble, and if we fail the Dark wins, setting back the establishment of the Kingdom of Light on Earth; so, a different approach was planned—a covenant between God and a chosen people. It was an astonishing idea and a deal: if you do this for Me, I'll do this for you.

God, in a vision, tells Abraham, the first patriarch, "You are to be the center of a monotheistic religion that will not allow injustice or war to hinder human progress. Your seeds will become the universal priesthood, a light to the world, and demonstrate the grace of the Creator. You are to worship me, your Lord God, and only me. You will obey me, and I will give you protection. I will protect you in peace and war, and you will never be conquered or enslaved. The children of Israel are to be an example to all men and women. At the end of our Covenant, I will send you My Son, and under the new Covenant, you will be the new nobility of the world." The Jewish side of this Covenant didn't work well, and they lapsed many times.

Why did they lapse?

The Powers of Darkness sowed discord to prevent the Covenant from happening. God's people strayed from the straight and narrow. Whenever they did, God removed or lifted the protection of the Covenant.

So why did God choose the Jews?

The land of Israel, like every other country on Earth, has three governing energies. All of them are Master energies. In Israel, they are El Morya, Kuthumi, and Lord Sananda. Israel is the only country where Lord Sananda governs. He selected the Jews because they are energetically at the center of the world for the reasons I previously explained. They were set apart to stop the Word of God becoming dissolved.

Mary and St. Germain play significant roles in the foundation of monotheism, and this will be the focus of this chapter.

She [Mary] must perfect her humanity over several complicated lives. She is preparing to be the mother of the Son of God, as promised in the Covenant, so she incarnates as Sarah, the wife of the unstable patriarch, Abraham. It is a difficult life but a vital and foundational one. Mary also experiences a life of drudgery and neglect as the unloved but fertile wife of Jacob; however, her life, as the beautiful Rachel, an aspect of Mary the Magdalene, balances these harder existences, preparing her to be the mother of Jeshua ben Joseph, or Jesus.

St. Germain's energy will be foundational. He will begin nations, discover breakthrough technologies, and work with other Masters to birth new laws, constitutions, and approaches. St. Germain takes on tough assignments and delivers results. In the Old Testament, the lives of Jacob, the father of Israel, and Jacob's son Benjamin, the forefather of the warrior tribe the Benjaminites, are both St. Germain energies. He is also Aaron, who established with Moses the priesthood, which governed and gave structure to Jewish religious life. However, his first significant life during this period was that of Noah. St. Germain's existence as Noah is substantial, for his outstanding technical skill improving the capabilities of grains and pulses and of all breeds of sheep and goats. We have already met him as the meticulous genius Imhotep, and who could be better to build an ark?

Noah (7th–6th Century BC), Builder of the Ark

As a first-grader, upon hearing Noah's story of rescuing the birds, animals, and family from a worldwide flood, I had one question: "Did Noah come to Australia to save the wombats and the kangaroos?"

The bewildered nun replied: "When you're working with God, He moves in mysterious ways, and there is nothing too hard for Him."

I later worked out that the kangaroos missed the boat!

No Biblical story delights children more than the story of Noah.

Noah, the hero of the Great Flood (Genesis: 6–8), was the ninth patriarch, the grandson of Methuselah. His father named him Noah, which means "rest" or "relief." By the time he was 500 years old, according to the Bible, Noah had three sons. Although God was displeased with the wickedness on Earth, he was pleased with Noah's goodness. He had no faults.

God warned Noah that He intended to destroy all humankind, animals, and birds in a great flood, so Noah built an ark, the largest boat ever constructed in antiquity until the 19th century. At the end of 40 days, Noah released a raven, then a dove, to see whether the water had subsided. When the dove returned with an olive twig in its mouth, Noah knew that his ordeal was over, and he gave thanks to God. A rainbow spread across the clouds as a sign that God would not destroy all life by flood again.

☀ Conversation with The Gatekeeper ☀

Is there any historical truth in the story of Noah's flood?

> Yes. There was a catastrophic flood around 7,000 BC. The Biblical flood story was limited to the Rift Valley of the Tigris and Euphrates. It included Northern and Eastern Turkey, Iraq, Kurdistan, and down to the border of Palestine and the whole Mediterranean basin. The Biblical Noah was called Nuah, and the Jews borrowed the Nuah story from the Babylonians. They heard the story and loved it. "Genesis" and the Sumerian epics about Utnapishtim describe the same flood.

Why did the flood occur?

> The flood was triggered by an earthquake and massive subsidence of the Rift Valley. The huge deluge that followed spread nutrient-rich mud and helped create the fertile crescent of the Middle East. It was, as now, the end of a climatic period.

Who exactly was Noah?

> Noah was exceptional—a keen agronomist, a mathematician, a bit of a Renaissance Man. We've already met him as Imhotep. He didn't knock the ark together in his driveway; rather, he employed boat builders from Nineveh, near the Caspian Sea, and Tyre and

Sidon, near the Black Sea, to construct his massive ship. It took two years. Noah was exact in his measurements. His expertise reading portents in astrology and astronomy and the increasing gaps in the dense cloud cover across Sumeria, increasing earth tremors and volcanic eruptions, led Noah to believe a catastrophic weather event was coming. God did not speak to Noah directly; instead, He used geothermal signs He knew Noah could interpret. God did not send the flood as the Bible claims. The forces of nature are neutral; there was no supernatural reason. The people rationalized the disaster as punishment in the aftermath.

Immediately after the rains, Noah quickly tilled the soil and planted crops to feed his family. He grazed his animals and built crude shelters and carts. To return to Sumeria, 1,000 kilometres away, would take him several years. Settlements were sparse because the death list was more than three million. He wasn't the only escapee, but he was the best organized to re-establish his livelihood. Noah was a good businessman, and after the recovery, as well as being a successful farmer, he became a banker sending huge deposits of gold and silver on guarded caravans to Greece. As a farmer, he used selective breeding stock to produce improved progeny. He bred bigger, fatter beasts that were strong for plowing. He improved the yield of his grain and saved the best strains of barley, wheat, rice, peas, lentils, and green beans to create dried beans for vegetable protein.

Did he live for 950 years as the Bible states?

He did live to be well over a hundred. Giving a long life to their patriarchs was a way of deifying Jewish heroes.

What did Noah bring into his incarnation from St. Germain?

He brought in his love of order as a codifier of information. He brought in observation skills, from which he drew deductions and conclusions. Noah would be the first to observe the simple repetitive pattern in genetics. He brought in St. Germain's trading and merchant abilities; Noah understood intuitively the possibility of trading his surplus of grain to achieve what he desired but didn't grow. He brought in his courage, strong libido, inventiveness, and love of a beaker of red.

Why did he have to incarnate?

Noah was to be the father of agronomy and animal husbandry. His contributions would lead to the establishment of the first urban civilizations. He was to be the progenitor of the next step to civilization, allowing humans to live in settled environments and develop a complex structure of tabular law needed in civilized societies.

Sarah (15th–14th Century BC), Wife of Abraham

Sarah was the barren wife of the Biblical patriarch Abraham, who, after God's intervention, became at 90, the mother of Isaac. Born in Mesopotamia, today's Northern Iraq, Sarah may have been her husband's niece or even his half-sister. Twice, it seems she was sold or traded by Abraham as a wife to powerful rulers.

Sarah was infertile, and knowing this, she gave her serving maid or slave Hagar to Abraham, who fathered Ishmael with her. Ishmael was, reputedly, the father of all Arabs.

The birth of Isaac was promised by God and predicted by three strangers who visited Abraham and Sarah's tent. Sarah, at 90, laughed at the possibility of becoming pregnant. Sarah died in Hebron at age 127. Her grave is in the cave of Machpelah, the second most holy site for the Jewish people.

※ Conversation with The Gatekeeper ※

Sarah seems to have had a tough life. Abraham was a disrespectful, calculating, and self-absorbed husband, who passed Sarah off as his sister, which she probably was, and sold her, for a barnyard full of animals, to a pharaoh as a concubine. Why did she choose this life?

Sarah's is the energy of Miriam or Mary, the mother of Jeshua. In this life, she is the half-sister of Abraham, a man you, understandably, don't seem to like much. Abraham is the first historical king in the Torah; and he didn't like independence in women. The Hebrew word for "wife" would eventually mean "property."

Did Abraham punish Sarah for her independence by selling her to a pharaoh?

It was her path to sanctity. God had her in training to be the mother of His Son. Great plagues swept through Egypt, destroying the animal stocks and the wealth of the people. The first sickness to descend on Egypt coincided with Sarah joining the pharaoh's harem, and he thought that Abraham's flocks carried the plague into his country. Sarah was blamed, and he nearly had her put to death until Abraham intervened, offering to take her back.

He was such an obliging bloke!

[My sense of grievance ended that discussion with The Gatekeeper, and it would be some years before I returned to the subject of Sarah. When I finally did, I asked if Mary could be present. I wanted to drop my bias against Abraham and capture Mary's assessment of one of her most challenging lives.]

Did Abraham love Sarah?

Although Abraham loved her before he traded her to the Pharaoh, Sarah did exasperate him, because she wouldn't be submissive. He couldn't win an argument with her, and she didn't want his children because she didn't trust him. Abraham had a madness about him; he had schizophrenia and his grip on reality was not firm. So, she used a natural contraceptive, a root used in the Middle East.

What was it?

A plant called pennyroyal. She made a tincture by boiling the root for long hours until, when concentrated to one-tenth of its original volume, she added alcohol spirit made from the lees [dregs] of wine to preserve it. She took it continuously. It's also an abortifacient, able to abort a fetus up to three months.

I will now return to my narrative. Sarah was furious to be sold as a concubine.

Why did she go back to Abraham?

She loved him deeply. She was independent, liberated, and a woman whose spirit was unbroken by her experiences.

Did Abraham put her aside because she had been with the pharaoh?

Being a queen of Egypt made her more desirable. She was an outstanding beauty: tall, five feet six or seven, with fair skin, dark black hair, aquiline features, light gray eyes, and white teeth. Her hands were long and graceful. Sarah loved music—she sang and was a mesmerizing dancer. She was brilliant and far brighter than Abraham, with a native intelligence unschooled in writing and reading. Sarah had a screamer of a temper, and when she let fly, everyone scattered. Abraham, well, he was wary of her.

The Bible is quite clear in saying Sarah could not conceive. Was Sarah infertile?

She controlled her fertility, but she was not infertile. An enormous maternal urge overcame her, and even though she was in a stuttering menopause she became pregnant with Isaac.

How did she react to Abraham's attempt to sacrifice Isaac?

Abraham was mentally ill, and his decision to sacrifice Isaac was during a phase of maniacal obedience to God. If God had told him to cut his own throat, he would have done it. Sarah, on the other hand, was against the Judaic practice of sacrifice. When Abraham took Isaac, Sarah was furious. She took a ram and anxiously followed Abraham as he prepared to kill Isaac. Sarah pricked the ram with a thorn to make it bleat. That was enough to distract Abraham, who believed it was God, who had sent the ram to him.

And this was the man whom God chose to represent the Jews when he formed a covenant with them!

Perhaps God has a different idea of his real worth than you!

How did Sarah react when Abraham told her about this Covenant with God?

She knew it meant trouble, and it convinced her of her husband's continuing mental instability.

Did Sarah have any particular accomplishments?

Staying married to Abraham was definitely one of them, along with raising her son, Isaac. She raised the standard of these wandering flock Masters and started their march to settlement.

Why did Mary choose to incarnate as Sarah?

To experience a life of unbelievable abuse regardless of the social mores of the time. Abraham's sale of Sarah to a pharaoh to gain his favor is appalling, and the greatest betrayal. And Abraham didn't do it once; he did it twice!

What qualities of Mary did she bring into this incarnation?

Her beauty, amazing endurance, and almost indestructible nature. Sarah ruled his household and his followers' households with a rod of iron in a velvet glove. She brought in Mary's capability, her intelligence, her feminism, her love of music. Sarah also possessed Mary's skills as an herbalist, and she also loved gardens and plants.

What was her life's purpose?

Largely to found Middle East culture and civilization. Sarah made Abraham's mission to start the Canaanites, Midianites, Syrians, and Armalites possible. She passed along her culture, values, and ideas about civilization to all the young females who passed the same traditions along to their families.

Sarah's treatment of Abraham's concubine, Hagar, the mother of Ishmael, comes across as vengeful jealousy when she maneuvers to have her cast out of their tent.

Sarah is revealing herself here, warts and all. Her defense of her son makes her so much more human. Abraham believed his two sons were equal, but Sarah refused to have a bastard sharing her son's inheritance. All Arabs are descended from Ishmael, Hagar's son with Abraham.

What was Sarah's spiritual challenge?

It was coping with Abraham's unblinking fanaticism. She opposed the brutal circumcision of children that gave rise to damaged penises and testicles. Whereas Abraham's God was vengeful; Sarah brought another perspective: one of kindness, love, and caring, all the yin values. Her gift to the Jewish people was her influence that led them to settle. Sarah wanted a house and changed Abraham's concept of wealth from the size of his flock to the size of his land. While it wouldn't change until Jacob's sons, the practice was set in motion by Sarah. And there was something else: Sarah gave to the Jewish people her argumentativeness.

Sarah, the Bible says, laughed when she found out she was pregnant!

And now you know why. She laughed when Abraham, ignorant of her control of her fertility, attributed her conception to God. This is the first example we see of Mary's feminism. She laughs on making a point!

Now, we've seen her as Maya, Buddha's mother, and there are more lives to explore—Leah, for example, long before she returns as Mary, Jeshua's mother.

Jacob (c. 1600–1540 BC), Founder of Israel

Jacob, an aspect of St. Germain, was the third Biblical patriarch after his grandfather, Abraham, and his father, Isaac. The second of twins, born minutes after his brother Esau, Jacob tricked his father into giving him his blessing and, therefore, an inheritance that should have gone to his older brother. Despite his doubts, Isaac blessed him and, in doing so, gave him the rank of eldest child in the family, a double portion of the inheritance, and the priestly office of the family. His irate brother denounced his trickery and vowed to revenge himself after his father's death.

Jacob fled immediately into Northern Mesopotamia, to his uncle Laban's house. He had two daughters, and there, Rebecca hoped her son would find a wife. On his journey, he had a strange dream of angels ascending and descending a heavenly ladder, where God spoke to him and blessed him.

On reaching his mother's birthplace, he was captivated by the beauty of his cousin Rachel. Laban told him he could marry Rachel on the condition he worked for him for seven years. Genesis (29:20) says that the seven years seemed to him "but a few days, such was the love he had of her."

Jacob finally married Rachel. Or he thought he did! In the morning light, he realized that he had been tricked into marrying her elder sister, Leah. Leah was described as "tender eyed," which could imply she was either plain or had weak eyesight. When Jacob protested, Laban claimed that the older sister had to marry first, but he would allow Jacob to marry Rachel if he agreed to another seven years of servitude. Jacob eventually married Rachel.

Leah bore Jacob four sons in four years—Rueben, Simeon, Levi, and Judah—and after every son, she prayed for her husband to love her. Unfortunately, Jacob's indifference continued unabated. Rachel envied her sister's fertility and offered her serving maid Bilpah to Jacob so that she could claim Bilpah's offspring, Gad and Asher, as her own. Leah conceived another two sons, Issachar, and Zebulun, and one daughter, Dinah.

Finally, Rachel gave birth to a son, Joseph. Jacob decided to return to Israel and brokered a new deal with Laban to leave with his wages in sheep and goats. A mysterious being appeared to Jacob in his prayers, he wrestled with him until dawn. When Jacob asked for his blessing, the being said that Jacob would now be called "Israel," meaning "one who has struggled with God."

Rachel would die giving birth to her second son, Benjamin, Jacob's 12th son. Benjamin was overshadowed by the radiance of his older brother, Joseph, and the love Jacob had for him. Leah's sons were also jealous of their father's love for Joseph, and, feeling alienated by Jacob's neglect, sold Joseph into slavery in Egypt. Eventually, a drought would draw Jacob's sons to Egypt, where, the Bible says, Jacob was reunited with his son Joseph, now the vizier.

Both Jacob and his son Benjamin are from the talented trickster line of St. Germain while Mary herself incarnated as Leah. Another aspect of Mary the Magdalene incarnated as Rachel. Lord Sananda incarnated as Joseph.

⁕ Conversation with The Gatekeeper ⁕

Jacob was nicknamed Yaakov once his personality emerged. His mother, Rebecca, saw him as a deceiver and a thief. A good St. Germain name!

Later God called him Israel.

On his way to Mesopotamia, Jacob had a vision that we call Jacob's Ladder. Can you tell me about his vision of ascending and descending angels going to heaven?

It was a dream vision. What he saw was the Hindu wheel of incarnation and reincarnation, which, if you had the same vision, you would say, "I dreamt of the double helix in hologrammatic form, but on the lines of DNA I saw people." Jacob translated what he saw into a ladder or a stairway reaching from heaven to earth, and while familiar with a wheel, he had never seen a double helix.

Did he see his future lives on the double helix? God supposedly also spoke to Jacob, telling him that He would give him numerous offspring and land equal to today's Israel.

God said nothing; instead, He put into Jacob's mind that he was the heir to Abraham, which meant he had an important part to play in the founding of a nation.

But was God commissioning St. Germain's energy as a pioneer or founder?

He was merely endorsing his latent characteristics.

Then why show him the Wheel of Life? How was that relevant to his commissioning?

How do you rehabilitate a villain? You rehabilitate him with a vision of something greater than himself, and you show his relevance to the vision. It was God's first step in teaching Jacob his future task. Up until then, Jacob's most profound thought had been, What's in it for me? The Wheel of Life is about transformation: to transform into a new being and be reborn as "Israel," a chosen man to lead a chosen people. At its foundation, the Torah is about justice, and Jacob would learn about justice and be "transformed" in the process. God expected Jacob to become the man the Creator knew he was and fulfil his task.

When Jacob reaches Mesopotamia, he sees the beautiful Rachel with a flock of sheep at a well. When she looked up from that well, what did she see?

A tall 23-year-old man, with dark curly hair, a thin beard, and a double-decker smile of beautiful teeth. Jacob had rugged features, a hawk nose, broad shoulders, and a lean, strong body. Rachel saw an impressive commanding presence.

And what did Jacob see?

A stunning young woman, voluptuous and tall, with blue-black hair, heavy brows, and long lashes. She had an olive complexion, sumptuous lips, firm jaw, and the most brilliant blue eyes. She was 18 years old. It was love at first sight for Jacob, and he rushed to meet her father. When Jacob asked to marry Rachel, Laban laughed. He was saving her for a prince, and she had a bride price. Jacob possessed only a few flocks of sheep and goats, and Laban made Jacob pay a high price for his love. Rachel loved Jacob at first sight, and her consent was spoken in her smiling eyes and otherwise, in the alchemical way of people in love. This is the first time we meet Mary the Magdalene.

Leah was fertile with Jacob, while Rachel was not. Why did it take Rachel so long to conceive?

Rachel had a sparse quality of eggs at ovulation and needed time to prepare herself for the reception of Lord Sananda as Joseph, although not with his Divine self; Rachel had to create the energetic stability to hold him. She was a beautiful, spoiled brat, and her energy needed to adjust, and that took time. Rachel was 27 when Joseph was born. Jacob was 35 when Benjamin came, about 10 years later.

How did Jacob assess the capabilities of Rachel's sons?

Joseph was not a farmer; he didn't like getting dirty, mucking out animal enclosures, or castrating sheep. Jacob thought Joseph was a failure. He did not know how to assess his son's high intelligence, facility for languages, reading, and writing. Joseph was Jacob's opposite, not only intellectually but physically. Joseph was pale-skinned, short, thin, beautiful, with humorous, gray eyes and the long thin hands of a scribe. And yet, Jacob loved his first son so much he ached when Joseph smiled at him.

On the other hand, Benjamin was more like Jacob, being from the same line of St. Germain. Benjamin was the charm of his life—a pretty young boy with bright blackberry eyes. Jacob adored him, too, while Benjamin lovingly crawled after his brother, Joseph, like a shadow. Jacob gave Joseph the famous cloak of many colors as a promise of his inheritance over his other male heirs. This gift set a series of tragedies in motion. Jacob should have given him the ring, too, because his brothers saw the cloak as a sign of inheritance not set-in concrete.

After being sold into slavery, Joseph became a special advisor to a Hysok king of Upper Egypt, the man who carried the pharaoh's seal. It was a meteoric rise.

Joseph asked for his younger brother, Benjamin, to be sent to him as an assurity of their commitment to Egypt. The brothers begged him to take one of them as hostage and leave their father his favorite son. Joseph, however, insisted on Benjamin and asked to see his father, Jacob. Jacob never came. He was 68 by then, and ill. His shamefaced brothers were afraid of Joseph, thinking he would manacle them as slaves. What they experienced instead was his loving forgiveness. Joseph triumphed over them all.

Was Lord Sananda's life as Joseph a practice run for his life as Jeshua ben Joseph?

Lord Sananda was also Isaiah, Buddha, Elijah, and Elisha, long before he was Jeshua. He would never desert his people. Everyone must obey the principles God has prescribed for incarnations on this Earth, and that includes Joseph. While the Master side of his divinity was perfect, he still had to perfect his humanity by removing, through his experiences, any flaws, just the same as we have to.

Returning to Jacob, what characteristics of St. Germain did he inherit?

Jacob had St. Germain's crafty trickster traits. An above average intelligence, he was innovative, bred animals, and built loyal teams to work with him. He had that start-up ability, founding Israel and establishing dynasties. Jacob was courageous, self-confident, and a leader, taking command easily with his plausible, convincing tongue and his charming and ruthless opportunism. He was simply a remarkable man; if he were any tougher, he would have rusted.

What was his life purpose?

The establishment of Judaism and Israel as a settled people rather than a tribe of wandering Bedouins. He achieved his life purpose.

What about his spiritual challenge?

To establish the Judaic tradition of wrestling with God.

Did Jacob actually wrestle with God?

Jacob was thrown to the ground by a force that broke his hip and left him lame, permanently in pain, and walking with a limp. Jacob became a symbol of all who have wrestled with God to discover their faith. At God's suggestion, he changed his name to Isra El, meaning "struggled with God." And so, St. Germain gave his name to the nation of Israel, as he did to many other countries, like Britain, America, and China.

What triggered this wrestle?

Jacob was performing what would become the age-old right of every Jew to argue with God. Everyone resists change in themselves; it's uncomfortable. The Creator forced Jacob to look at his problem behavior and how it prevented him from delivering his task. He was, as his Jacob name proclaims, a cheat and a conman, and he had to stop that behavior and open himself up to wisdom. He was a prisoner of habit, looking at every opportunity as an excuse to do somebody out of something.

From that point on, what did God expect of Jacob?

Newly named Israel, he became recognized as the living embodiment of wisdom and justice and taught those qualities to his people. Before he died, Jacob determined there would be 12 tribes in Israel, and was influenced to select 12 by his reading of the Kabala. The Kabala is the world's oldest, single, continuous, symbolic system. In it, there are 12 branches of the Tree of Life. His 12 reinforced an energy continuum: 12 houses of the solar system, 12 tribes, 12 men needed to establish a temple, 12 apostles, 12 knights of the Round Table, 12 members of a jury, and…

And the 12 Master energies for our spiritual DNA?

Jacob's greatest achievement was the establishment of Israel and a tribal structure that gave his descendants a welded identity as the children of Israel. He made great advances in selective breeding and farming, and established granaries for his surplus seed and silages for leaner years.

Leah (c. 1585–1535 BC), Wife of Jacob

※ Conversation with The Gatekeeper ※

In the novel, *The Red Tent*, Leah is described as tall, strong, and with vibrant eyes of different colors, one blue, and one green. She is blessed with full, high, shapely breasts and muscular calves. Does this describe her correctly?

She was the exact opposite, although I'll grant you, Leah was tall with a small, squarish face and clear sallow skin. She had poor posture and was nearsighted, with crooked teeth. Leah had no illusions about herself and had known since she was a small,

neglected child that she was a plain woman. Her pretty sister, Rachel, tormented her, and because Leah wasn't strong enough to be a shepherd, Rachel had to take care of the sheep.
Leah was Cinderella, running the household, cleaning, and grinding grain. According to custom, as the eldest, she had to be married first. As you know, Laban entered into a contract with Jacob only to hoodwink him. Jacob did not treat Leah well, even though she was sweet-natured, hardworking, and wanted desperately to please him. Leah's sons belittled her authority because they knew they would get away with disobeying her, while they encouraged their half-brothers to make fun of her. Jacob was tricked into marriage with Leah, an unforgivable treachery on Laban's part, both to her and him. He just wanted to get rid of Leah as fast as he could.

Why did Mary have to incarnate as Leah?

To learn to be ugly and short-sighted after her beauty as Sarah, and help Jacob achieve his mission. Once that ugly was enough!

What characteristics of Mary did Leah bring in?

Patience, kindness, compassion, boundless love, incredible loyalty, and Mary's capacity to see it through to the death: perseverance. Leah demonstrated that you could be strong without being aggressive.

What was her life's purpose?

It was to found, with Jacob, a dynasty. Leah's life was one of the most remarkable in the Bible. Betrayed by her father, despised by her husband, hated by her sister, rejected by her children, no-one was ever on Leah's side. Nobody. Ever! And yet, she unswervingly displayed all her beautiful inner qualities.

What was her spiritual challenge?

Leah's was a hard life, and her spiritual challenge was coping with a poor self-image, as an unlovable human being who did not have the authority a first wife should have. Despite all the put-downs, Leah remained humble, with a burning faith in God, and a loving wife to a neglectful and emotionally brutal husband.

What was her greatest achievement?

> Leah's triumph over all those circumstances makes her the mother
> of all those wives who suffer unfairness, neglect, abuse, and lack
> of love. She was a woman of great virtue. While it would've been
> easy to lapse into resentment, seek out revenge, or mistreat other
> women's children or handmaidens, instead of being destructive,
> Leah was a cohesive force. Mary acknowledges this as a life of
> spiritual triumph.

Thinking about These Lives

Each of these lives contributed to the founding of the belief in one God and
did so in remarkably different ways. It was a time of climate change, when
events that are typically rhythmical and renewing become catastrophic. The
deluge between 7000 and 6,500 BC, inundating the Rift Valley of modern-
day Iraq and spreading to surrounding countries, was devastating. It destroyed
the old and allowed the new to flourish into a fertile crescent.

Noah's role was not to preserve the biodiversity of the planet, or even of his
region, but precisely the reverse, to select and protect the best breeding stock
of recently domesticated farm animals and save the best strains of wheat and
barley. Noah was also to preserve his biological seed from his nine wives and
his son's nine wives, ready to become the distant ancestors in Mesopotamia of
Krishna and Arjuna, Abraham and Sarah, Jacob and Leah, and Benjamin and
Joseph.

The Noah of the Biblical account is a moral figure; the Nuah of The
Gatekeeper's account is far from it, without the unifying moral context of the
Biblical text. The Gatekeeper's account describes a purely physical universe,
and the moral universe, which he says was superimposed later, is absent. The
beginning of Western civilization would have been set back thousands of years
without Noah. His reconfiguring of his animals, plants, and seeds, influenced
a significant transformation of society.

Five thousand years later, Abraham was a wandering herdsman, and Sarah's
role was to restart the unifying process. These were the three sources of spiritual input in their lives: the first was the voice of God, heard only by Abraham;
the second was the mysterious Zarathustrianism priest Melchizedek, who
inspired Sarah; the third was the relatively weak influence of the Egyptian
culture and religion.

The spiritual message in Mary's life as Sarah was "endurance." She persevered with good grace for 75 years in an abusive, emotionally violent mar-

riage, living the injustices of being a married woman who twice was offered up as a concubine; yet, she could still laugh and enjoy life. She learned to forgive the unforgivable because God has already forgiven the inexcusable.

In her next life as Leah, she was hated but loved anyway. Rejected by her parents, her sister, her husband, and her sons, her status as the first wife of Jacob was never acknowledged. Although she patiently asked God for Jacob to love her, she was punished for her father's treachery; Jacob, named the deceiver, was, in fact, the one who was deceived—first by Rachel's bewitching beauty, then by Laban into marrying Leah, and finally by his blindness in not realizing Leah's true worth.

Leah's descendants are the luminaries of the Bible. They are her son, Judah, after whom the Jews were called; Levi, from whom all priests are descended, including Moses, Aaron, and David; Mary's uncle, Joseph of Arimathea; John the Baptist; the apostles Peter, Joseph, and Barnabas; and finally, Jeshua ben Joseph. All descend from her.

And then there is Jacob! God's choice of patriarchs is interesting. They are tough herdsmen, rugged individualists, sharp dealers, and enterprising men, who travel on foot thousands of miles throughout their lifetimes, walking from Iraq to Egypt, and back again.

Jacob's role was to create a new nation, and to do that he needed vision, leadership, self-confidence, and unbelievable physical and emotional toughness. He possessed all those qualities in abundance. While he lacked faith in God, he had copious amounts of guile. Despite being tricked three times, Jacob did not change his behavior. In a long night of tussling, he wrestled with God, and God won. Jacob acquiesced. Physically wounded, he acknowledged God's might and greeted his new name "Israel" with humility, finally acknowledging that wisdom and justice worked.

St. Germain's role as Jacob is the second example of a life-fathering Lord Sananda (his first being the Buddha.) He will eventually incarnate as his father a third time, to Jeshua ben Joseph, or Jesus.

Although we cannot access the problematic lives of Jacob before this significant incarnation, we can observe Mary's trials as she prepares for her most momentous life. As lives follow one another, the progress does not seem to be an even trajectory upward; instead, it appears to be a slow movement through dramatic setbacks and a tedious marking of time, interrupted by the occasional life of unbelievable challenge.

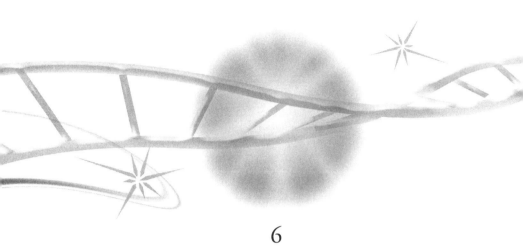

6

WARRIORS, HIGH PRIESTS, AND PROPHETS

When St. Germain and Mary incarnated as the early Jewish leaders, the purpose of their lives was to wander through the Middle East region of the world. They would eventually liberate, invade, and conquer, and establish their lineage in those lands. They were charismatic heroes and prophets who acted as the mouthpieces of God: Aaron, Joshua, and Deborah, the leaders of the Israelites, the priests, warriors, and judges.

The Jews had been in Egypt since the time of Jacob. His sons had migrated there in order to escape a fierce drought and had been held in servitude ever since. It was time to free them—time for St. Germain to step forward.

The Magician and High Priest would take the stage to create the political climate to force the pharaoh to release the Hebrews. Moses, the adopted son of the pharaoh, emerged as their stuttering leader, but it was his brother, Aaron, who conducted the difficult negotiations with the pharaoh, striking fear and surprise with his magic, predicting the Egyptian plagues, and performing the miracles until, finally, the Jews were freed.

St. Germain returns as Joshua, the take-no-prisoners-warrior, to conquer Jericho. Later Mary, in her Magdalene aspect, would return to fulfill her life as the judge, poet, and warrior Deborah, in one of her most impactful lives.

Aaron, First High Priest of Israel

Moses, Aaron, and Miriam led the Israelites out of Egypt and into 40 years of wandering before entering the Promised Land, as described in four books in the Bible: Exodus, Leviticus, Numbers, and Deuteronomy.

Aaron was Moses's older brother and had been born three years before the pharaoh ordered his soldiers to drown all Hebrew male babies. Historically Aaron has received a lot of lousy press, especially from Christian writers who point to one incident in his life for their judgment: Aaron is said to have aided the creation of a false god, the Golden Calf, an aspect of the god Baal.

This was considered treacherous, and for his sin, we are told that Aaron would die like Moses without entering the Promised Land and be buried with his sister Miriam at the edge of the desert. Moses stuttered and lacked Aaron's eloquence, so Aaron became Moses's spokesperson and served as mediator between the prophet, God, and his people. He was Moses's confidant and advisor, playing a role similar to his role as Merlin to King Arthur. Aaron is an example of the Comte de St. Germain's line of St. Germain, whom we have seen before as Krishna.

⁕ Conversation with The Gatekeeper ⁕

Aaron is hidden behind the sin of the Golden Calf, making it hard for us to understand and know him. Can you tell us about him?

Christian accounts downplay Aaron as the "eminence grise," but he was the brains, administrator, and salesman of Operation: Exodus. Although Aaron and Moses were brothers born in Egypt, they didn't look alike. Aaron was medium height, handsome with a full mouth, sensual lips, even teeth, heavy eyebrows, blue-black hair, gray eyes, and fair skin.

Moses possessed a sense of destiny. Aaron was fated to be a second in command. Life for him was either black or white. He loved music, was flamboyant in his dress and jewellery, while Moses was more understated. Aaron carried a staff carved of African ebony, inlaid with ivory, set off with a gold tip in the form of a cobra. "Get a plain staff!" Moses advised. Aaron ignored him.

While close, their relationship was complex. Aaron understood his mother's guilt over abandoning Moses, when his life as her eldest born son was threatened. Aaron grew up believing that he was the eldest. On her death bed, she begged Aaron to find his older brother, but when they were finally reunited their cultural differences were obvious: Aaron, a Jew, and Moses, a 40-year-old Egyptian prince married to a Midian; however, they worked together effectively. Moses was a strong, running, leaping man, in contrast to Aaron's studious nature. Aaron used guile, not strength, to assert his authority.

Did Aaron train as a priest?

Aaron trained with The White Brotherhood and advanced in that order as a workaholic scribe fluent in hieroglyphics. He was also an accountant and lawyer, and though married, he was wedded to his work. He wrote two books of the Torah, Numbers and Leviticus, and the first draft of Exodus, which were attributed to Moses.

And Aaron was also a magician?

Aaron was a conjurer of simple illusion, both sleight of hand and actual magic, learned from the Nubian uncle of his wet nurse. He mastered hypnotism to an advanced level.

Could you describe Aaron's contest with the pharaoh's magicians and his predictions of the plagues?

It was time for the Hebrews to leave Egypt, where they had been bonded servants working as manual laborers, artisans, builders, and artists. It was the first diaspora of Jewish people. Although they were critical to the Egyptian economy, providing cheap skilled workers, the Egyptians were very afraid of their potential, culling them whenever they could. Moses had avoided being a victim. It was a dangerous climate for the Hebrews, and Aaron was their fearless advocate. He, along with Moses, courageously approached the pharaoh, demanding an audience.

The pharaoh knew the Hebrews wanted to leave Egypt. He knew Moses was the adopted son of his daughter and that Aaron, considered a secret priest and magician, was his brother. The pharaoh also possessed magicians, who planned to out-magic the brothers; however, Aaron learned of the pharaoh's plan from his Nubian bodyguards and prepared for the pharaoh's trickery.

Aaron filled his cloak and sleeves with many hidden objects and animals. When summoned, Aaron turned water into blood, drew jewels from the noses of dogs, and frogs from the mouths of court officials, using all St. Germain's trickery to outdo the pharaoh. Still, the Egyptian king was unimpressed, refusing the Hebrews their freedom.

The Hebrews then resorted to threats of plagues and disasters, prophesizing disaster after disaster, but the pharaoh just smiled and refused to let the people go until the arrival of the last plague. This disease was so virulent and horrific, it killed almost 100,000 children. It was similar to Ebola. The Hebrews were protected from it by dosing their children with hyssop and marking their doorposts with lamb's blood.

Aaron warned the pharaoh: "The Lord, our God, will take from you the firstborn of every family."

"Then," said the pharaoh, "it will strike yours also." But none of the Hebrew children died.

In 48 hours, as horrific an Act of God as was ever to occur killed the Egyptian children. Hatshepsut, overcome by distress and anger, hardened herself for what was ahead. She had loved Moses as her grandson. How could he slaughter her grandchildren? Now, the Egyptians couldn't get rid of the Hebrews quickly enough. Some Hebrews took advantage of their grief-stricken employers and demanded all their gold jewelry. After their release, Moses went away for 40 days to receive the Ten Commandments while the Hebrews wandered the Sinai Desert and Aaron commissioned the casting of the Golden Calf.

Why did Aaron do that?

The casting of the Golden Calf represents a weakness in Aaron, who couldn't resist an opportunity to show off. Some of the Hebrews came to him saying, "Aaron, our people want a golden calf. Why not give it to them? Unlike your brother, you understand what it is to be a real man."

What do you think was Aaron's greatest accomplishment?

Aaron found ways, through the manipulation of rules, to help Moses govern an ungovernable people. It was Aaron who laid the foundations of Judaism. He was their chief priest, and he managed an unruly rabble of 300,000 Jews with 600,000 opinions and got them to do as they were told.

Was that Aaron's gift to the Jewish people?

By his codification of the law, Aaron told them precisely what to do. He said: "This is the box. Move outside the box, and God will strike you dead. Do this, and you will be happy. Do that, and you will be unhappy." He created the People of the Law. Aaron dictated the books of the Torah, and the provenance is still there. Someday it will surface.

What was his life purpose?

To be Moses's mouthpiece, to act as spokesman for a brother who couldn't be understood. He achieved his purpose.

And his spiritual challenge?

Aaron would have to learn to curb his vanity. Pride was Aaron's vulnerability amplified in someone who played second fiddle to a dreaming king.

Gatekeeper, I've been to Sinai. I don't believe you could lose 200,000 people in the Sinai Desert for one year, let alone 40. There must be another story here.

There is. The Hebrews wandered in the wilderness for 23 years, not 40 years. Their journey wasn't the accident of poor navigation. Moses commanded it, to eradicate their fixed slave mentality, created after 200 years of captivity. Moses needed tough and strong Hebrews, bred from marrying into various tribes and the freedom of living off the land. The journey is more important than the destination. By wandering the Middle East, they reacquainted with their heritage and married into the Canaanites. The story of Exodus is mostly accurate, written at the time of the Babylonian captivity. Remember, herders don't keep good records!

Why was the Egyptian bondage of the Hebrews allowed?

They went to Egypt as shepherds and cattle traders; they left literate and numerate. They learned from the Egyptians medicine, law, use of memory, and especially Egyptian religion.

What did they bring from Egypt into Judaism?

They took God—originally called Amun, they renamed him Yahweh—and the concept of priests, with an ecclesiastical hierarchy from one tribe that oversaw their liturgy, religious places, and became responsible for their ethical governance. They took the membership of The White Order and from them, male circumcision. They took Egyptian knowledge of herbal medicine and surgery, which put them ahead of others in the Middle East. They also took architectural concepts like the temple, with its various courts echoed in Solomon's Temple and the idea of the Tabernacle, the portable temple, containing their holy scrolls.

There is also the notion of Satan, which originated with Set, the wicked brother of Osiris. Although Satan is not in the Bible, he exists in their oral tradition.

What was Aaron's next life?

He needed to balance his idolatry and eliminate that vanity. He incarnated to do that as Samuel, the last judge. But first, we return to Imhotep's reincarnation, as the man of iron Joshua, the commando, who leads the Hebrews into Israel.

Joshua, First Commander-in-Chief of Israel

Joshua, the first commander-in-chief of Israel, was the son of Nun and a member of the tribe of Ephraim. Born in Egypt, he was selected by Moses as chief of security. Joshua had shown promise in defeating the Amalekites, so Moses chose him again as his successor to guide the Israelites into the Promised Land, to conquer the country, dividing it among their 12 tribes. The sixth book of the Bible, describing the 200-year conquest of Canaan, is called after him. Joshua is remembered best for his first successful battle and spectacular siege of Jericho's fortress.

This life reintroduces the important Imhotep line, whose spiritual DNA St. Germain relies on for the toughest jobs on Earth.

✳ Conversation with The Gatekeeper ✳

Why did Moses anoint Joshua, not Aaron or one of his sons, as his successor?

Aaron, as we have seen, was a man of dubious judgment, shown in his creation of the idol Golden Calf. On the other hand, although not a relative, Joshua was his prime minister, his most able administrator. He was Aaron's most trusted advisor, who enforced and translated the law for Moses. He was a graceful swordsman, a brilliant engineer, and younger than Moses by 40 years, a stocky, nuggetty man, five foot six tall with a broad chest, strong arms, sturdy legs, iron-gray hair, and a neatly trimmed curly beard. He was simply the best, infinitely better than any of Moses's sons.

Moses sent Joshua into Canaan to spy, and what did he discover?

The Hebrews were still in Sinai when Joshua left via the Gaza Strip, striking out for Jaffa on the coast. He traveled alone, living off the land as an itinerant herdsman. Later, he would skirt the Negev Desert and, seeing a mountain at the end of a rift valley, knew it was perfect for a fort. Joshua became the first Hebrew to see the site of Jerusalem and was overwhelmed with its grandeur. Over the 22 months he was away, Joshua collected the intelligence Moses needed to plan his invasion of Canaan.

Is it true that the invasion began with the crossing of the flooded River Jordan?

The Israelites started crossing the river with the Ark of the Covenant ahead of them. When Joshua stood the Ark in the middle of the river, its gushing waters went down in a day. Joshua had already sent a party upstream to divert the Jordan into a tributary. Putting a floodgate in first to allow the Ark to advance, he then built floodgates into the tributary. When he opened the floodgates, the waters fell in the Jordan and created the miracle. Taking five days to cross, this allowed Joshua to increase his hold over his people. He emerged as a stronger, less contradictable leader and filled the power vacuum left when Moses died—a simple feat for a man who had designed and built a pyramid as Imhotep and designed an ark as Noah.

We know Joshua for his commanding role in Jericho's battle, when the walls of the city came tumbling down. Joshua claimed God spoke to him. Is that what happened?

No, the battle plan was his inspiration. Joshua copied Moses: to ensure his arguments were accepted, he claimed they were God-inspired. Looked at another way, they *were* God-inspired: Joshua's governing energy was St. Germain, and through his prayer and contemplation, St. Germain, Joshua's higher self, inspired him.

Why were his soldiers told to circle the city for six days with priests blowing ram's horns?

Joshua's strategy was to make the army of Israelites seem bigger than it was to destroy any hope of resistance. It was not an organized procession. The men came and went, creating the impression of a huge army. The horns were war trumpets, sending the message "We're bigger than you." It was psychological warfare. Joshua's strategy created panic inside the city walls. Men buried their daughters to save them from rape and capture.

When the assault came on the seventh day, there was almost no resistance. The Israelite losses were small. They pulled down the walls and burned the city.

Was Joshua a great charismatic leader?

Yes, but in a terse, brief, no-nonsense, matter-of-fact way. His smile—oh, his smile!—it illuminated his face, showing his brilliant white teeth. When he smiled it was like a blessing. He was a man with a gift for leadership, but he was no orator.

Why did St. Germain select this life?

This was one of his how-can-I-resist-it lives! He had a chance to be an explorer of the Promised Land and to be a judge, a general, and a leader of an emergent nation. Yes, please!

What was Joshua's life purpose?

It was to establish the nation of Israel, to settle and grow its colony and unify these disparate people into a new nation. His spiritual purpose was to learn to handle power by overcoming his desires for increased power and wealth.

What characteristics of St. Germain did he inherit?

Joshua inherited his exploring nature, personal magnetism, intelligence, grace. His skill with the sword was what brought him to the attention of Moses.

What did Joshua have in common with Imhotep?

They shared engineering genius, as well as being logical organizers and inspirational leaders. They could get men to do their will gladly. Imhotep was a non-imposing figure, while Joshua was a charming, tough guy. When his line of St. Germain incarnates, it produces remarkable but largely unappreciated men of destiny. Look for him standing as Fauci beside President Trump.

It seems like this Imhotep line is saved for special occasions.

He is one of God's A-Team! Watch out whenever he has incarnated. It is because something essential and challenging has to be done.

Deborah, Judge of Israel

Mary returns as the fascinating biblical Deborah, the Judge of Israel, from the Magdalene line. The Bible first describes Deborah sitting under a palm tree, listening to and settling the disputes of her people. Not only is she a judge but she is also the commander-in-chief of Israel's armed forces.

Deborah rose to these positions during tough times, when gangs of thugs roamed the countryside, and a Canaanite overlord controlled her valley. Her people, the tribe of Ephraim, cried out to God for assistance.

In the poem "Song of Deborah," she described how God told her to instruct her general, Barak, to take 10,000 soldiers and fight the Canaanite general, Sisera, on Mount Tabor. Deborah outlined her military strategy to Barak, instructing him to form a coalition army with other tribes, but he was reluctant to act. His soldiers were vastly outnumbered and poorly equipped compared with the Canaanites, who had 900 armed chariots. Barak replied that he would fight—but only if she would, too. Deborah, not amused by his equivocation, agreed to accompany him to battle, but let him know that, due to his hesitation, he would have to share the glory of his imminent victory with two women: herself and another woman, Jael.

Deborah described a flash flood, which turned the soil of the battlefield into a quagmire, immobilizing the enemy's chariots. Overwhelmed with heavy casualties, the Canaanite army and their leader took refuge in the tent of Jael, the wife of Heber, where Deborah's prophecy was fulfilled. Jael drove a tent peg through the ear of Sisera as he slept. Deborah's savage victory hymn described in slow motion the violence of Sisera's death.

Why would Mary select such a life?

☀ Conversation with The Gatekeeper ☀

When we first meet Deborah, sitting outside under a date palm tree, how old is she?

When you meet her in *The Book of Judges*, she's sitting in the seat of a leader, at 25. A palm in an Israeli settlement showed that there could be a learned leader there, and it was very significant.

How did Deborah's life begin?

Deborah's origin is obscure. Her aunt, widowed twice, inherited two fortunes. She sent her brilliant niece Deborah, who was called Hannah at that time, to a Talmudic school, like a Hebrew university. From there, she graduated as a lawyer.

What did she look like?

She was plain, with beautiful, thick, auburn hair and fair skin that burned easily in the sun. Her grandmother was a freckled Celt, brought to Israel as a prisoner-of-war from the Caucus. Hannah was of medium height and inclined to be overweight. Although she was not pretty, she was absolutely brilliant. After finishing her studies, she ran away from home to become a warrior at 16, going into battle disguised as a boy.

It was then common practice for Judaic men to have long hair. A devout Jew of the time did not shave his face or trim his beard. Hannah artfully constructed a false beard to fool her comrades. Because she was physically strong and athletic, when a young leader of the army became injured, Deborah took over and triumphed in a small battle with Syrian troops. She was promoted until it was discovered that she was a young woman and a lawyer.

Which was worse?

Always the answer is the same: being a woman, of course. She had to convince many hard-line judges she was a capable lawyer. She constantly had to prove herself smarter and tougher than those around her. They made her a local judge in the north. By the time Hannah was 25, she was a senator and a national judge, of the status of someone sitting on the US Supreme Court.

Why was Hannah given the name Deborah, which means "she spoke"?

It was given to her after her triumphant stint in the army. She was made a lawgiver at 18, the equivalent now of a senior barrister, and her name, Deborah, was in common usage whenever she acted as a tribal judge.

What prompted Deborah to rely on such a seemingly limited man as Barak as the commander of her army?

Barak seems a weak, vacillating man, even though he was the commander. She had to promise to go to war with him to put lead in his spine. She did the real soldering.

Didn't Barak say, "I'll go if you go, but I won't go if you won't"?

That exchange occurred because when she called Barak before her, Deborah had said to him you are not going without me. She was 30 at the time, and her store of courage was enough for both of them.

What was a women's role at that time in battles? Were they on the sidelines barracking, or did they participate as fighters?

Women could be treated on equal terms in the archers. The women archers were as good as or better than men. The Hebrews not only had women as archers, they had whole regiments of women archers. They were great fighters!

What happened to her after the battle with Barak?

It was an amazing battle with an amazing result. She became the preeminent leader of Israel. Her life was her work. But there is something there . . . a secret?

She is a woman I respect. If she wants to tell us she will. I wonder whether she is one of the most perfect women in the Old Testament.

On reflection, I agree, she was the most perfect woman.

Deborah is an outstanding role model, but Mary, as a fiery warrior, isn't that unusual for her?

Deborah was an ice killer, cool and collected, not fiery at all.

What was her strength?

Deborah never behaved in ways women were expected to behave. She could, for example, maintain silence for minutes on end. As a lawyer, she would stare at a victim until they broke and revealed the truth.

Deborah didn't scare easily. Although she was capable of outrage, she never lost control.

What do you think of her poetry, "The Song of Deborah"?

It was an orthodox peculiarity of her nation to describe a battle in that manner. She was, as a person, infinitely more attractive than that great poet, David. But the song was not all written by her; some was added after her death. She was a sublime poet, and, in her future lives, she will demonstrate how beautiful her poetry is.

Why did she have to incarnate?

Deborah incarnated to give expression to the more combative side of Mary's character, and do this as a woman, not as a man. Remember Mary the High Priestess was a warrior as Arjuna, now as the Magdalene she's a warrior as a woman.

What qualities of Mary did she bring to her incarnation?

Her intellect, clarity of mind, and patient perseverance. Deborah only got impatient with nonsense. She had a clear vision of her part, a great determination, and a great strength of character.

What was her greatest achievement?

Her greatest achievement on a temporal level was her successful unification of Judah.

And her spiritual achievement?

To learn how to wield power without becoming intoxicated by it. That is so much harder than it sounds.

Did Deborah achieve what she set out to accomplish in that life?

Yes, she did. She harnessed her martial nature to her law-giving role and infused it from her large central core of caring. Her depth of caring was very Marian. It is right that she is well loved.

How did she die?

Of a massive heart attack at 90. It is often a reliable index of the success of a person's life by how much they are mourned. Deborah was mourned throughout the land, publicly and privately. It was hard not to like her enormously. She was a great woman.

There is a grave near Tel Kadesh in Israel that is attributed to either Barak or Deborah. Whose is it?

I am looking, just a moment. [The Gatekeeper paused and spoke quietly in Hebrew.]

I have been told one of her secrets. They are both buried there. They were secret lovers when they were young. Barak died first at 78; he was five years younger than her. She ordered that she was to be buried with him. He was the love of her life, and when he said, "I'll go if you go," what he was saying was, "If you're going into battle to die for Israel, you will not die alone. I will die with you." They knew that they could only be together in death.

That's sad! But what was her other secret?

Now you will think I am going to say that Barak returned as a president. I am not going to say that, although it might be true. She will return as whom do you think? Mary the Magdalene!

Why am I not surprised? I would have loved to see any of her lives.

And so you shall—in a most remarkable role . . . as Golda Meir!

Thinking about These Lives

Despite his failings, Aaron's life has the dash and flash, sleight of hand, guileful words, brazenness, and intrigue of some of St. Germain's great lives as Merlin the Magician, Benjamin Franklin, or Benjamin Disraeli. You will notice two of those lives share the same first name. St. Germain and Mary will repeatedly use the same names for their dual energies: St. Germain uses Jacob, James, Benjamin, Christopher, Julius, Jules, Claudius, Claudio, Claude, Joseph, and Joshua, while Mary uses Luke, Mary, Deborah, Leah, and Golda. Fortunately, neither of them has reprised Imhotep and Nefertiti yet!

Joshua is a surprise: strong, pragmatic, intelligent, a return of the Imhotep line. The Gatekeeper's rendition of him is closer to the Bible than his account of Aaron's. Aaron appears to have been entirely overshadowed by the charismatic deliverer and leader of the Jewish people, Moses. His contribution to writing the first three books of the Torah was even attributed to Moses.

In her life as Deborah, Mary is gifted with leadership, prophetic inspiration, creative ability, and wisdom. It is a life that will prepare her for life as Mary the Magdalene, the passionate lover of Jeshua ben Joseph, where she demonstrates the characteristics of Artemis and Diana: physically strong, intelligent, and articulate. In a time when women were subordinate to men, Deborah emerges as a wonderful model of a leader: courageous, firm, kind, wise, and humble. In her poetic song of deliverance, she calls herself "a mother in Israel." The story of Deborah raises interesting questions because neither the chronicle in Judges nor her lyrical outburst tells the actual story of her life, and The Gatekeeper attempts to remedy this. Deborah, who appears not to have the flaws of either Moses or Aaron, was the perfect woman in the Bible. Mary's incarnation as commander-in-chief and a wise leader is different from those seen in her previous life experiences.

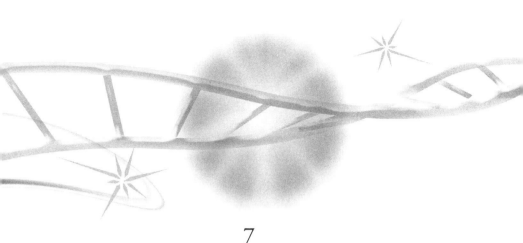

7

DEFINING
WESTERN THINKING

Greece, the mother of Western civilization, was a confederation of different city-states, each governed by two or more different energies.

Let's take one example here: Athens. Her governing energy was Pallas Athene, assisted by Hermes, the energy of governance, and St. Germain for its fine arts.

On the other hand, Macedonia, Alexander the Great's birthplace, was headstrong, violent, and vain, a state epitomized by its favorite son and reflecting its dominant energy of Hilarion.

Troy, the world's first city-state, was complex. Its dominant energy was Artemis Diana, whom we know as Mary the Magdalene.

Ephesus, in today's Turkey, was the city of Mary the Mother. St. Germain assisted her two aspects with his commercial trading and diplomatic best. Together, they spurred the Trojans, after their defeat, to migrate around the mighty Mediterranean and settle in Israel, Spain, Britain, and Ireland.

Finally, there was the city-state of Sparta, with two dominant energies: those of Hilarion and El Morya, who gave it its athletic rigor and military thrust.

St. Germain, the innovator, dominated Greek thinking when he incarnated as Homer. A great romantic, he blended the legends, the myths, and heroism, the three pillars on which Greece was founded. He integrated Greek music with drama, sculpture, architecture, and poetry. This music is unfortunately lost. He developed Egyptian medicine to new heights, while Kuthumi excelled in mathematics, logic, and philosophy. It cannot have been an accident that Socrates (Kuthumi), Plato (St. Germain), Aristotle (Serapis Bey), and Hephaestion (The High Priestess) were all linked.

Homer (c.1218–1135 BC),
Epic Poet of the Trojan War

Nobody knows anything about Homer's life. It's a blank slate. Scholars argue about whether a man called Homer existed, or whether he was just a legend, not one poet but many: a group of bards. So who was Homer? What role did he play? When did he live? How did his wondrous epic poems of such suppleness and scope come to be in the form they are?

In Greek, Homeros means "the one who did not fight but could, instead, remember the highlights of a battle for recitation later on." Scholars question whether the same poet could compose *The Iliad* and *The Odyssey* because of the inconsistencies in their language and storylines. Others argue that one could be the product of youth and the other of late maturity. A common joke about Homer is that his poems were not penned by him, but by another man of the same name!

There is also a tradition that says Homer was blind. This belief is reinforced by the marble bust showing Homer with his head tilted up and his eyes closed in a manner reminiscent of a blind pianist. Various cities in Greece claim to be his birthplace, but all scholars agree that if Homer existed, he was a genius, and *The Iliad* and *The Odyssey* are among the greatest works of world literature. The superlatives keep coming. Why? We have only Homer's written texts with no music or instrumentation to reflect their original beauty. We have to rely solely on the poetry of Homer's epic songs.

✳ *The Iliad* ✳

In *The Iliad*, tragedy defines its plot in its first line. It's the story of the power, fury, and wrath of Achilles, Greece's greatest warrior, and his dispute with his commander-in-chief, Agamemnon, King of Mycenae, the prime Greek power of the second millennium BC. It covers only 40 days of the 10-year siege of the kingdom of Troy, whose ruins are visible in today's Turkey on the Bosporus Sea.

Ostensibly, the Greeks were fighting to recapture Helen, the trophy wife of Agamemnon's cuckolded brother Menelaus. Many scholars are dubious whether this was the real reason for the 10-year war. Homer's description of the Trojan War, with its dramatic soliloquies and searing imagery is played out against an irreverent soap opera of the dysfunctional family of the gods and goddesses from Mount Olympus, making it the masterpiece of classical literature.

✳ *The Odyssey* ✳

The first line of *The Odyssey* reads: "Sing to me of the man, Muse, the man of twists and turns, driven time and again off course once he had plundered the hallowed heights of Troy . . ." [transl. Robert Fagle].

Odysseus, the man of twists and turns, was the first hero to use his brain to temper his bravery and physical prowess, and Homer shows how he schemes.

The Odyssey begins with Odysseus's scheme of trickery and deception in order to finalize the war that has exhausted both Greeks and Trojans. His plan is for all Greek ships to retreat out of sight and leave a massive wooden horse on a wheeled platform outside the gates of Troy filled with silent soldiers. Everyone knows what happens next. The epic poem tells of the 10-year homecoming of this sensual, smooth-talking schemer, King Odysseus of Ithaca, from the Trojan War.

Odysseus (or Ulysses in Latin) is simultaneously telling his story and listening to it as if Homer was performing it in front of him. It describes his fighting and romantic adventures, his manipulation by the gods, and his eventual reunion with his wife, Penelope, and his son Telemachus. Throughout his journey, Odysseus loses his colleagues, self-esteem, and ship, until he descends into the afterlife. Rising from the dead, he is stranded on the paradise isle of Calypso for years before he eventually returns to Ithaca.

These complex Homerian epics had a profound effect on Western civilization. Every Greek schoolchild studied them, and most of them learned them by heart. They were their major source of moral and practical instruction, as well as the symbol of Hellenic heroism and unity. Romans followed the Greeks in learning from Homer the heroic ideal and all its contradictions: its grasping pride, its animal strength, and its ultimate humanity. Hector's courage and valor were the models for the leaders of the Roman legions. A hundred generations of Europeans would closely study his texts and enjoy Homer's poetry.

But what is Homer's story? What is his role in the lineage that takes us back to God? I put these questions to The Gatekeeper.

✳ Conversation with The Gatekeeper ✳

Who is Homer, Gatekeeper?

Homer is the blind bard from Boeotia, a rural province north of Athens, born about 1218 BC. His father was comfortable financially, providing a tutor in formal Greek, rhetoric, and religious legends to his son. His name was Midas (pronounced Meedas) and his last name, Homeros, was both a description and a rank. Around the age of 22, he went to the later stages of the Trojan War as a war correspondent and "entertainer."

What caused his blindness?

It's not entirely clear. When he was six, he fell from his father's chariot and was concussed by a severe blow that damaged his optic nerve. His eyesight deteriorated throughout his childhood, but he did not go completely blind until 28. Homer was an alcoholic. One day in his desperation to get some alcohol, he drank fusil oil, which is an alcohol made from fermented wood. The poison affected his nerves and deteriorated his already weak eyesight. The question to ask now is: Why was the genius an alcoholic? This is typical of God's gifts. When God allows genius, He creates a shadow as a challenge. Alcoholism is a chemical disease; it is an inability to deal with disappointment, which triggers a descent into melancholy and a black heart.

Did his blindness give his poetry any unique insights or approaches?

His gradual loss of sight increased his competent tonic judgment to perfect pitch and increased the rhythm in his head, allowing him to think in rhythm and not be distracted by the visual stimuli that surrounded everyone else.

We have a bust of Homer. He seems a big man. Is it a true likeness?

Homer was a burly man, inclined to run to fat, without the extreme muscular development of the Greeks. He was physically strong and excelled in wrestling. With light brown hair with a fair gold streak, olive skin, a curly beard, a snub nose, his bust or statue flatter his blunt features.

Where did Homer get his front-line copy for his epics, especially about the Trojan enemy's intimate life?

Odysseus hired Homer as a chronicler and performer. Homer was a singer, played the lyre, but his primary function was to entertain Odysseus: reciting, gesturing, singing, and playing. He sang his compositions, glorifying those who were getting drunk around him, flattering whoever paid for his food and drink. He based his songs on what he overheard or was told by soldiers, slaves, or the heroes themselves.

A master of spin?

Yes, but Homer knew what he was doing. He was not on anyone's side. He sang of the Trojans in his lyrics, and because he played with the Trojan minstrels, they told him their best stories. Homer's poor eyesight led him to train his prodigious memory.

How did he gain the background for *The Odyssey*?

When a victorious Odysseus left Troy, he toured the Black Sea and the Mediterranean, taking Homer with him as his entertainer. He clothed, fed, and kept him in wine. Homer was promiscuous, with both men and women, but his true love was Odysseus. Their relationship lasted over 10 years. Reread *The Odyssey*, you will see his love there.

How significant was this love affair?

It was very significant for Homer, but not Odysseus. The only significant love in Ulysses' life was Ulysses.

What made Homer, Homer?

Homer poured everything into his poetry, in a constant state of creative passion, living on alcohol, a meager amount of bad food, and gallons of wine to wash down mouthfuls of dried fish. He didn't have enough discipline to control his drinking and carousing. Like Brendan Behan or Byron, he couldn't sustain the power of his creative spirit. He had an enormous creative urge to absorb all experience and reduce it to art. It was continual warfare between his intellect and his body. His body demanded he live healthily, eat, sleep, and exercise, but his urge wouldn't allow him. This is a commonality of all bards and writers as they struggle to create.

Homer was not a normal person. He was emotionally crippled, except in his fantasy world. Like Mozart, an aspect of Kuthumi, he had a minor form of autism. He was childlike and perceived differently to others.

Homer imbues his characters with moral dilemmas. Where did his moral consciousness come from?

He didn't have one. Nevertheless, in his poetry, Homer dramatically poses moral and ethical questions. Homer used them because he'd heard them argued and they stirred the emotions shocking his audience. They started arguments and provoked fights. He posed moral questions to make his drama more exciting.

What was Homer's spiritual challenge?

He would struggle with containing his incredible creative force over several lifetimes. And his use of alcohol would cripple him, just as it would in St. Germain's lifetime as Dylan Thomas.

And his most significant achievement?

The Odyssey, a polished gem. In writing it, he sacrificed himself to his creative force.

Why did St. Germain incarnate as Homer?

The energy of St. Germain finds it difficult to resist the allure of genius. St. Germain has so much to imprint on human culture and incarnating as Homer was the most effective way to do it.

What qualities of St. Germain did Homer bring in?

Let's tick off the positive qualities first: creativity, to forge beauty from words and music, to bring sensitivity to the shaping of social mores that will profoundly influence people's behavior after reading his work. It will become the cultural keystone of the Greek ethos. Homer was possessed with the spirit of divine invention. But he was a liar and overindulgent.

What was Homer's life purpose?

To lay the foundations of Western literature and the Greek ethos. Did he achieve it? Yes, absolutely; by paying a high personal cost. Everybody loved Homer. They identified with him, and in turn, people inspired him. Homer knew his human failings and didn't make excuses for them. He loved humanity. He laughed, he sang, and people wanted to be around him to enjoy him.

How did he die?

Homer died ignominiously at 83, in a drunken stupor. He choked on his vomit.

Plato (c.427–c.348 BC), Philosopher of Ancient Greece

Plato, one of the most influential philosophers, was taught by Socrates. Socrates, an aspect of Kuthumi, taught Aristotle himself, an aspect of Serapis Bey. Plato would inspire Augustine, Thomas Aquinas, and Francis Bacon, and invent the dynamic of philosophical argument in Western thought.

Born into a noble Athenian family around 427 BC, Plato was destined for political life. Critias and Charmides, infamous members of the Thirty Tyrants government in 404 BC, were relatives. His mother was descended from Solon, the Athenian lawgiver, and his father from Codrus, a legendary king of Athens.

Plato became disillusioned with his relatives' tyranny and was later devastated by the irrational execution of his teacher, Socrates, a man who greatly influenced him. Plato painfully concluded that future leaders needed to be educated in the study of philosophy and ethics to prepare them for their roles, but before bringing his school to fruition, Plato left Athens in 399 BC for 12 years of travel and study. Once established, Plato's Academy taught philosophy and mathematics to families of Athens.

Most of Plato's writing is in the form of a dialog with Plato's former teacher, the brilliant Socrates. A student would pose a question: What is justice? And after being subjected to a searching cross-examination by Socrates, he would devise precise definitions and reach answers to his questions.

In *The Republic*, the dialog answers the question "What is an ideal state?" followed by "Who is an ideal ruler?" The well-known answer to that question is "the philosopher king." Plato was invited to Syracuse in Sicily to train a young Dionysius as a philosopher king. It did not work out.

Plato developed a theory that everything has an unchanging reality that describes the form of an object. For example, a chair has four legs, a seat, and a back. Take the back away, and its reality changes to become a stool.

Plato taught the philosopher Aristotle for 20 years, but Plato's influence was greater than that of his teacher Socrates or his pupil Aristotle.

※ Conversation with The Gatekeeper ※

What is Plato's biographical background?

Plato was born, like Homer, in Boeotia, on his parents' estate. Plato was his nickname. It came from an infamous youthful adventure, when he was captured by pirates in Asia Minor and sold by a Persian satrap into slavery. He escaped disguised as a woman. He found a Greek ship in the harbor at Antioch, belonging to a smuggler. Plato promised him a reward from his father. This event, plus his natural inclination to homosexuality, meant he was given the slang name Plato, which meant "tart" or "a girl of loose morals."

Gatekeeper, Plato is kidnapped like the young Julius Caesar, St. Patrick, and Cervantes, all enduring similar episodes with pirates. Why does St. Germain choose these experiences as preludes to some of his most important lives?

When he is born with such a prodigious intellect, how else can he learn about being helpless? The greater the intellect, the more all-powerful the stature, the greater the need to be balanced by a humbling experience. He does not want to wield power without compassion. He can't lead men without understanding the experience of unquestioning submission to another's orders, and, most important for Plato, he can't teach about freedom without knowing its loss.

We have a bust of Plato. Is it a good likeness?

The bust is a good likeness. Plato was a handsome man with a slight build. He developed broad shoulders from wrestling. He was a good runner, kept his hair unfashionably short for a Greek. There was a streak of asceticism in him.

How would you describe his relationship with Socrates?

Plato became his student in his twenties. He loved Socrates intellectually, emotionally, and physically; he loved him completely. Devastated by his death, Plato couldn't attend Socrates's suicide execution. He couldn't bear it. He got drunk instead. His devastation impelled him to immortalize Socrates: both his thinking and method of teaching.

Was Plato's view of Socrates accurate or embellished?

When we love someone, we exaggerate their attributes, but Plato was accurate and embellished little. Plato kept notes on Socrates's teaching and collated them, aligning the time sequence and supplementing notes from memory after his suicide. Where he doubted his memory, he consulted other students. After Socrates's death, Plato wanted to travel but had copies made of every note and dialogue. He left the originals safely at the scribe's house. Plato traveled then to Egypt, and all Greek colonies where people spoke Greek. He was a bit of a xenophobe and liked to be with other Greeks.

On what principles did he found the academy?

The structure was loose—a gathering of students around a master teacher, a center of learning. If they didn't learn, they would drift away. The guiding principle reverberating through St. Germain's lives was investigation. Why is it so? "Why?" is always the most important word in his language, and the academy fostered a genuine spirit of inquiry.

Plato taught zoology dissecting animals and practicing taxidermy. This information about Plato, though, has been lost.

Is it true that the phrase "LET NO MEN IGNORANT OF GEOMETRY ENTER" was carved above a lintel on academy grounds?

Yes. The academy was a private estate, with an ordered garden, wooded glens, and small buildings containing Egyptian, Hebrew, and Greek scrolls, animal specimens, and gifts from ambassadors. Plato was the headteacher, with approximately 30 to 100 male students. The school was exclusive, serving only the brightest young boys and teaching rhetoric, logic, philosophy, botany, and zoology.

In Plato's Idea of Forms, he describes an invisible blueprint that pre-exists every pattern, object, or living being before it materializes into its actual form. Was he right?

Absolutely, because in that, he described the pattern of the universe. Plato developed this theory from the processes he followed as a scientist. As a naturalist, he couldn't study nature without seeing its patterns, the synergy of life, so he developed his theory to explain it.

What qualities of St. Germain did Plato bring in?

Plato exhibits his curiosity, ability to think creatively, to originate, and coordinate projects. He's a brilliant organizer, shrewd as an assessor of people and their capabilities, and possesses intelligence, clarity, and brevity of expression. He had the charm of St. Germain but, for him, a very low libido.

What was his life purpose?

To be a teacher and to refine and disseminate knowledge, a purpose he achieved perfectly.

What was his spiritual challenge?

Love! Plato suffered from something he brought in with him [from a previous life]. He was emotionally paralytic. He couldn't experience emotions because he was frightened of them. He had an extremely cold, distant, and austere father, who died when Plato was young. His mother abandoned him to an uncle. She claimed she didn't know how to bring him up. She thought he needed a male role model. His uncle was manipulative, cruel, and very sadistic. He not only beat Plato, he tortured him and sexually abused him. But from the age of four he penetrated him and forced Plato to perform oral sex on him and his cronies.

Plato was never able to free himself from the prison he built to protect himself as a child. He couldn't allow himself to be loved or to show love to anyone, so his spiritual challenge was to overcome his self-disgust and be able to express affection for others.

Because Plato never knew love as a child, he didn't know what it was. Socrates said, to talk to Plato about love is like talking to a blind man about sunlight.

Plato wrote *Symposium*, in which Socrates, Alcibiades, and Aristophanes discuss the nature of love. Did this dialogue occur as Plato described?

It did occur, as an after-dinner conversation. Plato, the only non-drinker among them, wrote it up the next day.

His history of child abuse triggering his inability to express love gives a cruel twist to the expression "Platonic relationship," doesn't it?

The only way Plato could hang on to his sanity and to God was to cling to reason. The terrible truth about abuse by a family member is that they are loved and trusted by the child. It is the ultimate betrayal.

It gives a fresh understanding of why he argued the supremacy of reason over emotion!

Plato had an innate distrust of love. His friends in *Symposium* did not understand, as he did, that love could lead to betrayal.

What do you think is his greatest work, and would Plato agree with your assessment?

The Republic flawed though it is. Plato was disillusioned with it. He thought The Dialogues was his greatest work. They contain more speculative philosophy and are more productive of discussion rather than holding the Utopian vision. The Republic, for all its faults, contains the building blocks of an ideal society, something we haven't managed to achieve so far.

Why did St. Germain incarnate as Plato?

To improve or perfect the philosophical facet of his nature. There's a point, you know, where the dramatist and the trickster, with his smooth tongue, can interfere with an ability to define issues, and he wished to strengthen his ability to define issues.

What do you think was Plato's most significant achievement?

I suppose it was the Platonic influence on Western philosophy, theology, and government and the imposition of the inquisitorial style that demanded you set standards and boundaries.

Gatekeeper, it can't be an accident that the incarnations of Socrates, Plato, Aristotle, and Hephaestion were all linked?

It wasn't. Look at the timeframe from our point of view. Egypt was in decline, and Greece had stopped the expansion of the Persian Empire, inspired by Homeric heroism. The Mongols were about to invade the Middle East, making it the perfect time for Alexander to advance and take with him, courtesy of Aristotle's tuition, the Athens School of Thought brought by Hephaestion, returning it to its source. This reimporting goes on and on throughout history. Athenian thinking Hellenized the whole of the Middle East, allowing Christianity to spread, and through that process, it could be reimported at the Renaissance to Europe and reinspire them.

Did Plato have any regrets?

Plato regretted not running away from his uncle and taking his chances. He thought it lacked courage. His misgivings are personal ones. He did not know how to share uninhibited love or how to go about it. A young widow called Lydia offered him love and comfort. He did not accept; he didn't think he was capable.

Legend says Plato died at a wedding.

It was a wedding feast, and Plato died of a heart attack at 83. He died sitting quietly. It was time to go.

Hephaestion (356–324 BC), Alexander's Lover

Hephaestion (pron. he FAIS ti on) stands in the shadow of the man who conquered most of the ancient world, overthrew the Persian Empire, and Hellenized it from Greece to Persia and from Egypt to India. Hephaestion, called by Alexander Philalexandros, meaning "the dearest of all Alexander's friends," remained at his side, his second-in-command, his closest advisor, and probably his lover for all of his life.

Born around 356 BC, in the royal palace at Pella, Macedonia, Hephaestion was the son of Amyntor, who was presumably a noble in King Philip's court. He attended school with Alexander, and was educated by Aristotle in rhetoric, science, poetry, drama, and philosophy. As an aspect of Serapis Bey, Aristotle was formerly the Egyptian god Osiris, married to the goddess Isis. In the schoolroom, he was united with his former wife as his male pupil, Hephaestion. Aristotle wrote to Alexander during military campaigns, offering ideas about infrastructure, language, roads, and bridges—all to facilitate trade.

At the beginning of their 20,000-mile military campaign, Alexander and Hephaestion visited the site of Troy—Alexander to pray at the tomb of Achilles and Hephaestion to honor Achilles's lover, Patroclus. Whether they were making a declaration about their relationship was unclear, but it underscored their admiration of Greek heroes and culture.

After the Battle of Issus, where they were victorious against Darius III's troops, Alexander and Hephaestion entered the royal tent to inspect their spoils of war. Darius's mother-in-law, mistaking him for the king, prostrated herself at the feet of the taller Hephaestion and was very embarrassed to discover her error. "Don't be upset, Mother," Alexander is quoted as saying. "He, too, is Alexander." Later, he would marry her granddaughter, Stateira, and Hephaestion would marry her younger sister, Drypetis, allowing the two friends to become brothers-in-law. The Roman historian Catullus describes their relationship thus: "Hephaestion was . . . the counselor of all his secrets. No one had more freedom to admonish Alexander. He was used in a way that his power seemed to have been granted by the king, rather than taken by himself . . ."

✳ Conversation with The Gatekeeper ✳

Was Hephaestion an aspect of Mary having a male life?

It is Mary the High Priestess who, as Hephaestion, was unlikely to be in military command as a general. He was a gentle, compassionate, brave, strong man, who loathed violence but loved Alexander. He was also previously Isis, the passionate lover of Osiris, who returns here as Aristotle. It's a partnership carefully orchestrated to ensure clear and frequent communication between them on the issue of Hellenization of Alexander's conquests.

What does Hephaestion mean?

It is a barbarian name originally meaning "a manufacturer of goods." Coming from the same root as the smith god Hephaestus, Hephaestion was a doer; an intelligent, practical man of action, a good organizer, and respectable tradesman.

What was his background?

Born in Macedonia the same year as Alexander, Hephaestion's father was a general and captain of the bodyguard. He was a close confidant of Philip, the king. He and Alexander grew up together around the royal palace.

It is said that they were lovers. Were they?

In their teenage years, they were friends experimenting with sex. Their love developed into passion. Remember, the only options for 20-year-old Greek men were whores or one another! Men weren't allowed to marry until they were 30.

Hephaestion and Alexander were opposites: Alexander loved Hephaestion's gentleness; Hephaestion loved Alexander's impervious belief in himself. Alexander did what he wanted to whenever he wanted. He was a born swordsman, a great rider, and handsome, with a classic Greek profile and curly dark blond hair, light gray eyes, and a stocky build.

Hephaestion had curly dark hair and a wiry, slender build, with significant upper-body strength. He was taller than Alexander; a brave man who never held back. As Alexander's counselor, Hephaestion agreed with him most of the time, which Alexander found most satisfactory.

Theirs was indeed a great love. They were building on their unfinished love as Ramses and Nefertari. Hephaestion was intelligent and strong, while Alexander was only interested in being a soldier. Aristotle respected Hephaestion's intellect and sense of responsibility; he would have loved a son like him. Aristotle knew that Alexander did not possess the same intellectual capacity, so he wrote to Hephaestion during military campaigns.

Alexander worshipped Achilles as a great soldier. War meant bravery, courage, daring, and Achilles exemplified all of that. Hephaestion, on the other hand, believed in Achilles's soldiering ability but considered him moody. His hero was Patroclus, Achilles's lover and a craftsman.

Hephaestion possessed the strategic brains, suggesting the creation of Alexander's elite household troupe as well as his famous flying wedge. Alexander is credited for his friend's inventiveness. Being the "wind beneath his wings" is a trend we will often see in Mary's lives when, as a devoted companion, she will set others up to succeed, allowing them to take the credit. It was always hard for her to find a companion brighter than her! Unless it was Mr. Razzle Dazzle himself!

When they reached Ephesus, they saw one of the Seven Wonders of the Ancient World, the Temple of Artemis, destroyed by an earthquake. Did Alexander ask Hephaestion, an aspect of Mary, to rebuild her own temple?

It is sort of a dance, isn't it? An historical choreography, in which a sacred structure was built, rebuilt, destroyed, then moved to Istanbul. Ephesus, where Mary will die as the Christ's mother, is one of her cities, and it will be of great importance to Mary in the future. There is an indestructibility about the place, and Mary's association with Ephesus is indestructible.

What was Hephaestion's greatest achievement?

His selfless and unconditional devotion to Alexander made Alexander a man the world could celebrate. Hephaestion's many brilliant inventions and suggestions credited to his lover were instrumental in building Alexander the Great's mystique. Hephaestion's love for Alexander made his greatness possible. Without Hephaestion, who was his adjutant, organizer, and administrator, Alexander would have been a military disaster, forging ahead and bashing on, regardless. He would have been dead in no time, with his supply lines cut. Hephaestion organized everything, quietly standing in the shadows. This is that Marian reticence at work. Don't you call it "setting them up to succeed"?

And his spiritual challenge?

His spiritual challenge was overcoming his strong distaste for violence and death, so that he could stay close to Alexander.

How is that a spiritual challenge?

It's a kind of sanctity in reverse, to totally subjugate one's nature to please the one you love. Hephaestion was Alexander's partner in the modern sense of the word, his closest confidante. Hephaestion understood and loved Alexander completely.

How did Hephaestion die?

He died of typhoid and pneumonia. The two maladies together made it impossible to diagnose accurately.

Is it true that Alexander had Hephaestion's doctor hanged or crucified?

No, neither. The physician was strangled, garrotted, on Alexander's orders. A wise physician would have called in a specialist, and Hephaestion would have been diagnosed and saved.

Did Alexander die of a broken heart, 18 months later, in June 323 BC?

People don't technically die of broken hearts, but they do die after they have lost the will to live. After Hephaestion's death, Alexander lost his emotional balance. He became erratic and weakened and just wanted to die. Somebody poisoned him with monkshood, given in massive doses fed to him over a couple of weeks. He wanted to go to be with Hephaestion.

Why did Mary select this life?

Mary selected this life because she loves Hilarion and to put steel into the backbone of a gentle soul. She wants you to imagine a submissive, anti-violent, devoted mother who watched her beloved son sacrifice himself in a barbarous, cruel way to fulfill God's will. That flower of a woman needed to complete her mission, and her life as Hephaestion gave it to her.

What qualities of Mary did Hephaestion bring into his life?

He brought in compassion, romantic love, and protectiveness; they were all in his nature. Not the least was his yin qualities: a passive, a nonaggressive toughness. He was steadfast and trusted, because he was honorable, and needed to improve aspects of his character to perfect his higher consciousness.

Why did Hephaestion incarnate, and what was his purpose?

His purpose was to be a devoted and trusted servant to others. Hephaestion achieved what he set out to achieve.

Was the Hellenization of the Middle East that Hephaestion fulfilled a necessary precursor to the spread of Christianity?

It was not essential, but, in the Divine Plan it was considered a bonus, conceptualized by Serapis Bey as Aristotle, implemented by Hephaestion, and used by St. Paul effectively. Mercantile Greek or Koine Greek became the language of the Mediterranean. It meant that Paul and his disciples—Timothy, Titus, Barnabas, Luke, and Priscilla—could freely preach gospels wherever they went. Even Julius Caesar used Greek for family intimacy, because it was a far subtler language than Latin; it was also the language of engineers and senators, so the Hellenization was very useful.

Thinking about These Lives

Each of the four lives explored in this chapter was involved in the elaborate Divine Plan to set the conditions for the birth of Western civilization. Homer and Plato represent the energy of St. Germain and contribute in some way to the emergence of the West. Hephaestion, Mary's High Priestess energy, incarnates as the brilliantly inventive and supportive lover of Alexander the Great, without whom Alexander would merely be called Alexander. His impact on Western civilization would not exist.

The myths sung by Homer are based on historical fact, and Homer's eventual blindness sharpens his ear, increases his sensitivity to rhythm, and schools his prodigious memory, allowing him to record and remember what he hears in both music and verse. The Gatekeeper's Homer is a lover of a vainglorious Odysseus and an entertainer who revels in and provokes audience participation. Homer is a spin doctor glorifying his masters because they provided him with corporate hospitality. In return, he puts the best spin on their pettiness, disputes, and grimy deals. His slight autism and eventual blindness contribute to his genius, giving him the gifts of perception, lyricism, and storytelling. Homer, who possesses the creative start-up energy of St. Germain, sings of the siege of Troy and the skirmishes between gods and warriors. His voice illuminated characters distraught by the slaughter and losses of war and ennobled them. As Homer, St. Germain struggles to control his creative energy with alcohol and sex. He fails. It seems that the price of genius is high, and difficult spiritual challenges tarnish its brilliance. It will be thousands of years before St. Germain could control his rampant creativity in a non-destructive way.

Homer is the firstborn of a creative storm: an aspect of the line of St. Germain I will call the Dante line, after the poet, satirist, philosopher, and diplomat who wrote *The Divine Comedy* for his idealized love Beatrice, nearly 3,000 years later.

Plato, who follows, does not disappoint. Burdened with an abusive childhood, he is emotionally damaged and unable to form any loving relationships. In a long life, he creates masterpieces of world literature, canvassing life's most essential questions and describing logic, dialectic, induction, and the classification of ideas.

Hephaestion is animated by Mary the High Priestess. Remember, we saw her as Arjuna, when St. Germain and Hilarion were together as Krishna. Multitalented Hephaestion exists for someone else in a symbiotic relationship. Historically almost invisible, his role was to make Alexander greater. Time after time, The Gatekeeper will haul out aspects of Mary's line to stress her importance during significant turning points in history.

Did an agreement exist among the masters before their incarnations to have outstanding lives close enough together to influence Western thinking? Kuthumi incarnated as Socrates, St. Germain as Plato, and Serapis Bey as Aristotle, birthing together with the summation of the truth and rational thought. After them, did Mary and Hilarion agree, as Alexander and Hephaestion, to spread Plato's rational thought through Aristotle's tutelage as they Hellenized the ancient world? Perhaps due to the close relationship of Mary to Serapis Bey, they just got on with it and credited Alexander!

The Gatekeeper told me that the time was right for this to occur, and it fitted the developmental pattern of the world. This coincidence of equals was one of the most important interlinked incarnations for the progression of the Light in our recorded time. It was a setback for the Dark, and Hephaestion's role was far more critical than we give it credit. Overshadowed by Alexander, he shared with Aaron the fate of being dominated by the bombastic, charismatic Hilarion as Moses. Unfortunately, this facilitating role has contributed to Mary's invisibility through the ages.

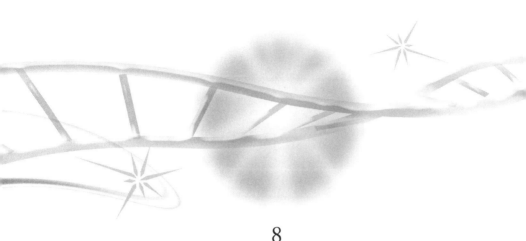

8

SHINING IN THE ROMAN SUN WHILE CREATING WESTERN EUROPE

Who were the governing energies of Rome? The Gatekeeper was adamant that Rome was governed by Mars and Minerva, the god and goddess of war, and helped the messenger of the gods, Mercury, together with a minor influence of the trickster Pan. We use their Master names: Hilarion, Pallas Athene, Hermes, and St. Germain.

These governing energies planned their domination of the Western world for 500 years. Their agenda was clear: tame the known world first, build roads and military camps, establish law and order, grow trade, teach Greek and Latin, spread Greek logic, venerate the Stoic philosophy, and foster civilized living.

But did the energy of the Roman gods maintain its influence after the fall of Rome? Hilarion removed himself, Mary arrived, and St. Germain became a major influence. Together, Mary and St. Germain encourage a more casual, laid-back, and artistic society, one that is almost ungovernable, pulsing with music and song, art, exquisite couturiers, and beautiful food. Meanwhile, Hilarion ensured its religiosity, often incarnating as a pope.

St. Germain shone in the Roman sun, enjoying his lives as Julius Caesar, Emperor Tiberius, the statesman Cicero, the poet Virgil, and the playwright and administrator Seneca. On the other hand, Mary was absent, because the Roman climate was not conducive to her energy. Rome was a place that adored the gods of war, a place where Mary could not thrive. Because of Rome's stifling corruption, she didn't even try any significant incarnations; yet, as the ruler of Egypt, she still played an influencing role.

This chapter explores St. Germain's lives as Caesar and Mary's Egyptian life as Cleopatra.

Julius Caesar (100–44 BC), Roman General and Statesman

> Why, man, he doth bestride the narrow world
> Like Colossus and we petty men
> Walk under his huge legs, and peep about
> To find ourselves dishonorable graves.

Shakespeare's Mark Antony used the imagery of a giant dwarfing everyone to convey the might and the magnitude of Rome's dictator, Julius Caesar. Caesar, a Roman statesman, was one of the most successful military commanders of all time. He extended the Roman Empire throughout Europe, marched on Rome, seized power, and eventually proclaimed himself dictator for life. He achieved his goals through courage, brilliant military tactics, beguiling oratory, political populism, and gold-standard charm.

Gaius Julius Caesar, thought to have been born in July 100 BC into a well-connected noble family, practiced as a lawyer and orator until he completed his military service in the despised marines. By 72 BC, aged 28, Caesar had begun his political career as military tribune and was responsible for bread and circuses. He borrowed a fortune from Crassus, Rome's banker, to buy his popularity. After serving as Spain's governor (61–60 BC), Caesar made a pact with Pompey and bought his election as consul. His debt to Crassus, about 830 talents (the equivalent of 17,500 kilos of silver), would need his own silver mine to repay it.

As consul, Rome's highest position, Caesar gained the right to command an army, but the conservative senate became jittery at Caesar's increasing political power and watched his ascension nervously. He sidelined them further, forming the first triumvirate with the conservative champion Pompey and Crassus, then headed off with the Tenth Legion to the governorship of Gaul.

Over the next eight years, he waged war against the Gallic tribes. Twice, he tried unsuccessfully to conquer Britain. He chronicled his success in the Gallic Wars, and as his own war correspondent, made himself the idol of the Roman people. Through his chronicles, he became the first man to write his history before anyone else could.

Refusing the senate's command to disband, Caesar trooped his legions back to Italy and crossed the Rubicon River in order to march on Rome.

A civil war began. Caesar confronted Pompey and defeated him in Greece, causing Pompey to flee to Egypt. While pursuing Pompey in Egypt, Caesar became entangled with the new pharaoh, Cleopatra, with whom he spent nine rapturous months.

On his return to Rome, Caesar appointed himself consul and hurriedly began reforms. He enlarged the senate, revised the calendar, and began construction of public monuments. Having experienced the burden of debt, he relieved the indebtedness of the poor. In 44 BC, Caesar made himself dictator for life. The senate was appalled, and two senators, Brutus and Cassius, assassinated Caesar on March 4. Caesar's appointed heir, his nephew, Octavian, succeeded him.

Now for the true story!

⁕ Conversation with The Gatekeeper ⁕

Where do we start with Julius Caesar?

We start with the following: Julius Caesar was one of the most magnificent lives of St. Germain, and full of contradictions. It's a life in two parts: Julius, the young general, and Caesar, the uncrowned emperor of Rome and its empire.

As a young man, Julius was brave and adventurous. He saw his father disgraced and his noble family cast into poverty. Julius was an illustrious young leader; he had great personal magnetism, was quick thinking, fast-moving, and a flashing swordsman. His men would do anything for him. He used his tremendous personal charisma to turn two disgruntled, incompetent Spanish legions into crack troops. His meteoric rise later degenerates, and he becomes a morose, moody, vengeful, epileptic man who manufactures his death. His losses drove the contrast between the younger and older Caesar.

Let's set aside his campaigning, politicking, the crossing of the Rubicon, the civil war, three wives, many lovers, the maelstroms of treachery, and political upheaval that swirled around him and his brilliant manoeuvring, because we will not concentrate on his victories; instead, we will study his losses. What was Julius's reaction when his family lost their honor? Or what was his reaction when he lost his heart, his health, his life, or his soul? You won't find these answers in the volumes of the Roman history.

What did Caesar look like?

Lissom, athletically graceful, a superb swordsman, with the perfect balance of Rudolf Nureyev, gray eyes, receding brown hair from an early age. He was a handsome man. His deep eyes were capable of an ardent look or freezing ice cold. He had large hands and solid wrists, sword-fighting arms. He was slim and slightly taller than average, at five feet nine. He possessed a phenomenal intelligence and was excellent at mathematics and engineering and a quick thinker. He could solve a problem before anyone had even grasped that there was a problem.

As a young man, what made him stand out?

As a tribune, Julius was an excellent support officer. He was the first legate to recognize the importance of the auxiliary troops, the non-Romans, soldiers recruited overseas. He treated them with respect. Previously regarded as expendable, Caesar treated them well and organized for them the privileges of citizenship and land grants on completion of their service—all the same entitlements as legionnaires.

Julius was a stickler for the essential things, not the dress codes. He insisted on proper fortifications being made every night before they camped. A brilliant engineer, he developed engineering in the army, and every legionnaire had to build roads, bridges, and administration centers as he conquered vast new lands.

Why did St. Germain choose to incarnate in this life?

St. Germain had form. He had founded China as Huang Ti, settled the Persian Empire as Darius I, and effectively built Egypt as Imhotep. Rome, the center of the civilized Western world, had to become an empire. In his life as Caesar, St. Germain was the only man capable of crowning himself dictator and leaving Romans delighted about it. The inefficient republic couldn't run an empire, but with Caesar creating a tiered, delegated government system, anything became possible. If Caesar had not incarnated, the history of Western Europe would have been different. He brought in cataclysmic change in delegations, in the provision of infrastructure and how leaders communicate. He facilitated the spread of Rome throughout Europe. His life goal was to create a Roman empire. His spiritual goal was to subordinate his desires to the larger purpose.

Did he succeed?

Yes and no. Only Caesar can judge whether he succeeded or not, but he was predominantly successful.

How were his exceptional gifts shaped and developed? Did anyone help the young Julius become who he was?

Julius formed a special relationship, in his teens, with Renius, who taught him swordsmanship and tactics. Renius was a one-armed gladiator, formerly a centurion, who demonstrated to Julius the highest standards of loyalty. Renius was Julius's role model, and because of him, Julius would expect loyalty from those around him and give them commitment in return. Renius, an aspect of Hilarion, taught Julius respect for blood and earth ties and an understanding of the love the common soldiers gave to one another. They didn't fight for the glory, the spoils, or the honor; they fought for their friends. Renius taught him what made the ordinary soldier tick.

Julius hero-worshipped Renius. He taught Julius about manliness, honor, and how to keep a part of yourself safe from treachery. He passed on to Julius his belief in the Stoic philosophy: Don't complain; just get on with it.

Caesar took him to Spain, Gaul, Britain, and back to Gaul, where he died, as Caesar planned his return to Rome to cross the Rubicon. Caesar was grief -stricken because he had lost his only father figure. Renius was 78.

How did Caesar's family losing its honor affect him?

Caesar watched the senate turn on his father and grandfather, creating the family's disgrace. It gave him his profound contempt for the senate, and he would support, instead, the people's assembly. He outmaneuvered the senate to his very end. Having seen political power at work, he formed the cynical view that it could be bought, and fame was fickle.

There must've been a metaphysical reason for this loss, or you wouldn't have singled it out for exploration.

This disgrace drove Julius's hatred of the senate and his fierce, burning anger to win a victor's wreath, a triumph that the senate had refused him for his Spanish victories. If Julius hadn't passionately hated the senate, he wouldn't have created this new system of governance necessary for his rule of an empire.

How did Julius lose his heart? Was it to Cleopatra?

Caesar gave his heart five times, twice to women—one, of course, was Cleopatra, in an intense but brief relationship. He lost his heart to his sons and to his standard poodle Germanicus, who he got as a pup, and it would run alongside his chariot. The first time he lost his heart is a long story. I'll give you the short version. Julius loved a manumitted slave—a courtesan called Servilia Caepionis (an aspect of Lady Portia). Servilia was tall, with black hair, full lips, unusual green eyes, olive skin, and classical features. She was beautiful, with a magnificent body, high breasts, and long legs; a talented dancer, and one shrewd woman—the Angelina Jolie of her time—and a great judge of men. She was a man's woman who lived by her wits, cunningly manipulating men.

Why was she the love of Caesar's life?

An aspect of Lady Portia, a frequent love of St. Germain. She could outmaneuver Caesar and bring him tranquil periods of happiness, as he, too, brought her. She loved and respected him. This was the love of his life. They were passionate lovers, not sweethearts, and there was a son born of this union. Brutus did not physically resemble Caesar in any way (so he doubted his parentage, given his mother's livelihood), but he too was deeply loved by Caesar.

Did Brutus know that he was Caesar's son?

Caesar refused to confirm that Brutus was his son, worried that if he publicly acknowledged him, Brutus would become a target for murder. Nevertheless, father and son loved one another deeply. Caesar even forgave Brutus after betraying him, when he fought with Pompey against Caesar in Greece.

Caesar married three times in search of legitimate heirs, but he didn't seem to be very fertile.

There was his daughter Julia by his first wife; his son Brutus by Servilia; and his third son, Caesarion, by Cleopatra. He also had a brief affair with a Balkan slave called Octavia, who gave him his second son, Octavian, whom Julius loved on first sight. Octavian looked exactly like him: aquiline nose, highbrow, and similar deep-set eyes. Renius had returned.

Who was Octavia?

Octavia was the concubine of a powerful senator. She could not admit her pregnancy with Julius, so she feigned illness and went to the country during the final trimester. Octavian did not know who his father was until after Julius's death, when Caesar left him a last testament, telling his son who he could and could not trust. Caesar praised Mark Antony, revealing that he had been his brother, deputy, and lover. He loved him still, but was not blind to his weaknesses. Octavian would later quote Caesar's assessment of Antony in a letter, not acknowledging it as Caesar's.

Who knew of Octavian's parentage?

Nobody. And Octavian would never reveal it, concerned that it'd raise questions of his legitimacy, despite being his true successor.

Lurid graffiti on Roman walls describe Caesar as "every woman's man and every man's woman." Is that true?

Caesar was bisexual, with a preference for women, and highly promiscuous, reinforcing his sense of power and confidence. His low sperm count produced few offspring. He enjoyed the intimacy of gay relationships. His primary lover, Mark Antony, was turned on by the attractive Caesar's power and charm; however, there was a remoteness to Caesar that made relationships difficult to sustain. He avoided anything long term. After a one-night stand with Cassius, Caesar rejected him, and this rejection festered his hatred.

Caesar hid ill health in the form of migraines and epilepsy and relied on Mark Antony to keep it secret and treat him; however, Cleopatra suspected Caesar's illness, and Egyptian doctors treated him for a drooping eyelid and slight tremor in his face. It was myasthenia. His growing disability led him to manufacture his death.

How did he lose his soul?

Thirty years of war curdled his soul. Ordering men to their deaths in battle, slaughtering millions of barbarian hordes, commanding crucifixions, floggings, and sacrificing his principles to maintain his power—all took an emotional and mental toll. Julius's life had become a life in reverse. An ideal life starts in puzzlement and moves through strife into hope. Caesar's life starts in hope, achieves strife, and descends into hopelessness. Nevertheless, he improved Rome's governance by installing merit, not seniority, for promotion in the army. He curbed the senate's power and initiated good financial reform giving taxation relief for the less fortunate. He gave his life's energy to Rome, literally, and not as we have been told.

What is the real story?

Historians will say that despite warnings about the Ides of March, Caesar went to the senate and was assassinated by senators stabbing him 23 times under Pompey's statue. The truth is that Caesar, wanting to die, manufactured a conspiracy to assassinate him. He made his tenure as the dictator unsustainable by refusing to retire and employing agents to spread anti-Caesar propaganda. He deliberately behaved so atrociously to those around him and provoked retaliation. Caesar had lost control of his bowels. Only his son Brutus knew what was going on.

Where was Mark Antony?

Away. Caesar insisted that Brutus lead the conspirators, begging him to put his father out of his misery. Caesar revealed the true extent of his illness: constant shaking, falling fits, collapsed face, and memory loss. During the assassination, Caesar says to Brutus in Greek "Kai su teknon" ("And you, my beloved child"), to encourage him to stab him.

You're saying that not only did Caesar go knowingly to his death, but he manufactured his murder. Why? Surely a quick suicide or unexplained accident would be a better alternative to a painful public death? [The voice and demeanor of The Gatekeeper now changed, becoming stronger and more resonant. He was Caesar, rising from the chair and smiling and speaking to me!]

My first objective was the continuation of the Empire of Rome. My death must weaken the senate; otherwise, there would be a clamor for the Republic to return. And they could have returned to it; they had enough support. I had to create a martyr of myself, to negate how the senate would vote later and discredit them. As a martyr, I could rely on two powerful forces: the *vox populi* of Rome and the great sympathy of my Praetorian guard, who would move behind my nominated successor. I wanted Octavian to be emperor, but either of my sons would be an admirable choice. I weighed my options: suicide, a contrived accident, or poison like belladonna to simulate a heart attack. But there was a fourth option. Dying as a public martyr, murdered in front of the senate, would deliver everything I wanted. A quick death would cast all those I despised in a bad light. I needed Brutus; the others could not do it. Of my 23 wounds, only two were killing strikes—those of Brutus and Cassius.

Gratus tibi vale, dictator perpetuo. But there was supposedly only one fatal blow among the 23 cuts.

Cassius killed me.

But by involving Brutus, did you not condemn him to the harsh judgment of history as a traitor. Dante calls Brutus one of the three great betrayers of history, in the company of Judas and Cassius. Isn't that a harsh legacy for someone you loved? [The Gatekeeper, possibly fearing warfare, took over the reply.]

Isn't there yet another question: Had Brutus thought through the consequences of killing Caesar? I'll answer my question. No, Brutus had not thought it through. Brutus was a great and brave swordsman, with leadership qualities superior to Caesar's, but despite his gifts, he lacked strategic intelligence. He reacted emotionally to everything. Now, I'll answer your question. By the time of his death, Julius had experienced 30 years of warfare. Exercising complete power erodes your humanity. In his core being, he had steely determination, never governed by emotion; he never, for example, confused lust with love. But Julius also had fairness and rectitude and an ability to arrange tactics beyond the imagination of most people, although he was incapable of double-dealing or blackmail to grasp power. Sadly, I must conclude he had thought through the consequences of giving Brutus a role in his assassination.

What else did Julius Caesar bring to this incarnation from St. Germain?

He brought from St. Germain an innovative and practical intelligence, a genius. He had a quick, logical mind, with the command to engineer, explore, envisage, and lead radical change. Caesar had St. Germain's bravery and courage, clarity, and fortitude, and a charisma that made him uncommonly attractive to men and women, along with a libido that could exhaust anyone else on the planet.

Why do you say this was one of St. Germain's greatest lives?

It demonstrates mastery of his gifts, first, for establishment start-ups, knocking a nation into shape. St. Germain sees possibilities and then builds them—that's his forte; he is the builder. Caesar possesses St. Germain's gift for engineering. He is also the writer, the war historian, and he possesses a highly developed sense of honor and mercy. Maybe he overdid the ruthlessness, but still, it is a St. Germain trait. There are other Germainic traits of the dramatist, gambler, womanizer, charmer, ruler, and in Caesar's case, the hero. By the time Caesar had arranged his death, he was remorseful. His life had become painful and bleak. He was ill, incontinent, and impotent. Caesar's superb mental facilities were declining into dementia, with increased epilepsy and advanced myasthenia gravis. He was experiencing karma already, with a deeper understanding of what he'd done.

Cleopatra (69–30 BC),
Last Queen of Ancient Egypt

Cleopatra VII was the last pharaoh of Egypt. Born in 69 BC, in the capital of Egypt, Alexandria, her father was the reigning pharaoh, Ptolemy XII, a direct descendant of the conquering Macedonians of Alexander's invasion.

Cleopatra was well educated by Greek tutors and proficient in many languages, including Egyptian. She would be the first of the Ptolemaic rulers in 300 years to speak their native tongue.

Her father, a weak and cruel leader, was overthrown in a popular uprising in 58 BC and fled to Rome. Her sister Berenice became pharaoh. When her father regained the throne with Pompey's help, three years later, Berenice and her husband were executed. Four years later, on her father's death, Cleopatra, now a ward of Pompey, ascended the throne. She was 18 and ruled successively for 21 years, first with her two brothers and then with her son by Julius Caesar, until her death by suicide in 30 BC at the age of 39.

Although she inherited an empire in decline, she effectively ruled it through a dramatic time of plagues and droughts, resulting in famine and war. Cleopatra is best remembered for her love affairs with Julius Caesar and his protégé Mark Antony, with whom she had three children. Was Cleopatra merely a wanton seductress? I put that question to The Gatekeeper.

✳ Conversation with The Gatekeeper ✳

Was Cleopatra beautiful?

Cleopatra had the look of a Grecian woman. She was not a classic beauty, but she was striking and sexy, with dark hair, olive skin, a straight nose, a narrow waist, long legs, and plump breasts. It was impossible to take your eyes off her!

The Roman historian Plutarch said that Cleopatra was not beautiful, but that her voice was musical, and her charm was such as to make her company delightful. Did he get it right?

Yes, Cleopatra had a musical voice and dollops of charm, and with her sexual desirability, she believed herself to be sexually invincible. She lost her virginity at nine to her older brother and, after a variety of sexual adventures, learned how easy it was to manipulate men and get what she wanted. By the time she met Caesar, at 23, she was a seasoned performer. As a royal princess, she was educated in logic, rhetoric, politics, and governance. She loved poetry, art, and spoke Greek, Latin, and Egyptian fluently and understood Kurdish, Farsi, and Parathion. She was the original drama queen. Cleopatra understood self-promotion; she was a megastar. In her mind, Egypt was Cleopatra, a woman dedicated to self-absorption and selfishness.

Was she an able ruler and administrator?

She got things done. But she played favorites, leading to a string of bad judgments and the alienation of the most talented in the royal house and government.

What happened at her first secret meeting with Julius Caesar, when she was smuggled into his apartment?

Cleopatra was rolled in a carpet and carried by her servants as a gift from the queen to Caesar. The guards fell for the ruse and unrolled the carpet in front of Caesar. There lay Cleopatra, a sexual creature in diaphanous clothing, covered in jewels and precious metal. She sat up, purred, and fluttered her eyes at Caesar. Cleopatra had the confidence to know that she could make Caesar her slave in 10 minutes. He became besotted with her. She promised him the kingship of Egypt.

Yet she suspected that he was ill?

Cleopatra consulted physicians to gain a complete picture of Caesar's failing health. She acted quickly. She tried to get him to put aside his wife and marry her so that when he died, she would govern both Rome and Egypt. Caesar, however, suspected Cleopatra's plans—he saw her coming. Caesar was a man with superb strategic ability.

What was the reason for her visit to Rome?

She wanted a triumph to parade her relations, particularly her son with Caesar, before the Romans. Cleopatra wanted to feel what it was like to be truly at center stage, the Empress of Rome, and hence the world. She thought that if she got to Rome, Caesar might formalize their relationship. The opposite happened. Caesar saw it as a pursuit, and it turned him to ice. Nevertheless, because he loved her, he placed a statue of her as the goddess of love in Rome. Caesar pandered to her vanity. He welcomed her with what was as close to a triumph as he could give a non-Roman: the Praetorian guard marched, flowers were strewn, flame throwers roared. Caesar knew it was impossible to overdo it where Cleopatra was concerned! Then he put Cleopatra in a palace where he could watch her. Caesar wanted to be the sole willing recipient of her favors. He wanted her for himself.

Was Caesar the love of Cleopatra's life, or was it Antony, as Shakespeare implies?

Caesar was the most exceptional man she ever met. Nobody ever knew him fully. Cleopatra knew him better than most. She met Mark Antony (an aspect of El Morya, later Napoleon) as Caesar's second-in-command; for her Antony was easy prey. For Antony, Cleopatra was sensual, desirable, fascinating, and, because she was Caesar's, his ultimate aphrodisiac. Cleopatra didn't know the meaning of faithfulness. The reassurance of her power over men bolstered her self-importance.

On the other hand, for Antony, this was his significant love affair; he would fall completely under her spell. Cleopatra did not hide from Antony that she had other lovers. She loved seeing other men jealous around her. Caesar assumed Cleopatra wouldn't have the nerve to be unfaithful to him, let alone with Marc Antony, his good friend and lover. He would never know, so he did not consider it when calculating Rome's fate or his successor after his death.

What was the purpose of her affair with Antony?

To build an inspiring relationship between them of great beauty that would last for lifetimes. Cleopatra would incarnate as Josephine to his Napoleon, Princess Margaret to his Peter Townsend. And who are they today?

After Caesar's assassination, what did Cleopatra do? There is that wonderful quote from Shakespeare's *Antony and Cleopatra*: "I found you as a morsel cold upon dead Caesar's trencher."

Briefly, Cleopatra was in shock, but recovered quickly. She moved to assess how to turn this tragedy to her advantage. She considered her options. First, she looked at who may inherit Caesar's crown. She deduced wrongly it could be Mark Antony. Secondly, she assessed Octavian and dismissed him. Thirdly, she looked at Brutus and Lepidus, and not knowing what you know about Caesar's other son, she wrongly brushed them aside, too. She opted for Mark Antony as her best prospect and tried to sell him her idea, during some serious pillow talk, of becoming, with her, co-emperor of Rome and Egypt.

Cleopatra offered to return to Egypt with Caesar's son to implement this plan. She wanted to see how Antony would fare in the political quicksand after Caesar's assassination. If he was going to sink, she certainly was not going to go down with him.

Antony would summon her to Antioch to see her military strength, which he had seen little of. While he was besotted with her, he found Cleopatra's promises were wearing thin. Then, in Antioch, Cleopatra realized that Octavian was a far better tactician than she had realized.

There is a supposition that after Antony's suicide, she tried to seduce Octavian. Is this true?

To seduce him with power, not sex. Octavian told Cleopatra that if he wanted Egypt, he would take it. She knew he was right; she had nothing new to offer him. Reassessing her options, she saw growing opposition and a potential rebellion at home. She had lost her main allies. She knew Octavian could snatch her empire anyway, and she was scared of two shadows: the humiliation of becoming a Roman trophy and the signs of age in her face and body. And then there was Antony. He'd made such a mess of everything. She'd thought he was more able until the colossal impudence of his suicide. Devastated, she returned to her palace and summoned the priestesses, the suppliers of asps. Suicide was a mortal sin in Egypt, sending you straight to hell. If you were clever you could hold the creature to your breast, and if it chose to bite you, it was the asp's action, not your own. So it was, that Cleopatra suicided and passed into legend!

What is Mary the High Priestess and the creator of Egypt as Isis doing in this life? What was its purpose?

First, there was Cleopatra's historical purpose. As Isis, we saw Mary the High Priestess open Egypt up, and now as Cleopatra, she had to close Egypt down. In her ancient world, there were three major powers: Rome, Carthage, and Egypt. Rome had extinguished Carthage, and Egypt was sick, and in her life as Cleopatra, Mary ensures Egypt's illness will be terminal.

Secondly, this was a significant life devoted to self-interest. Cleopatra was a dissolute woman who could not think of anyone except herself (although I suspect she did love Antony because she frequently went back to him in their future lives). She desired absolute power. She was vain and spoiled, and her purpose was to get rid of any of her selfishness, because selflessness would be demanded of her lifetime after lifetime.

Sometimes we have an incarnation in which our best qualities are subdued, and our major weaknesses amplified to get rid of them, to accelerate progression. This means that all three aspects of Mary, including the mother of Christ, will be able to share Cleopatra's progression. You can expect to meet Cleopatra and Antony again as Empress Josephine and Napoleon. By the time she's Queen Isabella of Spain, you'll see her in all her glory.

What qualities of Mary does she bring in?

She brought in her inflexible will, intelligence, libido, facility with languages, and charm. Cleopatra didn't bring in Mary's understanding of governance, which we saw in Nefertiti, Nefertari, and Deborah, or her capacity for strategic analysis, compassion, and maternal love. Cleopatra was no feminist. She had little compassion and did not care a fig for the Egyptian people.

And her spiritual challenge was?

Her challenge was to conquer her greed for personal power and to master vanity and bring in compassion. She represented Mary's darkest side; all her negative traits rolled into one person.

Thinking about These Lives

The Gatekeeper is a man of strong opinions, but never was he more dramatic than when dealing with the Romans and the Egyptian queen, Cleopatra. Julius Caesar was simply, in his view, one of the most significant lives of St. Germain. On the other hand, he judges Cleopatra harshly, describing her as unpleasant.

"The abuse of greatness is when it disjoins remorse from power," Brutus says in Act II, scene 1 of Shakespeare's play *Julius Caesar* at his end; perhaps Caesar understood the meaning of remorse; he had regrets certainly. The Gatekeeper's Caesar manufactures the circumstances of his death when he creates the illusion that he is preposterously abusing his power. Then he uses the senate's understandable reaction to contract his assassination and, thereby, dooms the murderous senate to future irrelevance. Caesar's death ensured the Roman Empire's continuance, bequeathing to it a rudimentary government system that his illegitimate son Octavian would rule and stabilize as the great Emperor Augustus. Later, St. Germain, incarnating as Claudius and Seneca, would complete the administrative and legal infrastructure necessary to ensure Rome's greatness. Caesar left Rome as an empire growing but just surviving; Claudius left Rome as a superpower, with the administrative structure to prosper and survive.

More than any other man in Western civilization, Julius Caesar imposed his will on history, ensuring his other son, Brutus, would be condemned by it. Caesar, who articulated his regrets, did not regret involving Brutus. The Gatekeeper insisted that we explore the reasons why Caesar lost his soul. His decline into sickness will reverberate across 2,000 years, as his descendants, who share his spiritual DNA, will struggle with the seductiveness of power.

Cleopatra, unlike Caesar, was born with exaggerated shortcomings in order to fulfill her purpose: to lose a fading empire rather than win a glorious new one. She succeeded. Here was Mary the High Priestess fulfilling her mission: Cleopatra, through her brilliantly dramatic suicide closed down the ailing Egyptian empire, making possible the expansion of Roman power around the circle of the Mediterranean Sea.

No matter how I tried to match my vision of Cleopatra as a warrior queen wrapped in perfumed silks, clever, strategic, passionate, but caring for her people, The Gatekeeper consistently presented a different and negative view. He loathed Cleopatra as much as he loved Caesar. It seemed that all the qualities I admired in her had been attributed after her death. Whether as a scheming manipulator or a sensual and enticing woman, she still makes good copy. What was Mary, the embodiment of Jeshua and the Christian values of humility, obedience, compassion, and maternal love, doing as Cleopatra? It seems she was working to rid her line of orgiastic sexuality, selfishness, shallowness, and manipulation. Her Marian characteristics—superior intelligence, understanding of governance, and strategic abilities—were deliberately withheld so that she could succeed in her mission to give Egypt to Rome with minimum loss of life; therefore, in her failure, she ultimately succeeded.

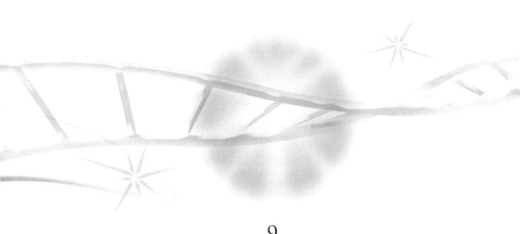

9

St. Germain and Mary's Role in Fulfilling the Law

Mary's story as the mother of the child who would change the world is an inspiring one of courage, devotion, and submission to God. Depending on the religious and cultural perspectives of the narrator, her story varies, but basically, there are three main versions: Catholic, Protestant, and scholarly. That was, of course, until The Gatekeeper provided a fourth version, one that presented a different Mary, but one consistent with her other lives.

Mary in the Catholic and Eastern Orthodox Churches

The Gospel of Luke is the scriptural source for all the great mysteries about Mary the Virgin, Mother of God. In his gospel, Luke tells of Mary's role in the Annunciation by the Archangel Gabriel, her visit to her cousin Elizabeth, the birth of Jeshua in Bethlehem, his circumcision, and her visit to the temple in Jerusalem. Matthew's gospel describes Mary's betrothal, marriage, the nativity, and the flight into Egypt from her husband's viewpoint.

The Mary of my Catholic childhood was demure, devoted, hardworking, and despite childbirth, never consummated her marriage with her older husband Joseph and remained forever a virgin. She ensured that her only son was brought up as a practicing Jew and encouraged Jeshua to enter his public life at the marriage feast of Cana, where, at her request, he performed his first recorded miracle.

Mary witnessed her son's crucifixion and suffered greatly as a result of her son's Passion on the Cross. This incident is the last mention of Mary in the Gospels. Tradition tells us that she would receive his tortured, dead body in her arms, an image captured poignantly by Michelangelo's *Pietà*. After Jesus's ascension, the Acts of the Apostles mentions her presence with his disciples at Pentecost, when the Holy Spirit comes to inspire and enable them to preach her son's message. One tradition has Mary traveling with John to Ephesus in Asia Minor, where she eventually dies and is assumed into heaven.

The Protestant Version

The Protestant version agrees with the major milestones of Mary's life but acknowledges Joseph as the biological father of her family. Jeshua's descent is traced through Joseph's line to King David, from whose house the promised Messiah would come.

Mary is, therefore, not the impossible ideal of a virgin mother of the Catholic version; instead, she lives in a sexually active marriage where she gives birth to James after Jesus and follows his birth with other sons and daughters.

The Scholarly Version

In the scholarly version, the picture of Mary is built carefully from the gospels and other historical texts, enhanced by archaeological discoveries and by the practices and rituals described in the Jewish scriptures. Scholars recognize that it is difficult to see Mary objectively because the gospels mention her rarely, and the Apocrypha, which glorifies her, was written between 200 BC and AD 400 by those venerating Mary as the Mother of God.

Scholars agree that Mary does not have a significant role in the gospels, and even if she attended special events like the Last Supper, she may not have been mentioned. In their view, Mary played a significant role, downplayed by the cultural perspective of the gospel writers and prevailing sexism.

Based on the Jewish scripture, the conventional age for a betrothal was 12 ½ years, and engagement lasted one year. Most accept that Mary was pregnant when she married. There is wide acceptance that the Virgin Birth was legendary. Paul never mentions it, nor does John or Mark. In Matthew, there is an assertion that she fulfilled a prophecy from the Book of Isaiah that the Messiah would be born to a virgin. However, recent translations from Hebrew use the phrase "a young girl", and although a young girl could be assumed to be a virgin, using the word "virgin" is simply an incorrect translation.

There is also a strong tradition that Mary lived in Ephesus in modern Turkey for about 10 years, although this evidence is circumstantial. Given the importance of Ephesus in Mary's other lives, such as Hephaestion, and The Gatekeeper's endorsement of it as Mary's place of death, it is reasonable to assume we'll hear more about it.

After meeting Maya, the Buddha's mother; Sarah, the feisty wife of Abraham; and Leah, the unloved wife of Jacob, three of her past lives, I did not know what to expect. Would Mary be a beautiful, argumentative woman like Sarah, a downtrodden drudge like Leah, or assertive and courageous like Ruth and Deborah? Instead, a lively Mary emerges, more complex and fun than I had expected. Someone must have forgotten to tell her that she was supposed to be the Mother of God!

☀ Conversation with The Gatekeeper ☀

The Gatekeeper's version of Mary's life story emerged over sessions in the leadup to Christmas. I interrupted with my usual clinical questions about statistics, dates, names, preferring a chronicle that either could or could not verify the story from the gospels. My questions included: Where was she born—place and date? Where was He born—place and date? Do we worship at the right site? Who showed up? Who were the eyewitnesses to the actual birth? What was the nationality of the Magi? What were their gifts? What was the bright star? How many angels were there? What were the animals? Was she a virgin? Was Joseph a widower? Were there any other children? Was Jeshua a difficult child?

These questions led to others about the five men: her uncle, Joseph of Arimathea; her husband, Joseph ben Mathias; her son, Jeshua; her protector in later life, the apostle John; and her biographer, Luke. I kept reminding myself that I was exploring her story not his. Jeshua's story could be told later.

Mary's Birth

Mary's parents, Anna and Joachim, lived in an Essene community, where she was born on 28 June 29 BC, near the settlement at Jimma, a town of Ethiopia. There was no angelic warning, and Mary was to be their only child. Joachim was a missionary for the Bahra sect, a more liberal branch of the Essenes. Traveling mostly by sea, he delivered pep talks, like an evangelist, to remote communities to enliven and inspire them. Mary's family would travel widely during her childhood from one desert community to another.

Joseph of Arimathea

Anna's family were well-off Levantine traders, a merchant family. Mary often traveled with Anna's brother, Joseph of Arimathea. He lived in a small village on the way to the port of Tyre in northwest Judea, not in the larger Arimathea, where scholars claim he lived.

Joseph was a powerful man and a member of the Sanhedrin. He was widowed with two children: Nicodemus, who later wrote a gospel, and Elizabeth, whom Mary visited when they were both pregnant. Joseph was tall, over five foot eight, with a shock of curly dark hair with a whisper of red, strong white teeth, pale skin, a full beard, and sidelocks growing into his beard (like a Hasidic Jew), which he plaited. He was a muscular man, always dressed in colorful clothes. An accomplished linguist, he spoke Hebrew, Aramaic, Greek, Phoenician, and Carthaginian, and enough Celtic to get by in Spain, Gaul, and Britain. He never learned Latin, because the Romans weren't traders, the Greeks were, and any Romans worth knowing spoke Greek. He was intelligent and well educated in the Greek classics. As a seeker of truth, he asked questions of himself and the universe. He was an excellent observer, able to do long-range weather forecasts based on his observations of birds and the elements. As an ornithologist, he kept records and wrote a fine book on seabirds. He is the most important man in Mary's young life, playing a significant role in the birth of Christianity.

Arimathea is St. Germain from his most crucial line, protecting and guarding Mary, as he had already done in their many lives together, especially as Boaz to her Ruth. He was also Aaron, a meaningful life for St. Germain.

Arimathea's Trading Enterprise

Arimathea regularly sailed to Carthage, Barcelona, Rome, Piraeus, Alexandria, Sidon, and back to Tyre. Mary traveled with him when she was old enough, hauling sheet anchors, setting sails. She was his favorite, a tomboy who loved adventure. Mary continued later to travel with him, disguised as a boy. She loved male clothing and wore it whenever she could, lifetime after lifetime, for its freedom and practicality.

Joseph traded in everything and anything: metals, notably tin from Britain and Spain, and lead. He married a Scythian Jew from the borders of the Black Sea, who mothered his two children.

When she died, their children were young. Mary became important in his life, his beloved favorite.

Mary's First Betrothal

Living in an Essene community on the border of the Sinai Desert, Mary became betrothed to Aaron. Good Jewish girls were expected to be married by 13, but by then, the travel-obsessed Mary was 16. It was usual to have intercourse during betrothal to test their fertility. After Mary fell pregnant, Aaron caught tuberculosis and becoming incapacitated, he reneged on their marriage. The community wanted to throw the humiliated Mary out, so her mother approached her brother for help. Arimathea urgently sought a husband for Mary within his extended networks. He found a 30–37-year-old widower with two children, who was a prosperous builder, living in Nazareth.

Joseph ben Mathias

Joseph ben Mathias was tall, with a lean, slimmer build, raven-black hair, gray at the side temples, and wore a whitening beard. He had a broad face, a hawk nose, a full set of glistening teeth, and large, strong hands. Joseph, an aspect of the Comte de St. Germain, came from the same line as Arimathea, Krishna, and Aaron. He was a serious, self-disparaging man who frequently doubted himself.

Before meeting Mary, he dreamed that the Archangel Gabriel spoke to him:

"You, Joseph, are to be honored. From your stem and branch will sprout the seed of David to be the Messiah."

"You are kidding! Why me?" he asked.

"Because of your steadfastness, virtue, and strength."

Joseph still had trouble believing Gabriel so did not speak of his experience.

Arimathea introduced his niece Mary to Joseph. This man trusted Arimathea, but when he met the heavily pregnant Mary, he became cautious. She was clearly soiled goods. He already had two children: 10-year-old Abigail and eight-year-old Simon. He didn't really need someone else's child. He thought Mary absurdly young. "I can't possibly marry her. She's my daughter's age."

But Joseph was what Mary needed: a rock, a taciturn man who didn't say much, with enormous moral strength. One word describes Joseph: kindness. If your daughter brought Joseph home, you'd say: "Well, thank God for that!"

Gabriel's Visit to Joseph

Their formal betrothal was to be a large ceremony in a temple. But Joseph had second thoughts, so Archangel Gabriel reappeared, saying: "Don't be afraid."

Joseph wasn't afraid. He just thought that this betrothal was past him.

Gabriel said, "Being as pious as you are, Joseph, you worry about taking this leap. Because of your virtue and strength, God selected you to father with Mary a son called Emmanuel." The name Emmanuel caught Joseph's attention, because it was used by Isaiah, saying, "He will be called Emmanuel," meaning "God with us." It isn't every day that an archangel tells you that you're going to father the Messiah. Gabriel pulled Joseph into line.

Mary's Second Betrothal

So when Joseph met Arimathea again, his friend encouraged him to invest Mary's large dowry into Arimathea's thriving business. That way, it would be invisible, and being a prudent older man, he knew that gossips would see the dowry as a bribe for marrying soiled goods. Mary would be hurt. Joseph did not need money; he had enough.

Joseph ben Mathias was in construction, building Roman villas and humble farmhouses. The word for "builder" and "carpenter" was the same in Aramaic. Joseph was not impoverished but an artisan, a developer, a solidly dependable, honest, moral, but vibrant man with St. Germain's love of dance.

Mary's Children

After Mary moved into Joseph's house, she gave birth to James, the son of Aaron. His father, a sweet and gentle man, died before James was one. Mary had to experience the humiliation of Aaron's betrayal to prepare herself for what lay ahead. Joseph, her protector, and provider, looked after the practical details, having extensive experience in raising children.

The Mother/Father wanted Jeshua to have older brothers, to be an idealistic revolutionary, because the youngest son was eager to challenge the existing order. So, Mary was to have two more sons, Judah and Joseph, before being pregnant with her fourth child, Jeshua.

Their Relationship

Their marital relationship was not an easy one; Joseph, a widower, was used to making every decision, and his strong-minded and strong-willed Mary wouldn't accept his authority. As Mary had three children in three years, there were settling-in difficulties. Mary was far more intelligent, more widely traveled, and better educated, but Joseph eventually grew to love her.

Gabriel's Visit to Mary

Four years after his last visit, Gabriel revisited Mary. Gabriel does not usually appear before women. He made an exception for Mary.

Gabriel begins, "Don't be afraid," and he tells her she is pregnant.

Mary is very indignant. "What, another one! Another child?" she protests. "How could this be, because I have not permitted a man within me?"

Mary and Joseph used a form of coitus interruptus, a notoriously unreliable form of birth control. She certainly didn't want another child. Nevertheless, Gabriel persevered.

"It is possible because the spirit of the Mother/Father has quickened life in you."

When Luke translated this from Mary's original Hebrew, he took it to mean that the Holy Spirit had quickened her womb in one who had not known a man recently; it sounded to Luke more miraculous. Later, in the Scriptorium, when copying the Gospel of Luke, they embellished the story to prevent it from being dull, and Mary became a virgin again, reworking the story of Jeshua's birth to make it sound heroic, believing that they were doing Christianity a favor.

As a pious woman, Mary accepted God's will, but it didn't mean she liked it. Later, when Joseph and Mary discussed Gabriel's visit, he finally told her about his dreams. Neither of them was happy. They feared, like sparrows, that there was a cuckoo crowding them out of their nest.

Mary's Pregnancy

In the spring of 13 BC, Mary, at 23, had an easy pregnancy, and leaving their five children at home, she accompanied 45-year-old Joseph to Bethlehem for the census.

Their Visit to Nazareth

In 13 BC, the Procurator of taxes decreed that all Jews had to return to their ancestor's birthplace to register for tax. The Procurator was always obeyed. Joseph tried everywhere to find accommodation, and eventually, someone took pity on Mary's condition saying, "You can share my animals' bedding in the stables underneath."

The Birth of Jeshua

It was a poor dwelling, a farmhouse, built in the Middle Eastern fashion of putting cattle downstairs to allow their heat to warm them in winter. They moved in with the ass, two draft oxen, a milk cow, and a guardian dog.

Mary had been in labor for two hours when starlight flooded the stable. Jeshua's spirit had entered, accompanied by his guardian, Archangel Raphael, and by the "Annunciato" Gabriel. They saw Gabriel as a tall, shining being with large, folded wings, but the spirits of Jeshua and Raphael were invisible to them, pulsating with golden light. Raphael remained holding a sword of fire, making sure the farm and the newborn were well protected. After a smooth delivery Joseph cut Jeshua's cord. Angels sang, but neither parent heard them. Sent by the Mother/Father as a gift of acclamation, triumph, and glory, it shook the foundations of Hell.

Gabriel said, "This is the one," gesturing to Jeshua. "I told you this would happen." He wanted to make sure that there was no doubt about whom they were the parents of. This was Emmanuel, the Messiah. Gabriel said, "This is the truth."

Raphael stood silent, watching, protecting.

Visit of the Magi

Shortly after Jeshua's birth, three strangers, all astronomers from the East, came to see the baby. These learned men, or Magi, had corresponded in Sanskrit for years: one from Iraq, named Belphasar; one from India, Sri Vishnamurti; and one from China, called Chang Tsing Pi. They anticipated an astronomical event, the massing of three planets— Jupiter, Mars, and Saturn—when the sun was in Pisces, and they knew that those same signs appeared each time a Great One incarnated. They knew that this life would have a tremendous impact on the world.

On approaching Bethlehem, the star emanated a golden light over the farmhouse. They saw it flare, its light pouring down as Jeshua's spirit entered.

After the men introduced themselves, Belphasar looked at the baby and said: "Zoroaster has come in."

Then Sri Vishnamurti looked at the baby and proclaimed: "Vishnu is born."

And Chang Tsing Pi said: "Lao Tzu has returned!"

Only one of them was correct.

They presented their gifts of gold, frankincense, and myrrh, then left to spread the word.

Herod's astrologers had told him that the child being born in Bethlehem that day would become King of Israel. A terrified Herod decreed that all males under two were to be killed. His decree prompted a mass exodus of families.

The Flight into Egypt

The family paid the farmer for their accommodation and traveled to Jerusalem, where the ceremonial circumcision took place. In a dream, an angel told Joseph about Herod's intentions. They rushed back to Nazareth to pick up the children and allow Joseph to salvage what he could from his business. With a donkey for Mary and the baby and a cart for their belongings, they hurriedly joined the convoy of pilgrims streaming out of Canaan, their baby boys hidden in camel saddlebags or in laundry baskets disguised as girls. Joseph paid for the passage of the family in a trading caravan swollen with refugees.

Their Stay in Egypt

Arriving in Egypt, the family rested in Alexandria's outskirts before joining an Essene community in the desert. They stayed there for three years, living in Thebes, where Mary gave birth to her last child: a girl, Rebecca.

Jeshua's Childhood

At the age of six, Jeshua broke his arm in a fight with this brother. Miraculously, he healed it. At 12, they discovered him in the temple in Jerusalem, discoursing with the learned doctors. Jeshua was a prodigy who walked like a king, possessing the calm authority and intellect to match any rabbi.

Joseph's Death and his Influence on Jeshua

Joseph, aged 58, died of a heart attack, leaving Jeshua grief-stricken. He would walk the Silk Road to India and Tibet after his father's death. When Joseph spoke, Jeshua would listen. His father was the one he most admired; his mother, Mary, the one most loved. Joseph was a humanitarian, shrewd, and always able to see to the heart of a problem. His son learned the value of brevity from his father.

Mary's Role in her Marriage

Mary was the dominant partner in the marriage and the moral and educational center of the household. She spoke, read, and wrote Hebrew and Aramaic, but Joseph also spoke Greek, which he taught his son, and the Greek language was vital to Jesus when he traveled to Tibet and Kashmir.

Mary's Qualities and Beauty

Mary was modest, self-effacing, always letting others take credit for things she did. She could be secretive. From Mary, Jeshua learned about humanity, the importance of kindness, and how to be around women. He had her compassion, devotion, warmth, and her ability to offer unconditional love, the kind of love he would share with his love, Mary the Magdalene.

Mary possessed a sense of the dramatic, as many gifted women do. She was a strong feminist and a natural leader, because Jewish women at that time were educated and listened to. You can see this at the marriage feast at Cana. The wedding was for her nephew, Arimathea's only son Nicodemus, and she, as a family leader, solved the embarrassment of the diminishing wine supply.

Mary was a renowned beauty: auburn hair with a hint of red, passed on to her son; dark gray eyes and fair skin.

Mary's Dreams for Jeshua

Jeshua's intellect was dazzling, and Mary hoped that he'd become a brilliant and charismatic chief priest; however, on his return from Kashmir, all she witnessed was Jeshua wasting his life with fishermen, laborers, whores, and innkeepers.

"Why don't you pick scholars, instead of rough fishermen and riff-raff?" Mary asked when he selected his apostles. But Jeshua knew that resourceful, strong-minded, and tough men, not academics, should be chosen. She was simply a Jewish mother who wanted the best for her son.

The Last Supper

Nearly 30 people gathered for the Last Supper, in a room above an inn on the outskirts of Jerusalem, not far from the Mount of Olives. There were 12 Apostles present with Jeshua, Mary, and Mary the Magdalene, together with various women who also numbered 12, the female disciples not mentioned in the gospels.

They ate the flatbread, black olives, cold meat, quail, salted oregano in oil and aromatic vinegar, salads of chicory, and greens. They drank wine. It lasted four hours.

Mary sat a sorrowful and silent observer. She, more than the others, knew of the mood of the Sanhedrin from Arimathea and Nicodemus. Jeshua did not have a chance. She ate little, silently observing his ritual of breaking and blessing the bread as his body and the offering of the wine as his blood.

Mary's Role in Jeshua's Passion and Death

Mary had to turn away as Jeshua, his back lacerated, his legs whipped, carried his cross in agony. Later, when she joined the spectators below the cross, Jeshua looked at her, not speaking to her directly until near his end. Her presence was a salve on his wounds. Their relationship, one of a master to a disciple and Jeshua's communication, was minimalist. It sounds callous, but loving-kindness could impede his disciple's progress.

When he died, Mary assumed the necessary role of the one person with unbending faith in him and his sacrifice. Without her, his mission would have been less effective. Her love brings him back. Mary was the surrogate for everyone on Earth. She offered her faith in him. This was an essential bridge to Isaiah's prophecy: "The serpent shall bruise your heel, but you shall crush its head."

Mary's Role in the Resurrection

Mary helped raise her son from the dead. Joseph of Arimathea told her Jeshua's wounds were healing, and she wanted to see this for herself. On Friday, Joseph and Nicodemus moved his body to his tomb in the garden of his Jerusalem home. There, Arimathea bound his body in bandages and had a dream in which letters of fire appeared telling him that Jeshua would rise from the dead— his healing wounds a sign the world could also be healed.

Mary led a party of Jeshua's followers to his tomb in the pre-dawn light of Sunday morning. She unwrapped his robe and unwound the bandages to examine his body. The wounds had closed, and some of the followers left to tell others who were in hiding. Mary the Magdalene remained outside the tomb, too distraught to enter. Now risen, Jeshua appeared to her, but she did not know him.

After his resurrection, Jeshua spent some time with the Magdalene and his mother. Mary, her eyes still red from her slow, steady tears, asked her son: "Why wasn't I told? It would have been easier if I'd known. I'd have been spared the hurt and misery I went through at your death!"

Jeshua knew that she needed not to be told, essential that she be kept ignorant, because she held his focus, and she was his way back to Earth. Mary was outraged on not being told the whole story, but she needed to propel herself forcefully through a gateway and move into acceptance of the wisdom of God. It was a forcible reminder to Mary that however much you learn at crucial points, or gateways, you will be completely alone when you go through them.

The first priest of all Christianity was Mary. Mary was Isis the High Priestess. She possessed the cup, she consecrated the first host, and she was descended from the first priest, Aaron.

Later, Mary left Jerusalem with her eldest son, James, and traveled, along with her uncle Arimathea, to Britain, then to France, and eventually to Ephesus.

Mary and Luke

Luke would visit Mary, now in her sixties, and crippled with arthritis, in Ephesus. Mary talked to Luke in Hebrew; he recorded her words in Greek. Mary was the main source of Luke's gospel, although some of the nuances of her stories were lost in translation. Luke witnessed Jeshua's death and his placement in the tomb. Luke also talked to Nicodemus and the women around Jeshua, but the misogyny of the time means that little of what the women told him finds prominence in his or the other gospels.

The Holy Grail and the Beginning of the Mass

[Mary's eldest son, James, speaks.]

My mother's prized possession was Jeshua's chalice, which she kept buried in a box close to her. Mary the Magdalene, now Jesus's wife, came to visit her in Ephesus. My mother would re-enact the Last Supper, using the chalice, whenever they ate together, as a ceremony for a group of devout people. When the Magdalene visited, there was John, Barnabas, Abigail, my stepsister, and sister Rebecca present. It was in a cave, where the walls were wet, trickling with water. She broke bread and blessed it and passed wine around in the chalice. Mary Magdalene took his cup home with her to France.

The Description of the Grail

[The Gatekeeper returns.]

What did the Grail look like? The Grail, as you call it, was a simple cup of wood carved by Joseph, with a slightly flattened base, completely unadorned. It had a clay insert, which could be taken out and washed. Later, it would be given a stem, scrollwork, and then the original cup would be inserted inside an elaborate chalice, not a simple one, but not excessive either. It would stay first in Spain and then in Provence until Helena, the mother of Emperor Constantine, returns it to Jerusalem.

Could you ask Mary if there is any particular message about her life, she wants conveying?

"Yes, there is. My life is my message," she says.

She has revealed to you through me her shortcomings and her strengths.

Was Mary warned of her death?

Mary was warned in a dream, by Mordecai, the angel of death. A creature of blinding light, he's often dreaded but comes with loving wings of comfort. He says: "It's time to join your Mother/Father at home. I will go with you."

On 18 July, Mary died of heart failure, at 68, in her cottage surrounded by her beloved stepdaughter Abigail and her stepson Simon, her emancipated slave, and the evangelists Luke and John. It was three months since Mordecai had warned her.

They lay Mary's body in a cave on a rocky ledge on Mount Bulbul. Barnabas, the disciple, came to see her the next day only to find her body gone, but her white grave robes were still there. There was an overwhelming smell of roses. Mordecai had accompanied her to heaven. Mary had ascended. Her resurrection and ascension were driven by her own will.

Thinking about These Lives

The Mary of The Gatekeeper's account is fresh, devout, loving, compassionate, strong, and adventurous. She is human and approachable, a woman we would all like to know. She is ordinary in her role as Judean wife and mother and extraordinary in her devotion to her son, Jeshua, during his Passion until his Resurrection, and later as his priest.

Her childhood is rich in adventure; she travels overland in Arabia, Sinai, Israel, and Egypt and by sea, across the Mediterranean, from Greece to Gaul, from Carthage to Cornwall. She speaks two languages and is an accomplished sailor. She is ready for life when her parents select her future husband, the gentle Aaron.

At 16, Mary is pious, intelligent, beautiful, and of proven fertility, a gift from heaven, only to be publicly rejected by her prospective husband and threatened with expulsion from her community. Mary's desertion by Aaron is a painful and humiliating experience. Arimathea, her uncle, shops her around the marital marketplace with a handsome price on her head until he finds Joseph, a widower, 21 years older. Joseph ben Mathias is such a reluctant bridegroom that he has to be prodded and pushed by none other than the Archangel Gabriel before he finally agrees, and only then with distaste written all over his face. Joseph's reticence is a good measure of his community's disapproval of Mary's condition.

Far from the picture of the divine virginal bride of medieval literature, this is a disgraced and humiliated Mary, a woman humbled by rejection. It seems that God wants to introduce her to the pain of betrayal, to toughen her resolve, increase her humility, and test her faith in preparation for her tragic and triumphant role as the mother of His son. Nor is the Mother/Father content with Jeshua being a first-born son or an only child. He is to be the fourth son and second last child. His birth order increases his tendency to be revolutionary.

When the Archangel Gabriel brings Mary the news that she will be the mother of the Messiah, she questions him closely before she agrees. She is not happy about a fourth pregnancy, which she has been trying to avoid.

When she discusses the archangel's visit with Joseph later, she discovers, after six years of marriage, that he has been previously visited and has been anticipating this event. At least, she can be reassured about the reality of her experience, although both parents seem uneasy about this alien pregnancy. When Jeshua is eventually born, Gabriel reappears to reassure the parents again and verify his identity. The angelic chorus of pure sound provides a wakeup call.

On Jeshua being the first son, The Gatekeeper maintains that this was a later embellishment. Its purpose was to increase the importance of the Messiah's birth and strengthen his direct line from King David, who, as a first-born son of the Israelites, was the sole heir to the dynastic inheritance. It was, he argues, part of Christian propaganda which, together with Mary's role as the Holy Virgin, sought to demonstrate Jeshua's superiority over the Roman and Greek gods and give his story divine credibility while making it seem more miraculous.

When Jeshua is six, Joseph has another visit from Gabriel. Mary is dreaming that her talented son could become a priest, hopefully, a chief rabbi, and Joseph is worried about whether his schooling will be scholarly enough to make his wife's dreams a reality.

Joseph, struggling to manage his gifted child, hopes that a selective private school for rabbis is the solution. Meanwhile, his divine Mother/Father has home schooling in mind to prevent the child prodigy from becoming too intellectual, and to foster his purpose to remake institutions and not be schooled in them. Joseph's decision about schooling presses a panic button, giving rise to one of the swiftest dispatchings of an archangel ever. I love this story. They could all live-in, school-obsessed Sydney.

Joseph teaches Jeshua brevity and clarity, and Mary reinforces his passionate nature, giving force in his teaching and encouraging his empathy and compassion, all elements that universalize his teaching.

In Mary, we have a woman who has experienced premarital sex, married a man 20 years older, has limited her pregnancies through contraception, reluctantly accepts her role as the mother of the Messiah, and completes her life as the first ordained priest of the new Church. She becomes the temporary guardian of Jeshua's chalice, the Holy Grail, from his Last Supper. Here we have many points of departure from traditional teachings on womanhood, sex, contraception, marriage, and priesthood.

There is a striking similarity between her life and that of the legendary Isis with Osiris. The most obvious one is in Mary's role in the *Pieta*, the grieving woman who cradles the dead Christ, just as Isis had cradled Osiris's body. Mary, Keeper of the Grail, is again like Isis the High Priestess. When Luke and John are in her presence, she blesses and consecrates the wine and the bread and shares her son's body and blood. She is the priestess: she does it; they watch.

Mary's death, although not as dramatic as some accounts, is dramatic enough. Visited first by the Angel of Death, giving her a three-month warning, Mary has time to bring her loved ones to her side and prepare for her death. Mordecai, the Angel of Death, is St. Peter, who accompanies her to her heavenly parents. After his annunciation, Mary dies, is buried, and 24 hours later, she rises from the dead and immediately enters heaven. No wonder her story has to be retold as an assumption not ascension! It could, otherwise, detract from the spectacle of her own son's Resurrection.

The misogynist writers of the gospels—and John and Luke in particular, who, being present at her death, had no excuse—failed to include this critical event in their chronicles. I can accept that the gospels were his story, not hers. Still, the omission of her death from the Apostles' Acts denies her recognition as his first disciple, denies her role as a priest, denies her recognition as the guardian of Jeshua's chalice, and most importantly, denies the recognition of her own ascension.

Mary has a multiplicity of different relationships with Jeshua. In his childhood, they are traditional—mother and son and teacher and pupil—but in his adulthood, He assumes the role of teacher and that of the disciple after she inaugurates his ministry at the marriage feast of Cana. Jeshua is a tough taskmaster, demanding that she accept his mission, even if that means she has to sacrifice her dreams and life. Jeshua controls the information he gives her, even when a forewarning of his Resurrection may have consoled her grief. He insists she join John, almost a stranger, despite an extended family. His decision means she will go into exile and comparative solitude to reflect on her life while preparing to ascend. At the same time, she will tell her son's story to Luke, and influence the composition of the Acts of the Apostles. Unlike the great images of Western art showing Jeshua helping his mother through colorful clouds into heaven, a stern Jeshua schools his mother through tough love into her mastery.

When I first heard The Gatekeeper describe the role of the Angel of Death returning for Mary, it reminded me of Serapis Bey singing as King Solomon: "Rise up, my love, my fair one, and come away. For lo, the winter is passed, the rain is over and gone." Mary had a hard and challenging life but won her right to ascend.

Our Mother/Father has the choice of the biological, intellectual, and spiritual diversity of all Ascended Masters for the parents of Jeshua. Why select

Mary and St. Germain? Once He has chosen them, why select the Kwan Yin aspect of Mary and the Count's aspect of St. Germain?

The answers to these questions are complex but rely on the following points. First, Mary and St. Germain were effective parents to a prior successful incarnation of Prince Siddhartha Gautama (560–480 BC). Mary, as Maya and St. Germain, as Prince Shuddhodana, provide him with the genetic input and spiritual guidance (or lack of it, in the case of his father) necessary for him to achieve his spiritual purpose: his enlightenment or Buddhahood.

Secondly, Mary is the most compatible with Lord Jeshua. She reflects his compassion and unconditional love and enhances these qualities through her teaching and example as a mother.

Thirdly, her role as Mary allows her to continue her role as Goddess in the West, a role that was unchanged in the East as Kwan Yin.

Finally, St. Germain, the father of Jeshua, becomes one of Christianity's sublime communicators. His lives as James the Apostle, Joseph of Arimathea, Patrick, Columba, Brendan, Christopher, Antony, and Francis Xavier will drive and inspire Christianity's growth. At the same time, his technological breakthrough as Joseph Gutenberg leads to the first printed copies of the *Bible* and the *New Testament,* thereby spreading Christianity's written message throughout the world.

St. Germain is selected because Jeshua requires a male guardian, a role model who is steady and practical. Being of a complex nature, he is also flexible, amenable, imaginative, and adaptable, as many-faceted as a jewel; that is why St. Germain is Joseph. Although he is a Taurean, he has the rising sign in Gemini, his moon in Capricorn, and these combined make him a defined but well-balanced figure. It is a difficult life but it is not his time to ascend; there is another path planned for him.

And Mary? The requirements for Jeshua's mother are also diverse. She has to be intelligent, compliant, but strong; a difficult tightrope to walk. Strong-minded women in a male-dominated society are usually rebellious and outspoken like Mary Magdalene or submissive in a passive-aggressive way. She balances between the two: submission to God but capable of assuming leadership when necessary. Mary is a modern woman.

Finally, what about St. Germain's role as Joseph? Based on The Gatekeeper's revelations, Jeshua has two hands-on fathers: one on Earth, one in heaven. While Joseph is the biological father, the Divine Father actively supervises Jeshua's spiritual and intellectual development. As a result, Joseph will deal with the Archangel Gabriel four times, more than any other human being until the Prophet Mohammed's experiences.

His contact with angelic beings, however, is not limited to Gabriel. Joseph has angelic visits and dreams to warn him to leave Israel at Herod's imminent slaughter of the innocents and to give him the all-clear to return home after Herod's death. Imagine the extraordinary difficulty of raising your son with God micromanaging your performance. In contrast, the son himself performs miracles and disappears from time to time to commune with what he calls "his heavenly Mother/Father." Imagine the complexity of skills, the balance of humility and assertiveness, and strength with flexibility necessary to inspire and teach Jeshua and his six other natural children and stepchild James.

Many Christian churches do not recognize Joseph as the biological father of Jeshua and instead, teach that it was the Holy Spirit. In doing so, they not only emasculate Joseph but diminish the complexity and difficulty of his role and that of all fathers.

St. Germain considered Joseph to be his most difficult life. You have to agree with him.

10

THE FOUNDING OF CELTIC CHRISTIANITY

Sixth-century Europe was sinking into darkness while Britain and Ireland flourished.

I asked The Gatekeeper where the impulse to inspire the flowering of Christianity in the British Isles came from? He answered slowly and thoughtfully, returning to the founding of Christianity and revealing a special relationship between Jeshua and Britain.

Jeshua himself sent Joseph of Arimathea to Britain to establish the beachheads for Christianity and asked him to return frequently to push them farther. Columba, Brigid, and Patrick were injected into Ireland to establish it as a place of Light, as the counterpoint to the Dark Ages. This decision was made by the spiritual hierarchy governing this planet. Ireland would become an impenetrable fortress of Light, not easily destroyed.

This chapter starts with the teenage Jeshua ben Joseph under the tutelage of his uncle, Joseph of Arimathea. It traces Arimathea's role in planting the seed of Christianity in southern England. Once we summarize the contributions of both St. Germain and Mary, we focus on their lives of missionary zeal as Patrick and Columba. Brigid's life will be discussed in the context of the kingship of Arthur in the following chapter.

✳ Conversation with The Gatekeeper ✳

Why were the Dark Ages necessary?

Western Europeans were far more advanced than the people in
Central Asia, but Europe's population was stagnating and Central

Asia's exploding. The stagnant Dark Ages were an essential part of rebirth and regrowth.

Why put a civilization so carefully constructed by the Greeks and the Romans into hibernation?

If you pour dirty water into a dam, it will eventually dilute with the clean water when the dirt particles settle. It is a more effective process than clarifying and refining every drop of water, liter by liter. The Barbarians had to be converted to Christianity and educated. The Dark Ages allowed the dirty water to settle in the dam. Scotland, Ireland, and the West of Britain were on the fringes of Europe, where this dark tide lapped them, but they were never overcome by it. The Light remained on this Western fringe, where the land was unattractive to the Barbarians. While the Roman Empire couldn't physically hold back the Huns, Goths, Mongols, and Turks, the rough seas around England, Scotland, and Ireland could. The Irish Sea made invasion difficult, and although the Danes made inroads on its West Coast, even they too were eventually converted. St. Germain's and Mary's lives were an investment against the Dark Ages but only just in time. Their work encouraged other intellects to pour into incarnation in Ireland.

St. Germain and Mary in Britain and Ireland

St. Germain and Mary have a particular investment in Britain and Ireland. These countries allowed the multifaceted St. Germain to incarnate in a vast array of essential occupations. Mary has also experienced a range of lives there, providing her with challenges to succeed. Both of them enjoyed their sheer freedom to explore and express his contradictory nature and her compassionate one. St. Germain flourished, because he loved the Celtic ethos, with its dynamic mix of heritages from Viking, Norman, Saxon, and Roman. Mary thrived because the blend of heritages gave her reticence and understatement and an opportunity to create quietly.

St. Germain's energy discovers, founds, and builds nations. He bursts in at the beginning, with the Herculean task of establishing the physical and conceptual foundation from which great countries can grow. In this role, he makes an extraordinary contribution to their development, sometimes as an authoritarian despot, sometimes as a privateer, but most often as a visionary leader. St. Germain has been active in the founding of Sumeria, India, Britain, Scotland, Ireland, France, Italy, China, Hong Kong, Singapore, Canada,

Australia, New Zealand, and the United States of America. In Britain's case, his role begins in a prehistory now lost in legend. The founding of Britain, according to Geoffrey of Monmouth, fell to Brutus, the great-grandson of Aeneas, a Trojan and the founder of Rome, a member of the vast family of Celts dispersed in the Trojan wars.

But is the legend true? Well, almost . . .

✳ Conversation with The Gatekeeper ✳

Who founded Britain, Gatekeeper?

The war-weary Trojans, who had well-devised escape routes from Troy, having had the best part of a decade of war to fine-tune them. When Troy burned, they fled, in disguise, on land and sea around the Mediterranean. These Indo-Europeans were a blend of cultures and people from Asia Minor and Greece, some originating from Sumeria. Their escape from Troy flowed in eddies around the Mediterranean to the farthest point in Ireland.

The founder of Britain was not Brutus but Britga, who was not Aeneas's grandson but like a godchild. He was a leader, a bard, and a warrior king like King David. As one of the displaced Trojans, he was one of the two forms of the migrating Celts: the dark-haired, narrow-skulled Celts who went into Spain and the red and fair-haired ones who went into Britain and France. Some of them founded Carthage; some settled in Barcelona. Others like Britga and the Tuatha de Danann in Ireland with their red or fair hair displaced the local Picts. Britga settled in Britain's southwest, naming it after his distant memory where his ancestors originated, Sumer, the ancient progenitor of the Trojans. His Sumer land today is known as "Somerset."

Although the Trojan War finished about 1190 BC, his clan's journey to the British Isles took a century. It left traces of this Indo-Aryan dispersion in the Irish language, with words in common with Sanskrit and a Celtic clan system that still follows the structure found in India today.

And Britga, who gave his name to Britain—legend says he conquered a land of giants when he arrived. One of the gene pools of southern England didn't allow thymus glands to cut off normally, producing a form of gigantism. Their size, helped by a plentiful supply of game, gave them such a high protein diet that they grew 8–10 feet tall, but their characteristics were eventually bred out.

St. Germain and Britain

St. Germain's relationship with Britain and Ireland is strong, persistent, and one of legendary devotion. His feminine aspect, Mary, also explores some of her most outstanding lives on British soil.

The British Character

[According to The Gatekeeper, the English have naturally occurring traits that endear themselves to St. Germain.]

Their Viking heritage makes them explorers. While some are missionaries, others are ruthless, with a playful tendency to lie to suit themselves. For St. Germain, truth is what he decides it will be at any particular time. The British are show-offs, while pretending to be otherwise, which means they underplay their part. While they are a race of merchants, many are artistic, and when you survey the breadth, the depth, and the brilliance of their artists, musicians, composers, singers, dancers, actors, poets, and writers, it is a disproportionate contribution for the size of their nation.

The British are inventors, and invention is part of the St. Germain character. His fellowship with the British means he can work through them successfully. St. Germain and Mary have contributed disproportionately to the standing of Britain in world history. Remember, they choose themselves what lives they want to explore, how they will develop, and what they will learn over successive incarnations.

St. Germain will incarnate as Alexander Pope and John Dryden and castigate everyone with his wit. He will engineer bridges, railroads, and steamers as Isambard Brunel and define logic as the philosopher Bertrand Russell. As the diarist Samuel Pepys he documents London life, and as Priestley, Faraday, and Dalton, spearheads discoveries in chemistry. He creates technological breakthroughs as George Stephenson and John Smeaton and makes surgeries safer as Joseph Lister. He will rediscover the blood circulation as William Harvey, beautify gardens and architecture as Edwin Lutyens and Christopher Wren, and build the nation as King Offa, lead it as George I and George III and as Benjamin Disraeli.

St. Germain will also contribute to Scottish life and history as John Logie Baird, the inventor of television; Alexander Graham Bell, the inventor of the telephone; Joseph Bell, the professor of surgery; and model for Sherlock Holmes as Arthur Conan Doyle, the author of Sherlock Holmes. As Walter Scott, he'll be a prolific romantic novelist, and as James Watt, he'll invent the steam engine. As Andrew Carnegie, he'll be an émigré industrialist, and philanthropist; as William Jardine, the first Taipan of Hong Kong; and as Stanford Raffles, he'll found Singapore.

The Scottish people share St. Germain's contradictory nature, while his Pan aspect savors the full force of their four seasons. The Scots are a wonderful mixture of Picts, of Iberian Celts and Celts from later migrations, and St. Germain adores their paradoxical nature, their devotion to education and their shrewd, prudent, money hoarding balanced by a warm generosity, philanthropy, and hospitality. Their vivacious conviviality and the warmth of their whisky balance their frugality. He loves Scottish inventiveness and pragmatism and admires their sense of humor—a humor cloaked in misery.

Mary and Britain

Mary's energy has a deep and lasting bond with Britain, growing from her relationship with Joseph of Arimathea and her son Jeshua's admiration for the country. Mary is St. Germain without the deception, a moderate version of his theatricality. She underplays her part, which is so British, as much as St. Germain overplays his role in his dandified lives as Benjamin Disraeli or Charles II. A perfect example is her life as the novelist Jane Austen, reticent and wittily observed. Mary energy delights in understatement.

As Jeshua's mother, she was an Eminence Gris, a role perfected by the English, that understated, read-between-the-lines diplomacy by political shorthand. She has made some remarkable contributions to Britain as Henry VIII's consort, Katherine Parr, one of the founders of the new Protestantism. She was King James I of England, who laid the foundations for the British Empire, and Edward the Confessor. One of her most enigmatic lives was the dashing Admiral, Horatio Nelson.

Mary shares St. Germain's love of magic and mysticism, which she uses in her darkest life as Morgana, where she explored what God was not. With her powers as Mary the High Priestess, Morgana matched Merlin's, practicing black magic and laying traps for another aspect of herself, Mary the Magdalene, as Queen Guinevere.

Like St. Germain, Mary chose incarnations as poets, including the British poets Percy Bysshe Shelley and Philip Larkin. She also searched for Canada's Northwest Passage as Martin Frobisher, experimented with the first English novel as John Lyly, designed romantic gardens as Gertrude Jekyll and Vita Sackville-West, and experienced madness as novelist Lady Caroline Lamb, triggered by the death of her St. Germain lover, Lord Byron. Mary's incarnation as Elizabeth Fry reformed women's prisons; as Annie Besant, co-founded theosophy; and as Marie Stopes, advocated family planning. She served Gandhi as Madeleine Slade and was executed as the World War I heroine Edith Cavell. She served Britain and its Commonwealth as the dedicated and much-loved Queen Elizabeth, the Queen Mother, described by Hitler as the most dangerous woman in Europe.

St. Germain and Mary in Ireland

Ireland is a challenging environment for both St. Germain and Mary because theirs are the Emerald Isle's governing energies. Mary's is the founding dominant energy of Ireland; St. Germain and El Morya assist her. Mary gives the Irish the gifts of her love of beauty and music, especially song and poetry, and the Irish affinity to sorrow, underwritten by their emotional courage. Mary the Magdalene incarnated as Deirdre of the Sorrows, giving the Irish people their instinct for political martyrdom and their quiet charm. St. Germain gives them a beautiful lyricism, recklessness, and humor, along with his mercurial charm, pioneering adventurous spirit, and adaptability. Both he and Mary provide a love of education by strengthening their will to establish schools, and El Morya provides a fierce pride, moral courage, everlasting memory, and toughness.

St. Germain, as Walter Raleigh, brought potatoes to Ireland, which allowed the Irish population to explode, and Mary mothered and taught the children. El Morya was responsible for the potato famine, which had two purposes: first, to trigger migration and populate the New World, and second, create a bitter memory and ensure that Ireland never completely united with England. The two countries must be separate and different.

St. Patrick, the national apostle of Ireland, was from the trickster line of St. Germain and christianized the Celtic country. As Ireland's founding father, he provided the nation with the physical and intellectual infrastructure to make them literate. St. Germain's love of mysticism, poetry, wit, and a warming drink found its most fertile ground to create the genius of the poet William Butler Yeats, the satirical novelist Dean Jonathan Swift, and playwrights Richard Sheridan and Brendan Behan. With the energy of St. Germain, St. Brendan the navigator, and the evangelist Columba, he will push back the boundaries of what was known and transport the Irish faith across the sea.

Mary's energy, St. Brigid, and Mary of the Gaels, a co-patron saint of Ireland with Patrick, would keep the Light alive during the Dark Ages of sixth-century Europe. They founded schools for girls. As St. Canice in a male life, Mary was a schoolyard friend and spiritual colleague of Columba and one of Ireland's 12 apostles. Canice traveled to Denmark to plead, unsuccessfully, with the Viking overlords to cease their raids on Scotland and Ireland. Mary would also support Yeats, as Lady Isabella Gregory, in founding the Abbey Theatre in Dublin.

Joseph of Arimathea (c. 50 BC – AD 40), Uncle of Mother Mary

Christianity begins in Britain with St. Germain as Joseph of Arimathea, Mary's uncle. By contrast, his entrance into all four gospels was solemn and sedate, a mysterious minor character in the drama.

Joseph appears toward the end of the Gospel's story as a rich and influential man from Arimathea in Judea. As one of Jeshua's disciples, a good and just man, he remained a secret follower of Jeshua, cautious of the Jewish authorities. Although he was a member of the Sanhedrin, the Jewish high court that condemned Jeshua, John's Gospel tells us that Arimathea did not agree with their decision.

After Jeshua's death, Joseph went to the Procurator, Pontius Pilate, and demanded Jeshua's body. This was a bold and courageous act for a man to openly request a criminal's body from Judea's most powerful man. Joseph claimed Jeshua's body from the cross. He and Nicodemus (who, although not identified as such, was Joseph's son) wrapped Jeshua in linen, anointed his body with myrrh and aloes, and placed him in a newly hewn rock sepulcher that Arimathea had built for himself. He left after rolling a high stone across the entrance of the tomb.

At this point, Arimathea disappears from recorded history and reappears in persistent legends associated with Glastonbury in southwest England. In one legend, Joseph is a towering figure: a wealthy shipping merchant, uncle of Mary, traveling companion of the Christ child, and founder of the first Christian Church outside Jerusalem as a missionary to Britain. Joseph is also the Grail's guardian, and a miracle worker capable of turning his staff into a flowering tree.

In writing his 1804 poem "Jerusalem"—first a hymn, now an oft-sung patriotic British anthem—English poet William Blake (1757–1827) built on the legend of the Christ's visit to Britain, asking:

> And did those feet in ancient time,
> Walk upon England's mountains green?
> And was the holy Lamb of God
> On England's pleasant pastures seen?

In the first verse of "Jerusalem," Blake refers to the tradition that a young Jeshua traveled with his uncle to Glastonbury on a trading trip for lead from the Mendip Hills in Somerset. In another legend, Arimathea fled Palestine, arriving at Glastonbury with 12 disciples. Supposedly Arimathea was sent by Philip the Apostle to evangelize the Britons in AD 63. Weary after his long journey, when he finally stepped ashore and prayed, he thrust his staff of thornwood into the earth. The staff miraculously rooted and burst forth into a thorn tree that still blooms every Christmas in Glastonbury.

Joseph met with the local ruler, Arviragus, and bought land at Glastonbury. There, Joseph built a wattle-and-daub church, and when Jeshua appeared to him to bless the church, Jeshua asked for the church to be named after his mother. Some years later, Joseph died and was buried beside St. Mary's Church. The Catholic Church canonized Arimathea and, in recognition of his role in Christ's burial, made him the patron saint of undertakers, for which he was, no doubt, eternally grateful. He shares his feast day, March 17, with St. Patrick.

☀ Conversation with The Gatekeeper ☀

What is the truth of Arimathea's story?

> When Jeshua was 14, Mary asked Arimathea to take Jeshua and his brother on a voyage of discovery. Mary hoped that Jeshua would be a rabbi, but there was always a safe career as a merchant. Jeshua saw the journey as an adventure, an opportunity to see Western Europe. Joseph had a long trip planned and a lot to teach his nephew, beginning with the basics of managing a ship. They sailed from Sidon to Malta, across to Rome, then from

Marsala (Marseilles) to Cartagena in Spain, and around Spain to land in Bordeaux, then to Lesser Britain (Brittany) to pick up blue rock ballast before going across to Britain.

Joseph owned 40 percent of tin mines in Cornwall at Carn Arthen and Carmarthen, south of Redruth, near its west coast. They anchored, in today's Falmouth, and picked up his tin, lead, and the blue dye, woad, while unloading the blue rocks. He pointed out Redruth, which he had named, inland from Falmouth. They went to Penzance (Hebrew meaning "Holy Headland") farther down the coast, which he had also named. Joseph was not the only Jew who traded in Cornwall and used Hebrew names when he talked about business to other traders. Cornish, an old form of Welsh, already had Phoenician words and letters, from the Phoenician traders who explored that area much earlier than Joseph.

Sailing around the coast of Cornwall into Bridgwater Bay, they arrived at Yniswyrddn, the Isle of Glass (Glastonbury). Joseph wanted to show Jeshua the holy Druidic site of Glastonbury Tor, the spectacular hill where the Druids had carved a dragon, winding its body around the hill to the top. In front of it, miles away, they built an earthwork zodiac of the heavens.

When Jeshua first set foot on the solid ground of Glastonbury Tor, it was full of peace and delight. He took Joseph's staff and planted it in British soil. He blessed it immediately, and it grew into a thorn bush, *crataegus oxyacantha praecix*. The thorn bush that grows there now is a descendant of the original tree. Jeshua wanted to leave his mark in Britain, he loved it so. Understanding the incongruity of planting a magician's wand in the earth of Britain, Jeshua chose a sacred energy point at Glastonbury to celebrate the mystery of the place.

Altogether they only spent seven months in Britain, Jeshua took away two values: fairness and independence. These concepts buried themselves in his mind and emerged in his teaching. The Celtic idea of justice gave all men the right to appeal above their chieftain to their king, to petition him personally. Jeshua was in constant and unremitting opposition to the priests of Jerusalem. In Celtic society, every man had the right to pray or talk directly to God, and they did not suborn their right to intercession to a priest; the priest's role was only to formalize ceremonies.

Jeshua used these concepts of independence and fairness in his teaching. He didn't and couldn't tell parables about Britain and

Gaul, because the Jews were intensely mistrustful of any foreign influences. His parables were about daily life in Palestine, as if he had never left Judea.

Did Arimathea participate in the meeting of the Sanhedrin that sentenced Jeshua?

Neither Nicodemus nor Joseph attended the meeting. Joseph had done the numbers and knew they couldn't avert the decision.

Was it a courageous move of Arimathea to claim Jeshua's body from Pilate?

Joseph was the nearest male relative, in Hebrew called the *go'el*. It was his duty to look after Mary's family, and he was therefore responsible for claiming Jeshua's body under Jewish custom. He paid a large amount of money to Pontius Pilatus: 500 shekels of silver, a considerable sum then.

If the sepulcher was in Joseph's private garden, do we celebrate the right tomb at the Church of the Holy Sepulchre in Jerusalem?

No. Joseph's house was on the slope of the Mount of Olives. The correct tomb was rediscovered by General Gordon and is near the Anglican and Baptist missions. It is plain and carved out of a grotto with a stone shelf.

Was Joseph a secret disciple?

His discipleship was an open secret among the apostles, although not widely known outside. Joseph was a closet rebel. To the Jews, he appeared a conservative man unlikely to have a relative executed as a common criminal. When he spoke to the scribes about his role in Jeshua's life, he was self-effacing and didn't want his name known. He also had been given secret information by Jeshua, which he didn't want to share.

Arimathea alone was given the vision, in words of fire, of how Christ would rise from the dead and how his wounds would heal to show that the earth, too, could be healed. Joseph needed to be informed of Christ's purpose in order to keep his body safe, cool at a constant temperature, free from rodent and insect attack, and otherwise secure while Jeshua was absent.

Was the voyage to Britain the last time Joseph ferried Jeshua?

Thirteen months after his resurrection, Joseph would ferry Jeshua and Mary the Magdalene to Marsala [Marseilles, France], from where they climbed to Braux, far above Aix-en-Provence, to be married.

A honeymoon trip—what did they talk about on that final voyage?

Joseph was a Celtophile—look at his flamboyance. They talked about the Celts in Gaul and Britain. Jeshua made prophecies about Western Europe, Gaul, and Britain, in particular. He prophesized how Gaul would help topple the Roman Empire and that Britain would be a world power, greater than Rome.

Did Arimathea convert Britain to Christianity?

After the Resurrection, Jeshua appeared to Joseph, showing him his healed wounds and, without speaking, transferred his love and understanding to his uncle about his life's purpose. Arimathea's experience at Pentecost heightened this. There, Jeshua was able to transfer his plan for Britain, not only for Christian priests but how he would need Arimathea to return as Patrick and Colum Cille. Joseph, believing himself called by Jeshua, returned to Glastonbury with seven disciples to establish the British Church. Later, five more, all Britons, would be called to serve, to make 12 followers. Wherever possible, Arimathea carried on Druidic traditions in the new Church.

Joseph loved birds, and in Britain, he had a jackdaw, which was odd because it was considered an ill omen. He believed it unfairly maligned. His love of birds is a St. Germain trait: we see it throughout his lives and in his return as Merlin and Colum Cille.

The Grail legend that runs through France and Britain features Arimathea. Is it true?

The legend of Arimathea bringing the Grail to England is partly true. The Grail, the cup used at the Last Supper by Jeshua, was carried on Arimathea's ship. Mary took care of it, and it remained with her in Ephesus until she passed it to Mary Magdalene before her death. Joseph carried the consecrated bread and wine from the cup to Britain, as a sample of Jeshua's body and blood. It is this that gave rise to the legend.

If Joseph of Arimathea played a significant role in the British Church's foundation, why aren't there records and references in church history?

If the British Church could produce evidence that a relative of Christ founded it, then all the Celtic countries would split off from the main body of the Church and form a rival block, a rival to the Roman pope. Such a belief had to be ruthlessly stamped out. Records were destroyed; Arimathea's epistles, monuments, any word of mouth were destroyed by order of St. Augustine of Canterbury. You won't find any mention of Joseph in the history of the British Church, but St. Germain, the trickster, if persecuted, leaves an indelible mark somewhere, and Jeshua had warned Joseph that the Roman Church would destroy the Celtic Church he founded.

So he must have outmaneuvered them in some way?

There is something—a tablet in lead, in front of Glastonbury Tor, in a long barrow. It is a memorial of Joseph. It is a long tunnel. It's his grave, and it will be found. It reads in Latin,

"HERE ARE THE MORTAL AND SANCTIFIED REMAINS
OF JOSEPH, EPISCOPUS PRIMUS BRITANNICA,
FIRST BISHOP OF BRITAIN. SENT BY GOD."

He's buried there. He died at nearly 90 years old.

Lies will dig their way out of graves eventually. Where exactly is his grave?

In the ruins of the first abbey, the church he built, under its East Transept, called the Church of the Mother. Jeshua appeared to him, as the legend states, to bless his work and endorse the naming of the church. Joseph saw Jeshua standing in all his glory in a cloud of luminous light. This occurred in AD 46, six years after Joseph went to Britain. The Church of the Mother was the first church of Christendom built in the shape of a cross.

The relationship between Joseph of Arimathea and Jeshua is not mentioned in the gospels or recorded by Luke or John. Why?

Both Luke and John mentioned the relationship, but it was removed at the Council of Antioch in AD 341. The Church was in the middle of a schematic power struggle, and they were terrified of Arimathea's influence. The council decided the bishops of the East and West would minimize this authority. Scribes in monasteries responsible for the liturgy and copying the gospels downplayed Joseph in the gospels, but the Arimathea legend lived and grew in the British memory until the Reformation. The triumph of King Henry VIII's battle with Rome, 1500 years later, was shared by the people, particularly in southwestern England, who believed deep in their national psyche that their Church was the Christ-appointed one, not Rome's.

St. Patrick (c.387–461), Patron Saint of Ireland

"I am Patrick, a sinner," St. Patrick declares in *Confessions of St Patrick*, an autobiographical account of his life as a runaway slave, outcast, mystic, teacher, missionary, and apostle of Ireland. It was the first written work in the history of Ireland.

Scholars believe Patrick was born near Dumbarton, Scotland, circa AD 387–390, the son of a Roman town councillor (decurio), when Christianity was the Roman Empire's official religion. Calpurnius, his father, was a man of standing and wealth. Patrick describes how, at 16, together with some servants, he was kidnapped by an Irish slave trader and sent into the hills of Northern Ireland to tend sheep.

Patrick said: "I would pray constantly, sometimes up to one hundred times a day." As a shepherd, he grew close to nature and his faith blossomed. Six years later, Patrick claimed, he dreamed that he heard a voice saying: "It is well that you fast. Soon you'll be going back to your country. Your ship awaits 200 miles away."

Seeing this as a sign, Patrick trekked across Ireland to find the ship and convince its sailors to take him aboard. After a three-day voyage, he disembarked in Gaul (France), a country despoiled by the Vandals, which he described as deserted by its inhabitants. Back in Britain, a much-changed Patrick heard another voice, pleading "Come back to us." A mysterious Wood of Foclut in Ireland beckoned him.

Patrick trained and became an ordained priest. He was in Gaul under the guidance of a different St. Germain, the great Bishop of Auxerre, when the Pope commissioned him to return to Britain to stamp out the heretical teachings of a Welsh monk, Brother Morgan (his Latin name is Pelagius).

Patrick traveled with the bishop to Britain and from there, returned to Northern Ireland. He was well prepared; he spoke the language, knew their customs, and understood their strong kinship allegiances. Supposedly he never left Ireland again, although a legend associates him with Glastonbury.

Using Armagh as his base, Patrick made missionary journeys into the rest of Ireland. Whatever he did in Ireland did not make him popular with the Bishop in Britain. His Confessio hints at self-justification like a plea before a judge. Later, when Patrick was proposed as a bishop to the English hierarchy, a friend revealed a youthful sin, preventing him being consecrated. It is unclear whether he was ever officially made a bishop, although traditionally, he is always depicted in a bishop's robes.

Patrick's writings are the first existing literature of the British Church and the primary evidence of Celtic Christianity. He wanted to abolish sun worship and paganism, and he made no distinction between classes. In a land where Celtic deities teemed all across the countryside, he melded the idea of a single, merciful God with the Celtic tradition. He often referred to himself as an unlearned exile and regretted that he had little education.

Patrick is said to have died at Saul, on Wednesday, March 17, AD 493. The site of his burial is disputed, but Glastonbury claims to have his relics.

The legendary Patrick stood six feet tall, wore green vestments and a gold bishop's mitre, and held a hooked staff that he commanded like a magician, pointing to snakes slithering around his feet as he expelled them from Ireland. Patrick explained the three-person God by holding up a green shamrock, the three lobes of a common clover leaf, to show that although each leaflet was equal in size, each was needed to make up the whole. Through Irish immigration, the legend of St. Patrick's magic reached the shores of Australia and the United States, and now there are school holidays and celebrations on his feast day, 16 centuries after his death.

※ Conversation with The Gatekeeper ※

Where was Patrick born?

He was born in North Wales to a Romano-British family, but the birthplace is no longer called by its original name. Patrick's nephew, Mel, built a church on the land where Patrick was born. He called it St. Patrick's Church, but it was known locally as St. Mel's Church. Today, it is called Kinmel, meaning the "Church of Mel."

What about his parents?

His father was a lawyer, a questor, effectively the minor ruler in Conway, not far from Merseyside (today's Liverpool). Patricus was baptized a Christian in the Celtic Church and sent abroad to study in Rome. He also attended school in Bologna [Italy], where he studied Latin, Greek, Rhetoric, Mathematics, History, and Philosophy.

But Patrick in his Confessions says he was uneducated.

He claimed that to humble himself. His Latin wasn't good; it was Romano-British Latin, a language in decay even in Church circles. As a schoolboy, he studied trickery and learned mass hypnotism from an Egyptian physician and various sleights of hand. He was well versed in the practices of Eastern magic, like Aaron, the brother of Moses.

When was Patrick ordained?

The teenage Patrick had been made a sub-deacon before his capture, which meant he could not be tried for a crime in Rome. He was ordained a deacon in France, where he met and became the lover of the Bishop Germain of Auxerre, another life of Master St. Germain. Germain returned to England, where the Roman grip was beginning to slip. Officially, his trip was to stamp out a so-called heresy, his true mission though was to destroy the Celtic Church. But Patrick supported the Celtic Church, and he and Bishop Germain parted ways. Patrick also supported Pelagius's belief that Christians should deal directly with God without intercession by priests, thus earning their way to heaven through their efforts. Pelagius's heresy is one of those Druidic beliefs that had appealed to Jeshua on his Glastonbury visit.

If Arimathea and Patrick advocate a Celtic form of Christianity, why does Bishop Germain advocate the opposite?

St. Germain will balance his lives around both sides; he is contradictory.

How did Patrick come to go to Ireland?

Patrick traveled to Northern Ireland, to Armagh, a more settled part of the country influenced by the Europeans. Fourteen years later, at age 36 years, he traveled to Rome to be ordained by a canon. When he headed back to Ireland, finally a priest, he was 37. His prime objective and divine purpose were to establish universities, libraries, and schools of rhetoric. He was spectacularly successful, and Ireland became a beacon of light in the Dark Ages. He set up his schools in Drogheda, Armagh, Lough Currang, Knock, Galway, Derry, and Kildare. His mission was to continue Joseph of Arimathea's work, and he converted western Britain, the Midlands, Wales, and Ireland into a peculiarly Celtic Christianity. He also established rapport with the Irish kings and established schools and monasteries for nobles and gifted commoners.

If the Irish were illiterate, where did he get his teachers?

Wales, Cornwall, and North Devon provided teachers, remnants of Arimathea's British Church. Patrick had seven sisters, six of whom he ordained in Ireland; two became abbesses of monasteries. They all spoke Celtic, but Patrick was not a teacher. From Jacob's line, he was a trickster, a superb leader, a gifted administrator, and organizer, and a devout but complex man. He ran his mission like a university president or vice-chancellor—exhorting, arm twisting, establishing, tricking, cajoling, but not teaching.

What traits did Patrick inherit from St. Germain?

Patrick possessed his intellect, pioneering spirit, capacity for innovation, adaptability, and mastery of magic and trickery. He had a regal demeanor, with considerable moral and intellectual clout, and walked with kings and negotiated with the rulers of Ireland. Patrick had St. Germain's communication skills; he was a linguist and an orator, only somewhat slippery.

How was he able to inspire such a following?

Patrick was a leader with vision and presence, a powerful force. Many people had incarnated waiting to be envisioned by him or by Brigid as part of their destiny. Patrick selected, or allowed to emerge, those he had baptized and educated as Celtic Church leaders. While an educative mission takes longer to build than an evangelical mission, it fastens better. It took time and patience, not typically St. Germain qualities.

What about St. Germain's magical abilities?

There are many stories about the wonders Patrick performed, and to an illiterate and gullible Irish, he amazed. Patrick reportedly tapped a stone with the metal tip of his staff, and clear spring water gushed out. He had competitions with the Druids, where they tried to out-magic one another. Patrick's basic skills were superior to the Druids, but he was no Merlin. He understood water divination, knowing which stones to tap. He used a mixture of primitive science and mass hypnotism. St. Patrick's wells sprang up all over Ireland. One of his favorite tricks was conjuring doves from his sleeves, which struck awe in the Irish. But there were never any snakes in Ireland. He didn't banish them. He won the war against the Druids, who were tattooed with snakes, because their chief weapon was fear, and education removes fear.

Patrick founded literacy schools, where scribes could be trained. There was a hunger for learning among the Irish, which gave him a tremendous advantage for converts in his newly established schools.

What did Patrick look like?

He was tall, thin, slightly stooped, with an aquiline nose and large tufted eyebrows. He looked exactly like the Roman Celt he was. He had undeterrable perseverance and was a charming but cunning negotiator who could smooth things and be placatory. He could also renege on his word later, if it suited him. He had an air of tremendous authority. People did as he asked.

What was his spiritual challenge?

Pride, which, to a certain extent, he overcame. He spent a long time in penance and sorrow, mourning, trying to suppress his baser instincts and sexuality. He had no further sexual contact after the experiment with Bishop Germain.

And his greatest accomplishment?

He almost single-handedly would leave Ireland a Christian country, and he cemented its learning tradition. Seventeen hundred years after his death, his work in Ireland lives on. The Shamrock story was not part of his legacy; it was added later. St. Dunstan imposed the sun sign on the Celtic cross, but Patrick was responsible for bringing it to Ireland.

Did he condemn the slave trade?

Patrick, who had been a victim of slavery, attempted to convert the kings of Meath and Wexford, who'd grown fat on piracy and slavery. Patrick made it a condition of their conversion that they renounced slavery, and Ireland remained slave-free thanks to him.

Is Patrick buried at Glastonbury?

Patrick visited Glastonbury when he was quite old, well into his sixties. But he did not die there. He died in the northwest of Ireland, on the border of Mayo and Donegal. His body was transferred to Armagh after his death.

Did St. Germain as Patrick leave his mark? Are there any traces of him?

St. Germain was more secretive as Patrick than in other lives. However, he left a footprint in primitive concrete beneath the altar of a ruined church near Ballymena. There might be some doubt now as to where the altar is, but its foundation is still there.

Thinking about These Lives

Whenever I meditate on St. Germain, the words of American poet Walt Whitman (1819–1892) rise to the surface: "I am large, I contain multitudes." (*Song of Myself*, 1855.)

In this chapter, St. Germain is three different saints from one branch line. If Joseph of Arimathea brought Christ's message and purpose to Britain, it is from Jacob's line; Patrick, bringing enlightenment through education to Ireland, is from the same line. St. Germain of Auxerre lives as the only counterbalance. He is from the Imhotep line. But St. Germain again as Patrick and Merlin are identical to each other. From Patrick comes a sense of identity, a love of literacy, and learning.

Joseph of Arimathea was the iridescent thread running through the lives of Mary, Joseph, and Jeshua. As in many St. Germain lives, it is hard to grasp all of his accomplishments. He was a surrogate father to both Mary and Jeshua. At Arimathea's son's wedding at Cana, Jeshua inaugurated his ministry. Arimathea was the caretaker and preserver of Jeshua's body after his death, ensuring that he had a safe vehicle for his Resurrection. Some years after Pentecost, Joseph carried the Christian faith to England as its first missionary. His missionary expedition was the first that grew from a trading mission, allowing him to found the first Christian Church in the world.

If one accepts The Gatekeeper's revelations about Arimathea's role, then it gives a new perspective on the claims of the Roman Church as the one true Church and sheds new light on Henry VIII's success in establishing the Anglican Church. Whenever I reflect on Arimathea's accomplishments, I return to the wonderful holiday he gave Jeshua in Cornwall and southern England, showing him the magic of Glastonbury and Stonehenge. It became such a special place in Jeshua's heart that he ensured Christianity would be established in Britain first and that his mother would be honored in its first church, in Glastonbury.

Arimathea, as a typical St. Germain life, was a frontiersman. He took Christianity outside Roman civilization to a country without Jewish settlement. Like Patrick, Brendan, and Columba, who followed him, he established the cradle of Christianity in the West.

But what happened to Arimathea himself? He returned twice to Britain to continue spreading and preaching Christianity, until he finally ascended—first, as Colum Cille, then as John Donne, the metaphysical poet, evangelical preacher, and dean of St Paul's Cathedral in London, one of the contributors to the King James's Version of the Bible. His nephew, Jeshua ben Joseph, charged him with the mission of converting Britain, and he converted it three times over 1600 years.

Patrick was a magician and mystic, an exterminator of slavery, a victor against the Druidic priesthood, a hard-nosed negotiator, a diplomat, a brilliant administrator, a builder, and an inspiring evangelist. He was a man who converted a whole nation without producing a single martyr, a feat not accomplished anywhere else in the history of religious conversions.

It is hard to grasp the magnitude of Patrick's accomplishments. He was called to enlighten Ireland using English-, Welsh-, and Breton-trained teachers directly descended from Joseph of Arimathea's Celtic missionary efforts. He created an Ireland that would save Western civilization as Darkness fell across the Greco-Roman world of Europe. Ireland's Light shone in learning and literacy, while it powered Western literature and philosophy with its multitude of monasteries and schools. Patrick was not a plaster-of-Paris saint!

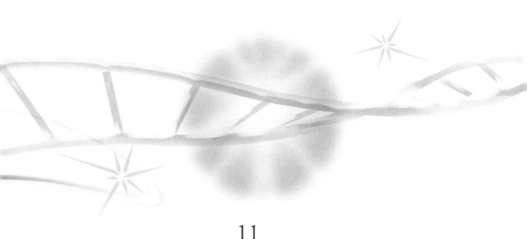

11

THE FIRST BATTLE
OF BRITAIN

The times were turbulent and gloomy when, around AD 400, the Romans abandoned Britain, leaving its civilized life to crumble. The retired legionaries in their sprawling villas in English valleys were left to fend for themselves. At the same time the petty Celtic kings in their hill forts squabbled over the boundaries of their fiefdoms.

Approximately 55 years later, a warlord, Vortigern, seized the opportunity to expand his territory and invited, as his tactical support, the German Saxons into Britain. When the Saxon invasion began, the true story of Britain's fierce defense by its Celtic and Roman inhabitants disappeared into Welsh ballads sung by the firesides of the vanquished, leaving the Saxon victors to write the "official" history of Britain.

In this chapter, I'll describe what I learned from The Gatekeeper about the first battles between adversaries of the Light and the Dark. It was the time of the reign of Artoris, the high king of Greater Britain. The Gatekeeper will answer the question: Why are some people born evil? But he will also pose new questions, such as: If there were 12 apostles led by El Morya as Peter, why are there now 12 knights of the Round Table led by El Morya as Arthur? Surely, we've seen all these knights before. If so, why are they returning, and why now?

St. Germain will frequently incarnate during this important time, but in this chapter, we will concentrate on his engineering genius and magician, Merlin. Mary will embody three lives, using each of her three aspects: first, as Arthur's queen, Guinevere, where she will use an aspect of Mary the Magdalene energy; second, as Arthur's half-sister Morgana/Morgaine, where she will use her Mary the High Priestess aspect twice; and third, in her life as

Brigid, an Irish saint, Mother Mary herself will incarnate, her first life since her sad but triumphant life as the mother of Jeshua ben Joseph.

Merlin (AD 430–540), Magician of the Light

We all know Merlin; he is the most famous of wizards. He is the tall, robed magician with the wild hair and the long white beard, the wise enchanter who will become the prototype for Gandalf and Dumbledore.

Merlin was the confidant of King Arthur of Britain in the fifth century and the designer of the Round Table for his 12 knights. Together, they lived in a legendary utopia called Camelot. St. Germain, the great showman and trickster, claimed that Merlin was his favorite life, so when Merlin inhabits this legend, he'll be a brilliant sorcerer; however, he is a person of dubious provenance and far more interesting when he inhabits history.

Our first glimpse comes from Geoffrey Monmouth's *History of the Kings of Britain*, where Merlin is described as the son of a nun raped by a demonic spirit, from whom he inherited his prophetic vision.

The story of Merlin goes something like this:

The legendary King Vortigern had a problem constructing a tower. His druids told him that if he sprinkled the blood of a fatherless man, the building would not collapse. The young Merlin was brought before Vortigern and immediately argued with his magicians. He correctly identified that underground water beneath Vortigern's building was causing its collapse. Merlin prophesized that there were two sleeping dragons below the water: one Saxon white and one British red. These two dragons would awake and fight. Merlin foretold the destruction of religion and churches until a boar of Cornwall trampled their necks under his feet.

Bored by the tale, Vortigern interrupted, wanting to know his future. Merlin then predicted the invasion of Vortigern's land by two brothers, Ambrosius Aurelius and Uther Pendragon. This was fulfilled upon their arrival with 10,000 men the next day. With his accuracy proven, Merlin became Vortigern's prophet. He was described as "the brightest genius," for his ability to both predict the future and construct mechanical contrivances. He would, however, eventually join the tall, red-haired Uther Pendragon as his special advisor.

King Uther Pendragon fell passionately in love with Ygern, Duchess of Cornwall, considered the most exceptional beauty in Britain. Merlin's enchantment allowed Uther to seduce Ygern while disguised as her husband, and from their lovemaking a boy was born who, at 15 years of age, would succeed his father as king and Merlin would become the new king's advisor. The king was King Arthur.

As legend records, it was King Arthur who succeeded in repelling the Saxon invasion of Britain. The final battle supposedly took place at Mount Badon near Bath, Somerset, in AD 542, at which Arthur was mortally wounded by his nephew Modred and was cared for on the Isle of Avalon near Glastonbury until he died.

It was not until the 17th century that the authenticity of Geoffrey of Monmouth's imaginative writings was questioned. In the interim, Welsh balladeers, French poets like Chretien de Troyes, and English poets like Malory and Tennyson recreated the lives of golden-haired Arthur, his knights, and his wise wizard and told of one of the world's greatest romances. We don't know whether Arthur and Merlin existed, which has allowed us to believe whatever we want. Now, The Gatekeeper will separate truth from legend, with surprising results.

✳ Conversation with The Gatekeeper ✳

Who was Merlin, and did he really exist?

Merlin was a wonderful human being, an aspect of the Comte de Saint-Germain himself and a twin soul of Patrick. Merlin spent his youth as a soldier, encouraged and guided by his Roman father, a Roman military commander from a senatorial family. His father, Marcus Fiddelius Cotta, owned a large Roman villa near Okehampton in southwest Britain. It was a fort really, around which he had built his village. He was not a king, but a ruler of a local area. Where is it? It is in North Devon. His mother was a Welsh Celt called Ingraine (pronounced In-gran). He was born about AD 430 and died about AD 550, having lived for 120 years!

Was Merlin his real name?

His father called him Ambrosius Marcus Cotta. Ingraine used his Welsh name, Myrddin. His last name was Cotta, a noble name because Julius Caesar's mother was a Cotta. His name alone would guarantee his father, a seat in the senate. He was known as Merlin because the British found it hard to say the Welsh name, and another important reason: in the Romano-British language, a small falcon was called a merlin, and our hero had one perched on his shoulder. He could also shapeshift into this falcon.

How did Merlin learn his magic?

He learned magic from his Welsh mother, who was an arch-druidess, an accomplished magician. She taught him elementary projection of his will and word commands and all the basic spells. Let me give you an example. He learned from her how to send forth his chi body to achieve his will. You look puzzled. Here is a lesson in St. Germain's magic. Imagine a king-fu master wanting to smash bricks with his hand. He breathes in and out to build his chi, creating as he does a course of energy. He will cry out at the point when the energy has become explosive and bring his hand down. His chi smashes the bricks, not his hand; his hand only creates the illusion.

It sounds more Eastern than Celtic. How did he learn the other standard St. Germain tricks?

His mother procured a Welsh tutor, a druid, who taught him Welsh ritual magic. All the tricks! He could turn a staff into a snake, a great crowd-pleaser, followed by pulling worms and maggots out of ears and noses or frogs out of a woman's cleavage. He would punish the pompous by pulling spiders out of their ears. Merlin, like his twin soul and contemporary, Patrick of Ireland, was an accomplished hypnotist, with mastery of mass hypnosis. Merlin mostly learned science from the druids. He was a keen observer of nature, and he used the clever application of fact to make him appear all-powerful. The druids were mostly scientists; only their shamans could do the super-normal. The little real magic Merlin did was like alchemy, the transmuting of metals. He was a good armorer, knowing metallurgy well, and he could command energy fields.

You said that he had a twin soul. What is that?

Everyone, before incarnating, can replicate their soul and plant it into a different body. There are a few rules. Each soul must be a minimum of a decade apart in birth, each in a different country, each with very different physical DNA, a different life purpose, and a different guardian angel. It is unusual for a twin soul to meet his or her twin soul, but St. Germain often sets out to break the rules.

You said that Merlin was a shapeshifter. How did he learn shamanism?

When Merlin was 12, he was taught by a Pictish shaman, a war captive of the Romans. He started as a slave at his father's villa and stayed on as his chief huntsman. The shaman taught Merlin to move without sound and stalk, be invisible in the stillness, and move with the light and shadow in the woods. Merlin could shapeshift and hypnotize any animal so that humans and animals were unaware of his presence. Merlin's pet jackdaw sat on one of his shoulders; it was his partner in magic. The bird understood Latin commands, and Merlin could shapeshift into it to scan the territory and spy on others. He had a succession of these jackdaws. On his other shoulder was his merlin, which he used for hunting.

This sounds like a movie script for a child's fantasy. How can we understand Merlin in our scientific world?

Think of Merlin as Leonardo da Vinci with a touch of showmanship and a wand! He also had some of the brassiness of his former life as Aaron. Merlin trained as an engineer, building siege engines, ditches, fortifications, roads, and fortified walls. He was a brilliant military tactician. On voyages to Brittany, he discovered the Frankish stirrup, an invention that allowed soldiers to stand. By standing in the stirrup, soldiers could get purchase to wield a sword. Arthur's victories in battle would rely on his revival of heavy cavalry helped by the stirrup.

Merlin was a talented mathematician, military engineer, chemist, metallurgist, architect, and builder. After he left the Roman army, he went to work for Uther Pendragon as his military engineer and strategist. He was intellectually curious about whatever gave him power. There, Merlin used his knowledge to predict eclipses, droughts, and deluges, allowing him to advise when to store grain and water, useful in the military camps he designed. He converted this information into his prophecies. Altogether, it was impressive. He protected the purity of Arthur with his magic, outmanoeuvring the darker magic of Morgana.

Why do you say "purity of Arthur"? It's a strange comment to make about a warrior king.

Artoris was there to lead a legion of Light against the Darkness of the invaders. I will return to this theme later.

Well, is it true that Merlin predicted Ambrosius and Pendragon's attack on Vortigern, as the legend describes?

This story is true. Merlin had an efficient network of informers and spies. He could observe troop movements through his fox and jackdaw, using his shamanic skills.

Did Merlin play a role in helping Arthur's conception, and was Uther Pendragon really his father?

Uther was tumescent with lust for Ygern, the wife of the Duke of Cornwall. He asked Merlin to help smuggle him into the hill fort in Cornwall. Uther entered through a secret passage to find Ygern waiting. Her husband was older and sexually inactive. Uther, the handsome flame-haired warrior, was the match to her tinder. Arthur was the result.

With flaming red hair to match his father. Were there other children?

No, Arthur, born in 453, had, as a child, his mother's ethereal beauty but with her coal black hair, and there were no more children. Uther was a fine soldier, a great and cunning general of total ruthlessness, and he kept the Saxons to a thin coastal strip. This meant that Uther was away for the next five years fighting. Ygern already had two daughters, Margaux and Morgana, by Gorlois. He was murdered; poisoned by his wine taster.

In the Arthurian legend, Uther murders Gorlois.

Uther was an adulterer, not a murderer. Gorlois's death allowed Uther to marry Ygern. Merlin concocted a fanciful story about Arthur's conception to look virtuous in others' eyes. This was particularly important for Ygern.

Was Arthur conceived at the medieval castle Tintagel in North Cornwall as the stories say?

It was in a place that no longer exists: an iron-age fort on the Rumps promontory.

What happened to Uther's son Arthur?

After Gorlois's death, Ygern chose Merlin as his tutor. He taught him Welsh, Latin, and some Greek, as well as rhetoric, logic, mathematics, and military tactics. Later, Arthur was sent to King

Cole, that merry old soul, his father's oldest friend. While in Cheshire, at the Roman fort Deva, Arthur learned tactical warfare, diplomacy, and the art of sovereignty. When Arthur's training was complete, Merlin hatched a plan to make him king. He built a sword in stone and placed it outside a coliseum.

Did Arthur become king because only he could pull a special sword from a stone?

It was expert showmanship from Merlin, crafting the most sublime selling of Arthur as king. One day, a stone was discovered with a sword embedded in it, outside the circus entrance of Cirencester, a Roman city. The mysterious stone was inscribed:

"WHOSOEVER CAN WITHDRAW THE SWORD FROM THIS STONE
WILL BE KING OF BRITAIN."

All men, young and old, passing by tried to pull it out without success. Arthur, just 17 years old at the time, was finally coaxed into having a go. Arthur stood above the stone, waiting. Merlin facing the crowd, nodded slightly to Arthur, and crossed his fingers behind his back, signaling his apprentice to release a lever, which held the stone's clamp. It was operated by a cable buried in the ground, and when the apprentice stood on a small lump of earth, it released the spring, which released the clamp, and out came the sword in Arthur's hand, like pulling a knife from butter. Arthur waved the sword above his head. "Behold, the future king!" Merlin yelled. It was not unlike one of Aaron's tricks!

Did Camelot exist?

Yes. Merlin designed them as part of Arthur's strategy to repel the Saxons. It was a series of four Camelots, Roman-style hill forts naturally shaped like a camel and used for water storage and troops. They were strategic garrisons at key vantage points and used to move troops by ship or land wherever they were needed. The main stronghold was near Cadbury in Somerset, the second near Strathallan in Scotland; the third garrison was southeast of York. The fourth, near Chester, where they conducted ship repairs and organized supplies. Merlin's strategy meant that Arthur's army could stay put while he and the closest knights moved around the coast or used the Roman roads.

What was the purpose of the Round Table?

Merlin dispensed with the tradition of head of the table and created the now-famous Round Table as a sign of egalitarianism, a hallmark of Arthur's government. Arthur shared his power with his council of 12 men, each having an equal voice. It's one reason we know so much about his knights and little about the knights of other kings. Every one of his 12 main knights was a returned apostle, except Sir Percival, who was Jesus returning as a Briton without his divine self, and Sir Lancelot, who was John the Baptist. Merlin was not present at the Round Table; his role was always one of adviser. He designed it with 13 places, leaving one seat (or siege, as it was called) vacant. The Siege Perilous was where Judas should have sat.

Twelve (and 13) are the numbers of Jacob's sons, or the apostles plus Christ, or the members necessary to establish a Jewish temple. Where did this idea come from?

Twelve represents the apostles with whom the knights shared a sacred mission. Merlin also took inspiration from the pagan Wiccans and the Babylonian Zoroastrians, for whom 13 was a critical number. Twelve is the oldest monumental survivor of the solar system's astronomical chart. Each of the Round Table knights, each son of Jacob, represents one of the Zodiac houses. Each knight was a reincarnation of one of the 12 apostles, hence Judas's empty seat. Arthur was Peter.

The Gatekeeper then explained which Apostles experienced lives as Arthur's knights: (*Indicates one of the twelve apostles.)

| Lancelot Grail Hero | Lanfranc Lancelote (Name given to protect his identity in Britain). Previously John the Baptist. Not in the Round Table | Lord Essarion of the Way, John the Baptist | The Frank from Burgundy, very close to Arthur, warrior of renown, great fighter called Lothar. Agrees to be Galahad's father, very handsome, very chivalrous. |

*Gawain (The Wolf) or The Hawk of May	Gowain	St. Germain, St. Bartholomew also known as St. Nathaniel	Lot and Morgause's son, second in command of cavalry. Arthur's first cousin. Very talkative. Hero of Chivalry. Will go on to lead many countries, most recently India as Jawaharlal Nehru.
*Kay (The Bear) Grail Hero	Ce pron. Kai -	St. Germain, St. James the Apostle	King Coel's son, very loyal to Arthur, his foster brother, quarter-master.
Percival (The Hare)	Parsifal Peredur –	Jesus. Jeshua ben Joseph, Rangy, strong, agile, tough	Celt with Jute father he followed Arthur around like a lamb. Spiritual. Walked the dragon lines of Wales to create Excalibur.
Bors (The Fox) Grail Hero	Borholt	El Morya, St. Mark, the Evangelist	King of Devon's son, immense size, black hair, very devout, prior lives as Achilles' lover, Patroclus, Scipio, Mark Antony. Will also be Duke of Wellington.
*Bedivere (The Stallion)	Bedwr	Hilarion, St. Andrew	Seschenal, Kay's assistant, twin brother of Lucan the butler. Very loyal, Welsh speaking. Dies before Arthur. Leads Britain as Henry VIII and USA as George Washington.
*Lucan	Lwchan	Mary the High Priestess. St. Phillip	Welsh, Breton, and French speaking. Twin brother of Bedwr. Leads Britain as St. Edward the Confessor, Queen Elizabeth, the Queen Mother, King James I. Leads France as Anne of Austria and Pakistan as Benazir Bhutto.
*Yvain The Knight of the Lion.	Yves	Pallas Athene, St. James the Less	Leads Britain as Elizabeth I and Margaret Thatcher.

*Arthur	Artoris	El Morya, St. Peter	Leader of Apostles and Knights. Son of Uther Pendragon and Ygern. Cornish, Welsh and French speaking. Fathers five children including Galahad. Killed by his own son with Morgana, Modred.
Guinevere		Mary the Magdalene	Welsh beauty, inspired Camelot. Wife of King Arthur. Briefly lover of Lancelot.
*Tristan	Tristram	Kuthumi	Son of King of Devon, brother of Bors and Lionel. Lover of Isolde.
Morgaine Morgana		Mary the High Priestess. Dido, Queen of Carthage	Daughter of Gorlois. Sister of Morgause. Half-sister of Arthur, Mother of Modred. A dual soul of Light and Dark.
Modred	Modred	St. Germain. Judas	Incestuous son of Arthur and Morgana.
*Lionel	Leonel	Hilarion	Brother of Bors. Fought Percival & lost.
*Gareth		Djwhal Khul. St Mathias or Mathew	A Frank from Alsace, lover of Morgause.
*Lamorac	Lamorak	St. Thomas. Serapis Bey	A prince from North Wales near Cheshire border. Chief of Intelligence, Danish, Saxon, Welsh, Romano British speaking. Frequently undercover in Saxon or Danish settlements. Manager of network of spies. Future lives Thomas Aquinas, Walshingham, Conan Doyle, Isaac Newton and Albert Einstein.

*Delleas	Dellynys	St. Germain St. Thaddeus known also as St. Jude, Hope of the Hopeless	
*Galahad Grail Hero	Gilead	Kuthumi. St. John the Evangelist	Arthur's son, 14 years younger, bad stutterer, Jewish. Mother: Mariana, brother Nathaniel. Previously King David, Finn McCool, Ulysses. Leads shock troops and cavalry. Gallant and pure, dies a virgin. Intellectually impaired. Future lives will include Leonardo da Vinci.

Why wasn't Arthur's military role and Merlin's contribution to it canvassed in the historical chronicles?

Did Arthur ultimately win? No? Who did? Wasn't it the Saxons? His enemies won, and the victors write the history. Arthur disappears. He disappears into Welsh legend, and so does Merlin. Legends are interesting, pointing the way, but not ultimately reliable.

Did Merlin play a role after Arthur's death?

Modred mortally wounded Arthur, and the king's body was secretly taken by boat to Glastonbury. Once there, Merlin threw Arthur's sword into the Sea of Glass. The ceremony conducted by Bishop Clannard resembled a requiem mass. Arthur was buried near Joseph of Arimathea in the wattle-and-daub church Joseph had built. Later, Merlin, afraid that the Saxons would desecrate Arthur's grave, had the body reburied in a secret place.

What did Merlin look like?

Much as imagined. At the end of Merlin's long life, he had a beard and white locks. As a young man, he was clean-shaven. He was tall, patrician with an aquiline nose, and thick bushy eyebrows. He looks like St. Patrick, with a classical Greco-Roman face, but he was squarer, with fuller lips. He threw more to his Roman than his

Celtic side. He had piercing, bright, periwinkle blue eyes and skin of pale, translucent whiteness. His hair was crow black.

Was being a shaman his greatest accomplishment?

In a metaphysical sense, Merlin's magic was critical because the times were Dark, and he had to protect the Beings of Light: Arthur, Guinevere, Galahad, Gawain, and Percival. In a practical sense, he brought the stirrup to Britain and reconceived heavily armored equestrian soldiers, allowing them to be mounted on Clydesdale-like horses. He rebuilt the harbor at Chester and a sea wall, all silted up now, although archaeologists may still find remnants. He reconstructed Roman siege machines and refined them.

Merlin created the myth of Arthur by creating the magic around him: his mysterious conception, the sword in the stone, the Round Table. He created Arthur as a king about whom people were in awe; otherwise, Arthur would have been a general and unable to unite other kings whose infighting might give the Danes more than a toehold in Britain. Merlin created a new form of a sword in Arthur's sword. His two technological achievements, the sword, and the stirrup, transformed warfare and made the medieval knight possible.

What was his spiritual challenge?

Merlin's spiritual challenge was to find God, but he was agnostic, so he never found God. He consciously never created any evil. There was so much to like about him. He was an intensely kind man. Animals came to him, hence the pun in his name: the Merlin. He always had animals around him, a raven (regarded as an omen of death), jackdaws, a pup fox playing at his feet, and field mice in his pocket.

Was Merlin buried at Marlborough College in Wiltshire?

No, Merlin's body is in North Wales—in Snowdonia, near a waterfall called the Swallow Falls, above Betws-Y-Coed. His bones lie in a cave sealed by a rockfall. Merlin will reincarnate as a great spiritual leader in Britain, and in the best tradition of his trickery, his remains will be discovered when needed. When Merlin reappears, watch for the warrior Arthur at his side. The new Arthur's father is already here, flame-haired of the Pendragon line. It could be as soon as 2020 or as late as 2030. Merlin will say no more.

Guinevere (c. 460–520), Neglected Queen

Wrapped in French romances and Irish and Welsh ballads, Guinevere is the ideal of courtly love, but in another role, she is ultimately the faithless queen whose love affair with Lancelot causes Camelot's downfall. In literature, Guinevere is the daughter of King Leodegrance (Lleudd-Ogrfan) according to Malory in *La Morte D'Arthur* tradition and the daughter of a Roman noble according to the Welsh Geoffrey of Monmouth.

While writers will disagree about Guinevere's pedigree, they agree on her beauty, desirability, and accomplishments. They also agree that she came from a noble family, that both Arthur and Lancelot loved her, and that she was unfaithful and childless. In some romances, she is devout and condemns herself for her unfaithfulness, isolating herself to a convent in Glastonbury, where she dies. Guinevere supposedly shares a grave with Arthur near Glastonbury Abbey.

✳ Conversation with The Gatekeeper ✳

Her biographers agree on her beauty. Just how beautiful was she?

Guinevere was so stunning; she took your breath away—think of a young Margot Fonteyn. Guinevere was tall, five foot seven, with nut-brown hair, hazelnut with copper tinges, soft and gentle dark brown eyes, and an oval face with full lips. She had thick, strong eyebrows. Her voice was low, a mezzo-soprano, melodious and rich. She played the lyre and Welsh harp and was an accomplished artist in watercolors.

Where was she born?

She was born in south Wales to Davydd, the daughter of King Leo de Graunce. Her correct name is Gwynhwyffawr, and his name is Lleud Ograffan. She had a sister who married a petty king in north Britain and a brother who inherited her father's throne.

How was she educated?

Guinevere could read and write and complete elementary figuring. She sang, spoke Breton, Welsh, Romano-British, and Latin. She was well educated for a woman of the time.

How did she and Arthur meet?

King Arthur was 25 when, during his progress through Wales with his court, and accompanied by Merlin, he met Guinevere. She was 18. For Arthur, it was love at first sight. Her immediate reaction was indifference, but he grew on her. He pursued her with zeal, courting her to the point that his traveling companions complained. He had loved her in his life as Peter the Apostle, when she incarnated as Mary the Magdalene, but his best friend and Lord loved her, too, so Peter stood aside. His love for her in his life as Peter was his strongest memory. Guinevere did not feel the same, but Arthur fell desperately, deeply in love with her.

Peter and Mary Magdalene! Where has that come from?

It has come from King Arthur, who is advising me.

Well, that takes my breath away! What happened next?

Merlin arranged the marriage, while Arthur beat back the Danes in the north. They married six months later. Lancelot escorted Guinevere. Bad move! Lancelot and Guinevere fell for each other during the procession, just as the legends say. There was no impropriety on the journey, but Lancelot, the Frank from Burgundy, was a charming novelty, a foreigner who spoke Celtic and Romano-British with a quaint accent, you know as only a suave Frenchman can. Ultimately though, Arthur and Guinevere were married near South Cadbury, in a Christian ceremony with several priests attending.

Was Guinevere childless?

To her great sorrow, yes.

Then who was the mother of all Arthur's children?

He fathered seven children with an Irish princess, a Jute captive slave girl, and a Jewish woman. He also had two children in Scotland.

From which line would the Tudors claim descent?

From the Irish daughter of the princess called Dymphna. She had red hair, and so did one of her sons. He took the name MacArthur, which became McCarty in some places. Arthur's descendants today in Scotland are from his Scottish children. Their names are Lyon, as in the former Queen Mother, or they are called Spencer, as in Churchill and Lady Diana; Tudor is the name used in England from his English-born children of Dymphna.

So Henry VIII's claim was correct?

Henry Tudor, better known as Henry VIII, was tall and red-headed, a Pendragon through the Tudor line. Look at Henry Wales, Prince Harry, tall and red-headed, twice a Pendragon through the Spencers of his mother's side and the Lyons of his father's grandmother.

Guinevere is represented as a two-dimensional character, but I suspect there's more to her.

Guinevere was responsible for the happiness of the main Camelot. She was a gifted woman, who made a home out of the iron-age fort at Cadbury or the summer Roman fort at Caerleon. She breathed life into any dwelling, asked about the servants and soldiers' families, and established, with Merlin's help, a health clinic for all the retainers, the servants, and their children. Surgeons were brought from Syria and Egypt to a military hospital, the first in Britain for battlefield wounds. Guinevere went on to create traveling field hospitals. Guinevere founded a free school, first at Cadbury, taught hygiene, and emphasized a clean water supply. She created an oasis of light and civilization. Caer Leon was a great place to come home after a campaign, with its heated floors and medical care. It was clean, ordered, and happy.

We've often seen that St. Germain's role was to protect Mary. Did this happen at Camelot?

Merlin was her great ally. She had ideas; he made them happen. He liked her, was even a bit in love with her, but it was truly a father-daughter relationship. He protected her. Guinevere was brighter than Arthur, as so often happens in Mary's marriages, with way above average intelligence. She was feminine and sensual, and Merlin enjoyed her company intellectually. He saw her loneliness, and knowing how to make a Marian energy happy, brought puppies from Brittany, spaniels that followed her everywhere, ate at her feet, and slept on her empty bed and protected her.

There are stories about Morgana and Lancelot. In one, she cast a spell on him; in another, he admits his secret love for Guinevere.

Morgana, disguising herself as a widow of a Scottish king, visited the Court at Cadbury. In Arthur's absence, she plied Lancelot with drink until he admitted his love for Guinevere. It was a secret she used to her advantage, seeding Lancelot's mind that Guinevere returned his affections. Morgana also planted small fragments of teasing information with the queen's waiting women.

Their betrayal of Arthur was never purposeful, no conscious urge to betray the man they both loved. They shared an enormous physical attraction, and Guinevere was a neglected woman besotted with Lancelot. Their passionate affair was brief, consummated merely three times. It ceased by mutual consent.

News of the affair went to the poisoned ear of Modred, who told Arthur. Arthur wept. He had lost his two closest friends. In the ensuing weeks, he attempted military suicide through insane personal displays of courage. Arthur drove the Danes back from Essex and then rode home to Guinevere. It was a meeting of the greatest sadness. She wished to enter a convent at Glastonbury.

Meanwhile, Modred fomented a rebellion, bringing together an army of northern tribesmen, Danes, and Scots. A final battle began. Lancelot survived but was hurt. Modred mortally wounded Arthur, who died in Galahad's arms on a boat taking him to Glastonbury.

What was the lesson we can learn from Guinevere's life?

Her life expressed an eternal truth. What we do, we do, and it's irreparable, and it has consequences. She survived 26 years after his death—a whole lifetime of regret, guilt, misery, and repentance.

What was her spiritual challenge?

To forgive herself, which she never did.

Where was she buried?

Not in Glastonbury Abbey, where tradition claims she was buried. Guinevere was buried in the convent's grounds, close to the abbey. Her body was then moved to a convent at Shrewsbury, nearer her family, known as the Convent of St. Walzeal in Saxon times; today, it's known as St. Winifred.

What do we know about Guinevere's past lives?

She was the only one we'll ever see of this line: the Pieta line of Mary. First, she was Mary the Magdalene; second, she was the Irish Deirdre of the Sorrows—the beautiful Deirdre, promised to a king, who falls in love with Naoise and escapes to Scotland. The king induced them back to Ireland on a false assurance of safety. On their return, he had Naoise killed. Deirdre, in her grief, fell on his murdered body, smashing her head on a white rock, and died.

And Naoise is a past life of Lancelot?

Lancelot was Naoise!

They were set up to fail. The tragedy of their love affair was preordained. Why did Guinevere agree to be part of an eternal triangle that would destroy all participants?

Without the eternal triangle, Arthur and Merlin would have won and driven the Saxons and the Jutes out of Britain. Their love triangle contained the Saxons, not defeated them. They were necessary for the genetic mix of future Britons.

How should Guinevere be remembered?

As a beautiful woman of great moral strength who was sweet-natured, sensuous, intelligent, and humorous. She adored music and dance. She was a man's woman, compassionate and generous, who created the values of Camelot, egalitarianism, helping and teaching others and spreading happiness wherever she went.

Let her be remembered for the sunshine she brought to Britain and not for her guilt and misery. She was a good queen. To understand Guinevere's legacy, we have to discuss Morgana. And I do this reluctantly.

Morgana,
Magician of the Dark

Cryptic, dark, and intelligent, Morgan le Fey comes from the hidden side of the moon. As King Arthur's adversary and his half-sister, she is portrayed in French and English literature as both an evil enchantress who encourages her son to slaughter Arthur and the fairies' golden-crowned queen.

In history, Morgana was the daughter of Ygern and Gorlois of Cornwall and, therefore, older than her half-brother Arthur. Geoffrey of Monmouth first mentions Morgana in the Latin text *History of the Kings of Britain*, where she is married to King Lot.

In legend, her story has all the intrigue and passion of a French movie, containing sibling rivalry, an unfaithful wife, a decaying marriage, betrayal and seduction, and the mastery of the dark arts, with the underlying pungent smell of incest. In actuality, it was the quintessential English melodrama, without the breezy Hollywood happy ending.

Morgana is a character who fascinates most people who read the Arthurian romance, but she does not captivate The Gatekeeper. He did not want to talk about her at all. In deference to Dr. Litchfield's Christianity, he would use a sign of the cross to open and close any sessions about her. He advises readers of this section to use whatever protection you consider appropriate when reading through our conversation. He made it clear that whenever he and I examined a life and employed the person's name, we called them to us, and that person was immediately present. Unseen, they could approve or disapprove the release of private information about their lives. The Gatekeeper was tough enough to deal with when it came to Jacob or Julius Caesar and took no nonsense, but Morgana was different. He believes that when you mention Morgana's name, you call the Darkness to you. She was the Lord Voldemort of Camelot legend.

✳ Conversation with The Gatekeeper ✳

Describe Morgana.

> Morgana was beautiful. She was born five years before Arthur, on the isthmus near Polzeath in Cornwall, with the sea crashing around. She was named Morgana, after the sea goddess. She had crow-black hair, pale skin, green eyes, and was tall and voluptuous, with a deep voice for a woman, a contralto. She had even white teeth and long, slim, graceful hands, which she fluttered when she spoke or sang. Until Arthur she was an only child. Gorlois, her father, became impotent after her birth.

How did she learn enchantment?

> Morgana learned the Dark path from a nursemaid, a slave from Egypt, but not Egyptian. She was a light-skinned, fair-haired Berber, taken slave when the Goths invaded North Africa.

Legends tell us Morgana learned magic from Merlin. Did she?

Morgana, disguised as a young man, became Merlin's apprentice to learn his magic. She fooled Merlin, but because his magic was 95 percent advanced science, she didn't comprehend it. Morgana was intelligent but not educated enough to understand chemical reactions. She believed that he was a true magician. Morgana was an accomplished herbalist and a poisoner, skills she learned from her Berber maid. Merlin became instantly sexually attracted to his pupil, the disguised Morgana, but they both resisted their impulses. This potent sexual attraction quickly turned to mutual aversion. Merlin observed Morgana and put proper protection around himself and Arthur. Merlin always went to sleep with a silver thread across Arthur's door.

Was it an actual or real thread?

It is a thread of psychic awareness, like a tripwire. The disguised Morgana planned to seduce Arthur. She took his sentries a sleeping draft but tripped the silver thread. Merlin awoke instantly and performed real magic, in the form of a bolt of energy. It scared the living daylights out of Morgana, and she ran to escape.

In the morning, Merlin's pupil was gone.

Who was he? Where did he come from? Merlin's network of spies traced his pupil fleeing northward. Merlin told Arthur, still not knowing the proper name of the spy. Morgana escaped, and outmaneuvered Merlin. It wouldn't be the first time.

Morgana desired power over others and learned the spells to give her that. Her Dark Lord assured her that she'd have a son to replace Arthur as king, so she hatched her plot to make her dreams come true.

In her second attempt to seduce the young Arthur, she appeared as a lady, a new guise. Merlin was on a trip to the Pictish kings when Morgana approached Arthur's castle at Caerleon. Calling herself Ilana, after Lana, the goddess of the underworld, she used her Dark arts to infiltrate the one weak spot in Arthur's character, his innocence. It was his most spiritually attractive attribute.

Arthur did not recognize Morgana because they had grown up separately, nor did he know she was his half-sister. Something about her green eyes reminded him of his mother, which made her even more alluring. Morgana's sense of humor made him laugh.

Lancelot watched the dinner party scene with growing unease and dismay. When everyone retired, Morgana slipped a sleeping draft into the guard's wine, and her treacherous seduction began. Nineteen-year-old Arthur was innocent about women, while 24-year-old Morgana was at the top of her allure. Once her seduction was complete, Morgana slipped away and, despite Arthur's entreaties, disappeared. He did not meet her again, but the memory of that night haunted him.

Their son was born nine months later. She named him Modred, which means "the inheritor" in northern Welsh. Morgana protected him from Merlin's vision by building a huge power shield around him so that Merlin did not know of his existence. Once again, she had outmaneuvered Merlin, producing an incestuous child, whose evil purpose was to destroy Britain.

When Modred was three, Morgana married an Irish chieftain named Anigus. He was a small tribal king, and with him, she had also a son and two daughters. At 10, Modred was sent to Scotland, where King Lot fostered him. Legend suggests she married Lot. She did not; however, they had an affair, and she learned of Lot's consuming hatred for his mortal enemy, Arthur. Morgana wanted Lot to educate Modred in the military and fill her son with his hatred for Arthur. Modred never knew Arthur was his real father.

This is an old story, isn't it—a woman hiding her true identity to seduce a man? Merlin must have recognized Morgana's trickery.

Merlin suspected it, but it was not apparent until Modred himself was at Arthur's command. At 22, he came as a member of the Round Table, looking like a slender version of Arthur, with his dark hair and his almost black eyes, with a lithe build, quite tall. His parentage was obvious. Morgana hid in invisibility; Merlin was unable to detect her motives or her movements. She outmaneuvered him for 22 years. She was a high-order black sorcerer who effectively tricked him. She came from Mary's High Priestess line and was a dual soul.

Was Morgana evil?

Morgana had given herself to the Darkness. If you give yourself to the Light, you will grow more of yourself; the Light expands you. If you give yourself to the Dark, you grow less and less. The Dark suborns you, and you end up a husk possessed by Darkness.

Why did Mary choose a life working with the Dark?

This choice is available to everyone. A small step starts you on the path until you are enmeshed, your willpower decreased, and the will destroyed to ask for help. The path is slippery. Isn't it easier to fall down the mountain than to climb up one?

Was this Mary's first evil life?

Her life as Morgana is her first and only life of evil. As we will see in Morgana's past lives, she has been on the fringe, but there's only one evil life. Remember, this is the negative side of consciousness, and without the negative, the positive is impossible. And Morgaine was there to be a counter-balance.

What was Morgana's spiritual life?

She had no spiritual life; instead, she lived consumed with self-gratification. If she was born evil, why would she have a spiritual challenge?

Why did she so hate Arthur?

She was mad, totally given over to the Darkness, which gave her an unreasoning hatred of whatever served the Light. Arthur was the brightest star, an innocent, pure man, and her obsession was to destroy Arthur's kingdom.

Does she ever reincarnate?

Morgana's soul was totally possessed, overpowered and merged by the Dark. She suffered soul death. She ceased to exist.

How did Morgana die?

Morgana became completely unbalanced and committed suicide in Ireland. The energy of the land unbalanced her.

How do we come to know Morgana's story, if there was no one to tell it?

Merlin exposed her when Arthur died. He confided the details to Kai, King Coel's son, and the commander of Arthur's cavalry, Bedwyn. They passed the story on, and that's why scraps survive in Welsh legends and songs.

Was Morgana the personification of evil?

Morgana was a murderer; she killed several men, inconvenient ex-lovers. She was an expert chemist and poisoner who killed easily, poisoning any female rivals for her lovers' affection. She murdered her female lovers, too. Her treatment of Modred was repugnant. He was the product of her incest with Arthur, and she played with him incestuously.

Did her darkness build over many lives, or was she just born evil?

She was born with a propensity to evil, but at all times she had choices and could have drawn back from it. As a priestess of Babylon, she plotted to assassinate King Nebuchadnezzar. It misfired; she blamed a Jewish captive only to escape to Nineveh to become a prosperous brothel keeper. Later, she was a temple whore in Athens, besotted with intrigue and sexual politics.

But it was her life as Dido, Queen of Carthage, where she really explored the Darkness. In that life, she had a capacity for unbelievable cruelty, when she ordered mass executions and human sacrifices, while at the same time, she was a brilliant strategist, an intelligent and educated woman. But Dido was as courageous and brave as she was cruel and corrupt. Consumed with a desire for power, she acted in total opposition to all that Mary stands for, performing the ultimate human sacrifice on her newborn baby. Before the fires of Moloch, she sacrificed her baby son, cutting his throat on the altar before consigning him to the flames. Can you see her spiralling fall into Darkness now?

Yes, but how does someone from a Dark path in past lives shut out the influence of Mary's Master energy and her gift of a second balancing soul?

The second soul was a risky, last-ditch effort to save Morgana, an attempt to absorb some of her karma. It failed. Morgana was already lost to the Dark. It is unlikely that anyone with their feet set firmly on the path of Light would suddenly turn to the Dark. It is erosion from their selfishness over many incarnations. The Dark is like an illness gradually taking over the metabolism.

The more Light is shut out, the less influence it has on your character. Morgana did not shut out the influence of her Master energy, Mary, or her second soul. It was not a conscious process; it was a reaction made inevitable by her vile, corrupted behavior.

Thinking about These Lives

The Dark Ages were turbulent and gloomy. There were two battles. One fought in what we would call Heaven, which resulted in a setback for the Light. Later, after the life of Christ, there was to be a battle fought on Earth led by King Arthur. This time the Light took no chances. Arthur was well resourced and the battles well planned. Gathered around the Celtic lord were Merlin, Galahad, Lancelot, Bors, Kai, Gawain, and Percival, all beings of Light fighting the invading Saxons from Germany.

Merlin brought the stirrup to Britain, allowing Arthur to use large, heavy horses to carry heavily armored men. The stirrup also allowed its rider to stand up, freeing both arms for a sword thrust. Merlin modified four strategically placed Roman forts, complete with standing armies, intelligent war machines, and armories of weapons. Britain, united under a charismatic king, used Arthur's Celtic culture's egalitarianism to give every grumbling warlord an equal voice.

What was at stake? The preservation of two cultures: Roman Britain and Celtic Britain. Roman Britain valued law and order, engineering, and a Spartan education; Scotland, Ireland, Wales, and Cornwall, in other words. Celtic Britain valued liberal law, the right to petition the king, poetry, song, and the Round Table's egalitarianism. Britain needed to retain both cultures to temper the harsher Saxon law of the invaders.

The Romans gave Britain a unique gift by encouraging Rome's best legionnaires to retire there. Their steadfastness, stamina, stubbornness, and ability to ignore privation were needed to create the British character and defeat the Saxons' next invasion—during the Second World War. Under the leadership of the red-headed Winston Spencer Churchill, a reincarnation of the knight Lamorak and carrying the spiritual DNA of Serapis Bey, he inspired his people to fight and win the second Battle of Britain.

The Celts had two other significant contributions. Their form of Christianity was fostered by Arimathea and spread by the Welsh-born Patrick to Ireland. This Christianity was needed to ignite the flame of the missionary zeal in the next generation. Brigid (Mother Mary), Columba (St. Germain), and Canice (Mary the High Priestess) would keep it blazing and spread it back through Scotland and eventually into the Continent.

The Celts' other significant contribution was their druidic love of plants and wilderness, represented today in their beautiful gardens. It would be critical during the Age of Exploration. Unlike the Spanish, who saw the New World as a quarry for precious metals, many Britons saw the New World as a Garden of Eden. James Cook, an aspect of St. Germain, took Joseph Banks, the botanist, an aspect of Mary, to Australia, while Walter Raleigh brought back potatoes. The British spread commercial plants, such as coffee and rubber, throughout the world.

Tradition claims Camelot's idealism, with the Round Table, failed because Guinevere's and Lancelot's love destroyed Arthur, allowing the Saxons to win. The Gatekeeper's revelations make it clear that the truth lies elsewhere.

The Dark gave it their best shot. Morgana, temptress and murderer, defiled Arthur in incest, and through that act, Arthur sowed the seed of his own destruction with Modred. Morgana manipulated Guinevere's and Lancelot's love and ensured that their betrayal was conveyed to Arthur graphically. Arthur died broken-hearted, losing the will to live after suffering his best friends' betrayal.

Mary countermoved—she reincarnated across the Irish Sea, well protected energetically as Brigid. She used her light to balance Morgana's darkness. She prayed for the man who was her son, Sir Percival, trying to fulfil her uncle's dream for a Celtic Christianity, one that honored equality and women's participation in all levels of the Church. Morgana never got close to her, but nevertheless, Brigid's energy unbalanced her, causing her to commit suicide

As Percival, Lord Sananda used his Light to stabilize the Celtic countries so that monasteries could flourish there during the Dark Ages. He empowered and balanced his warrior friends to achieve their purposes. Why didn't they win? It was not their purpose. The Saxons were needed to create a vibrant ethnic mix that would become Britain with the later-invading Normans.

Arthur, Merlin, Percival, Lancelot, and Galahad achieved their destinies. Their achievements bought Roman Britain time to stem and contain the German invasion to the East Coast, thereby ensuring that the Celts were saved to re-Christianize Europe, tempering Saxon law, and adding poetry, mystery, and song to British lives.

The consequences of Morgana's corruption, Guinevere's infidelity, Lancelot's betrayal of trust, and Arthur's early death were limited to personal tragedy. Arthur's victories were necessary to establish a balance in the racial blend of people who would make up Britain and eventually seed America, Canada, Australia, New Zealand, and South Africa.

While scholars debate the existence of Camelot and cynics denigrate people's fascination with its ethos, children have always known the truth. Camelot lives on in the Magna Carta, the Declaration of Independence, and in most democratic nations' constitutions. Camelot inspires chivalry, decency, and equality, and Camelot will enable the once and future king and Merlin to reincarnate when the world needs them most.

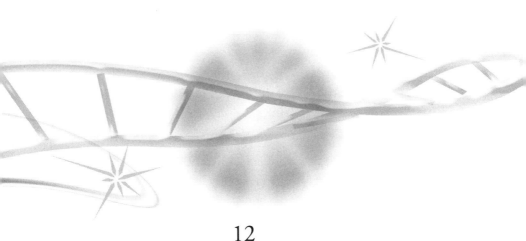

12

LOVE IN ACTION

This chapter spans 200 years and focuses on the incarnations of Mary and St. Germain as Pathfinders: men and women who often did not know where they were going but ultimately found their way home. Together they sow love in action.

Dante Alighieri (1265–1321) and Beatrice (c.1266–1290), Poet and Muse

Dante Alighieri wrote the first masterpiece of Italian literature, *La Divina Commedia* ("The Divine Comedy"), which describes the journey of his soul into the depths of Inferno (Hell) through Purgatorio (Purgatory), and ultimately, to a reunion with his love, Beatrice, in Paradiso (Heaven). Because his journey begins in misery and ends in happiness, Dante satirically calls his poem a comedy.

Dante was born in Florence in 1265. In his first work, a series of love poems called La Vita Nuova, he tells us that he is a Gemini. He introduces his ideal woman, Beatrice, a woman he first met as a 10-year-old child and then again at 18. He sees her briefly one more time on a Florentine street, and she looks away. Beatrice dies in her twenties, and Dante immortalizes her brief life in his poetry. Beatrice always seems remote, mysterious, wise, and good. She is an ideal woman, a distant sexual object. It is hard to understand how, with such brief encounters, Dante could fall so deeply in love.

The identity of Beatrice became one of Western literature's most famous literary puzzles. Was she Bice Portinari, the wife of Simone de Bardi, a banker? Or was she a fantasy of Dante's ideal love? Or was "Beatrice" a name he christened some unknown love? Italian women made up their own minds. The tomb of Bice Portinari, almost opposite Dante's house on a narrow Florentine street, is adorned with their love notes, invoking Beatrice's help to find them a sweetheart.

Beatrice's death devastated Dante. Looking for consolation, he turned to philosophy and theology, and combined with his poetry, produced his epic journey through the afterlife. The poem is in a language of his own creation, written in Italian not Latin.

Dante was politically active but, unfortunately, on the wrong side of a factional war, forcing him to live in exile from his beloved Florence for most of his life. He married, fathered five children, and died in Ravenna in 1321.

⁎ Conversation with The Gatekeeper ⁎

Who was the historical Beatrice? Did he first see her at nine? Did she greet him at 18? Later, did he conceal his love? Did she withhold her greeting creating his anguish, and finally, did she die in her twenties prompting him to immortalize her?

Beatrice Portinari's family were friends of Dante's family. She was one of six daughters. She first met Dante at a salon and hardly noticed him. He was nine, she was 12, but he developed a crush on her. When Dante saw her next, it was as if he was struck by lightning and wallowed in her wake.

Beatrice looked like a pre-Raphaelite heroine. She had raven hair, light gray eyes (although Dante insisted that they were emerald), a classic Greco-Roman profile, a slight double chin, white skin, and a voluptuous figure. Her Rubenesque carnality was attractive at 12. She didn't notice Dante, and two years later, at 14, she was married to a banker double her age.

They would meet again at a wedding after she'd been married a year. They briefly spoke because Dante was tongue-tied in her presence.

When Beatrice looked at Dante, what did she see?

Dante was a man of shortish stature, with a slight build, and handsome to the point of prettiness. He suffered from receding wavy hair and, after 25, became almost bald. He had small, neat ears, a pretty mouth—almost a cupid's bow, light eyes, a high forehead, with an aquiline nose. He had a restless mind; he was a visionary, not a raconteur, and not interested in trivial matters. He had a mordant wit, with an element of grimness. As a lampooner, he'd write anonymous lampoons of people in verse and stick them up around the city.

Was his meeting with Beatrice at the wedding the beginning of their relationship?

They didn't have a relationship! That's why she became a perfect focus for his idealized vision of womanhood and the vehicle for his salvation. They met again—he was 24 and she was about 27—at a civic function, where they'd enjoy a long conversation. She was already ill, pale, with dark shadows under her eyes, yet vivacious and enthusiastic. They talked about music, writing, and poetry. She was delighted by his attention and decided that they were going to meet. They set up a tryst. Dante was an accomplished seducer and read his poetry to her in the garden. Eventually, they moved to the bedroom.

When Dante finally made his move he was nearly caught *in flagrante delecto*. Beatrice's husband burst in, only to see Dante's bare behind disappearing out the window, his wife's maid under the covers, and Beatrice in her drawing room, asleep. Dante and Beatrice cleverly deceived the husband. Dante idealized Beatrice and learning of her death, he collapsed into a broken heart.

Did Dante ever write to her?

Sensibly, Beatrice forbade him to speak her name or write to her. She adored having this handsome young man in love with her, and she vacillated between moments of enjoyment and fearful despondency. It fitted with her depression cycles, and her blowing hot and cold just incited his ardor.

Did the lovers ever meet again?

Beatrice never saw him again. They almost met on the street. She looked away, and they never spoke. She remained a vision of *virgin intacta*. She'd been born with tuberculosis and, as it worsened, Beatrice didn't want him to see her looking so ill. She died two years later.

How did Dante react?

As any poet—with great drama, wounded to his very core! He professed the idea of entering the Church and went to a seminary in Rome! That did not last; the hypocrisy and corruption in the Church revolted him. Still, he stayed in Rome, drifting into life as a young man about town, fascinated and repelled by the intrigues of Rome's upper nobility life. This formed the basis of the *Divina Commedia*, particularly *Inferno*. What a nice fantasy to consign all that you despise into hell! It gave him a chance to populate heaven, *Paradiso*, with adorable fantasies, especially of Beatrice. Her death prompted him to start writing properly.

You said that Dante idealized her. I'd agree, but in *The Divine Comedy*, she inspires his wisdom and loves her deeply.

I take a more jaundiced view of Dante. There's a powerful strain in the Italian ethos to glorify women. They believe the female nature to be the highest expression of humanity. This focus on idealistic worship allows them to have sex with lesser women and removes them from the responsibility of looking after them. Beatrice stood on that pedestal, and if their "relationship" were consummated, she'd have fallen off that pedestal. It allowed him to roister with other women while keeping his love for her pure.

Why did Mary select this life as Beatrice?

There are two reasons. Remember, as Cleopatra, she wished to triumph and achieve a discipline. It was a balance between the temptation of privilege and the temptation of the flesh and the development of the spirit . . . to learn during a lifetime that you can't always have what you want. Her second reason was her pre-life agreement with St. Germain to allow both her existence and struggle to achieve purity inspire him to create his masterpiece.

Had they been together previously? Your reply suggests these aspects of Mary and St. Germain had a prior relationship. Dante's reaction to their first meeting, when he was "struck by lightning," suggests a previous deep attachment.

Those two, who as Boaz and Ruth, had loved one another since the beginning of time, but their particular influence was a 20-year relationship, when Dante was the French medieval poet Chrétien de Troyes and she, his lover, was Anne Marie Sans la Ville, whom he called Isolde. On seeing Beatrice, Dante had an unconscious memory of Isolde, a lightning bolt. As Chrétien, he had written the story of their love affair as the story of Tristan and Isolde. Our friend, St. Germain, is never clear about the boundary between truth and fiction.

Can you give me a little more about them?

I can't. There is a lock on their lives. But I can tell you that when Julius Caesar returns as Dante, they all share that same unconscious memory of the lost love, and of Cleopatra. Nothing is lost whenever St. Germain revisits his love affairs!

What was Beatrice's life purpose?

It was part of Mary the High Priestess's detailed journey to explore her humanity, her love for St. Germain, and to curb her self-indulgence. Not being in love with Dante, although she had loved him before, she was playing with love, but she had to stop to fulfill her purpose to be the focus for his creative genius. Dante had to be in love to write; love had to infuse his work. Remember him as Homer in love with Ulysses, writing his masterpiece, and when he meets the beautiful Nefertari he promised her a poem. Well, almost 2,000 years later, here it is Nefertari! *The Divine Comedy* is a detailed picture of medieval morals, thought, philosophy, theology, and politics. Dante was a mirror of his times, when every aspect of life was dominated by the Catholic Church, and his *Commedia* was a genuine mirror of his time!

Did Beatrice achieve her life purpose?

Yes, but she learned that a human being is not an island and that her self-discipline had costs for others. When she incarnated as Queen Isabella of Spain those issues were evident once more, in the form of her obligations and outcomes of regality; with an opportunity to meet her Dante again, this time as Christopher Columbus.

What qualities of Mary did she have?

Beatrice had Mary's strong will, sympathy, and empathy for others, her capacity to try to please everybody, and her ability to separate the important from the less important, leaving her great capacity for love untapped.

What was Beatrice's life achievement?

Inspiring Dante. Beatrice spent most of her life sublimating her will to her father, then to her husband, and then to Dante. This Beatrice line is from Isis, able to move into and out of the underworld to rescue loved ones. It is a line of devotion to others and through them to God.

What was the meaning in Beatrice's early death?

It was her gift to Dante; her death allows him to imagine her in heaven, guiding him on his other-world journey. Her life had to be the embodiment of a tragedy. What's the point of an ideal if it's not eternally tragic?

The Beatrice you have revealed and the Beatrice of _The Divine Comedy_ are quite different. It seems the poetical Beatrice was more a figment of his imagination.

No! Dante saw into her soul, into her spiritual core, but she was the ideal woman: because his love was never consummated, she never left her pedestal. All of their mutual desire and disappointment, along with her self-discipline, were necessary for Dante's gift to the Italian people. Without Dante, there wouldn't be the Italian language. He started writing _La Divina Commedia_ in Sicilian, then moved to Latin before using Florentine with some Romano and some Urbino dialects to complete it. Almost single-handedly, he invented the language. Dante could tap into the Divine Mary while dreaming of his Beatrice.

Why did St. Germain choose to incarnate as Dante?

St. Germain loves being a poet, creating things, and here was one of his greatest start-ups: the introduction of the Italian language, with its lovely cadences and beautiful lyricism.

What qualities of St. Germain does Dante bring in?

His sense of sardonic amusement, great determination, love of lyricism, charm, intelligence, great Romanticism, and his deep abiding love of Mary. And one last thing: St. Germain's love of birds. Dante would spend his money feeding them and emptying their cages to see them flying free.

What was his life purpose?

To celebrate Mary, his divine love. Dante had two great achievements. One was creating the Italian language—he wrote in a decayed Latin, cleaning it up, polishing and blending it as he wrote. And his second achievement was also as a writer. He brought elegance to satire. While the *Divina Commedia* was part satire, part idealism, Inferno was pure satire. He wrote poetry of such beauty and elegance, while still being satirical; no one had married the two as successfully as Dante. So the anger and repulsion he observed, which he could've expressed spitefully, he used instead as barbed humor reflective of his good nature.

And his spiritual challenge?

To keep his faith and moral purity in the face of his total disillusionment with the Church. He succeeded in a peculiarly Italian way, by concluding that a cultivated and intelligent person's religion was an intensely private matter between himself and his God.

Dante spent a good deal of his life writing about life after death. How did he die?

Dante died as a result of an infection in a wound that made him susceptible to other infections, and he caught pneumonia. He was terrified of death because he'd imagined the worst when he created Inferno, but he saw Beatrice in his delirium. His vision of her inspired him to reach out toward her, and he died of heart failure as she took his hand. To where? To Paradiso! Who said life (and death) don't imitate art?

Isabella of Castile (1457–1504), Powerful Queen

Queen Isabella I of Castile ascended the throne at the age of 25. Before her coronation, in 1474, she married King Ferdinand of Sicily, now Ferdinand II of Aragon, who became Ferdinand V of Castile by marriage. They united their kingdoms and, as joint rulers, created today's Spain. Ferdinand and Isabella's Christian forces resumed the long-running war to expel the Moors, who had occupied Spain since the 700s, and in 1492, succeeded in forcing the last Moorish kingdom at Granada to surrender. To create a Catholic

Spain under one religion, Ferdinand and Isabella expelled all Spanish Jews and Moors who had not converted to Catholicism, thereby bleeding Spain of its professional classes and other talented citizens. The Inquisition ensured the religious orthodoxy of those forced to convert.

Isabella sponsored Christopher Columbus's first voyage to America. Her three daughters and one son sat unhappily on the thrones of Britain, Portugal, France, and Spain.

⁕ Conversation with The Gatekeeper ⁕

Imagine we could see Isabella as a young woman, how would she present?

For a woman, she was quite tall at five foot seven, taller than Ferdinand, with chestnut hair with a red hint. She had a good figure, full-breasted, long legs, and startling blue eyes that would change to the color of ice with anger. Isabella's manner was fierce and imperious; she did not brook fools. She was a good scholar, fascinated with law, and would have been a very clever lawyer if she had been a man. She had a full mouth and was very sensual and conscious of her womanhood. She flirted discreetly, brilliantly manipulating men. She was impatient of the silliness of women in her court. If you could see king and queen standing together, Isabella was taller by an inch, older by a year, and smarter by a country mile than her co-monarch.

What qualities of Mary did she bring in?

She had a regal imperious quality that we have only seen before in Nefertiti and Nefertari. It was displayed unconsciously. Isabella understood governance, used charm, and was enormously sympathetic, which she learned to moderate (yet it's still there in her last testament). She was intelligent, interested in theology, talented in many languages, practical, and being both frugal and generous, she would leave money in her will for poor women who couldn't marry, not having enough money for a dowry.

Interestingly, she is endowed with so many Marian qualities compared to Beatrice! Why did Mary select this life?

Mary needed to test her character against having great power. She'd succeed in that test, and again in her next life, as the king's [Henry VIII's] consort Katherine Parr. Later she would retrace her steps to correct some imbalances around regality as James I of England. There she would be out of balance sexually: James was a bisexual and emotionally crippled, a man developmentally disabled and raised without parental love. Where Isabella was scrupulous in her fair exercise of power, James was not. He rewarded favorites, particularly his male lovers, with extravagant estates.

And Mary agreed to do this?

It fulfilled both her purpose to remedy imperfections and the purpose of history, which was to begin the British move to republicanism. James started the rot in order to destroy the royal family, allowing Cromwell to move Britain toward a constitutional monarchy. These moves saved Britain from the revolution that France experienced.

We are told that Isabella picked her husband Ferdinand from a line-up of hot prospects for her.

Ferdinand was her second cousin, and she was intensely attracted to him when she first met him. He was Ulysses to her Penelope, but she was irritated by his insufferable macho male supremism. Nevertheless, she approached her choice rationally, asking lots of questions before agreeing to his offer.

Isabella and Ferdinand gave the impression that they shared a single mind. How did they manage running two kingdoms together in harness?

They worked out a rough three-part verbal agreement never to disagree with one another in public on important matters and never to abrogate the other's authority. Ferdinand was to be the consul-general, responsible for external and military affairs and appointments in defense and foreign affairs. She was the one responsible for law, administration, and the economy, and for appointments in civil government. It worked stunningly well, although it would result in some harsh judgments of Isabella by historians as we shall see.

What made Isabella, Isabella?

A simple motto—"I can do that!"—while she politely remarked to Ferdinand, "Brains and ability do not reside in your codpiece!"

What was her life purpose?

Her purpose was two-fold: to be largely instrumental for the foundation for a united Spain. Her need for religious unity helped deliver her first purpose. The second was to be the iconic role model for future female sovereigns. She was the role model for Queen Elizabeth I. She delivered on both her life purposes.

And what about Ferdinand? He's been described as devious, amorous, game playing, and unfaithful. Are these accurate?

He was a cunning general, and he played games with the lives of his daughters, using them as disposable political pawns. A man of enormous charm, he may have been unfaithful physically, but not emotionally. It did upset Isabella, but not as much as it would a woman today. It may be an accurate description of Ferdinand, viewed from your perspective, but not in his time.

Her role was to be seen to be a figurehead. She rode beside her husband, astride her Andalusian horse, in specially made armor and culottes. She insisted on going through the hardships of campaigns to motivate the troops and support Ferdinand, who was very happy about her role and respected her for doing it. She made rare strategic suggestions but remembered their agreement. Isabella did not want her husband transgressing into her fields of responsibility, so she did not transgress into his.

They conquered Granada and insisted that the Sultan of Granada abandon his palace, raising the Spanish flag on the Alhambra on January 2, 1492. What was it like when they entered Granada for the first time?

It was an amazing time. There was still the stink of burned bodies, blood, and excrement everywhere. Above them was the Alhambra, this white-veined marble citadel, this Islamic heaven on Earth. They rode side by side. People came out of their homes, commoners, and nobles alike, and laid out bolts of cloth under their feet as they dismounted, the church bells pealed, and everyone cried and praised the Lord, for although the Moors were tolerant and fair, it was still a triumph: the expulsion of the 800-year-old conqueror. They rid Granada of its foreign devil, even though his yoke was light. The Moors were the White Light of the Dark Ages, and the royal Moorish family knelt and kissed the hands of Isabella and Ferdinand. Above them, was this palace made of living stone, arabesque arches and lacework, a poem in marble, full of glancing light but not their Catholic view of Paradise. Soon their royal standards would flutter over the Alhambra.

Yet, from a modern perspective, there are three stains on Isabella's reign: the imposition of the Inquisition in 1478, 14 years before the conquest of Granada; the expulsion of the Jews; and the expulsion of the Moors! Why did Isabella agree to the Inquisition in her region of Castile?

Isabella agreed because the Pope said it was her Catholic duty to do it, saying if you don't do it we will insist on canonical law. Today, that would be like saying to a prime minister, "Agree to this, or we will impose Sharia law." Her agreement to the Inquisition was a *quid pro quo*, in return for allowing her to keep Spanish civil and criminal law intact and free from ecclesiastical supervision. Its implied threat about the Inquisition and the later expulsion of the Jews was clear: the Inquisition or canonical law ("Do as we say, or our militant arm will displace you with more malleable rulers"). Isabella and Ferdinand regarded this as a severe threat.

But what would have happened if she had stood up to the Vatican?

Portugal would have invaded from the west, Austria from the north, the Franks from the east. Royal Spain would have been decapitated, a puppet prince put in their place, Isabella would have been executed or exiled, and France would have picked over their bones. Later, Isabella would argue against the expulsion of the Jews.

Isabella has the reputation of being anti-Semitic and anti-Islamic. Are you telling me otherwise?

Historians establish reputations. They present their own opinions as facts, but there is no concrete evidence. Isabella, with her considerable intellect, was neither anti-Semitic nor anti-Moor, but as a super-Catholic, she felt sorry that they were denied the one true faith. She argued all the economic reasons for the Jews' retention to Torquemada. It was a tragic mistake for Spain, bleeding its talent and investment. Next were the Moors. Jews or Moors ran all the schools for physicians, surgeons, and doctors. After Spain drove them out, Europe lost Moorish medicine, setting back European medicine for 500 years.

Isabella could see this and the loss of Spain's business acumen, so she argued vehemently against it in private. Ferdinand made it plain that going to war with Austria was the only way of saving the Jews and the Moors. Isabella had borne the blame for both atrocities because she was the high-profile identity responsible for civic government. Ferdinand thought that the expulsion was a good idea, because he was all for cuddling up to the Pope. He knew, militarily, that if the Pope ordered an attack on Spain, Spain wouldn't withstand it. Besides, much of the war's cost against the Moors was covered by Jewish bankers and expelling them would erase his debt.

Isabella wouldn't split Spain by leaving Ferdinand, and she wouldn't break her agreement with him. It was the greatest disappointment, the fundamental disagreement with Ferdinand, and she hated losing an argument. Look at her alternatives: either split from Ferdinand or split from the Church. She fought as hard as she could, and she had to preside over its unfairness. Her anguish couldn't be shown in public, but let me stress, it hastened her death.

I suppose that it is hard to believe now that an educated, compassionate woman, who probably had Jewish blood herself, would agree to the expulsion of Jews.

The Inquisition was concerned that most Spanish families had been "infiltrated" by Jewish blood. Over 70 percent had either converted or covert Jews in their blood lines, and the Inquisition decimated many families. In the Inquisition's eyes, all Jews and Moors were unbelievers. To understand Isabella the Catholic, understand that most of her options would lead to her excommunication, and it meant, at that time, to be cut off from God for eternity! Heaven and hell were not abstract concepts; for Isabella, they were real places waiting around the next corner.

I am still finding her difficult to understand.

Isabella was sexy, charming, and powerful. She lived a full-throated life of a sensual and intelligent woman. Her Achilles heel was her susceptibility to flattery. Curiously, in 1492, when Columbus appeared before her and her husband, his initial refusal to flatter her made her trust him; that, of course, and the unknown connection between them.

Was she a good administrator?

Isabella was the stabilizing administrative force in Spain; she united the two governments, integrating two sets of royal servants who were immensely suspicious of one another. She cleaned out the licentious behavior in the court. She ordered new combined standards of law. She strongly opposed the Church's demand that Spain adopt canon law, with heavy penalties for spiritual sins like adultery. They wanted adulterers stoned to death.

What did she die of?

High blood pressure leading to heart failure. Isabella's frustration and internalized grief at her son and daughter's death drove her ill health, as did the manipulation of her daughters as marital pawns. She remained angry about the Jews' and Moors' expulsion during the Inquisition and the execrable life of Catherine of Aragon in her second marriage to Henry VIII. Isabella died tired and in anguish. In her insight into her own mistakes, she was very harsh on herself.

Is it right to place her in the 100 most influential people of all time, and one of the greatest queens?

Yes. Queen Isabella's life is still an iconic example of good women in power, and that's her main legacy. She reformed the court, brought back chivalrous behavior, built schools, developed a great art collection, and in her will insisted on the fair treatment and rule for the indigenous populations of Spanish territories in the New World. Not only did she sponsor Columbus but she also started the Spanish golden age of exploration, which made Spain, after Imperial Rome, the world's second superpower.

Christopher Columbus (1451–1506), Italian Explorer and Navigator

The Columbus joke goes something like this:

They say Christopher Columbus had to be the first economist. When he left to discover America, he didn't know where he was going; when he got there, he didn't know where he was; and all this confusion was done on a government grant.

In the 1960s, in a US high school, Columbus Day was still celebrated as a patriotic pause before Thanksgiving amid autumn's vibrancy of color. By 1992, the 500th anniversary of Columbus's "discovery" of America was met with boycott, contempt, and division. The former hero was now branded a cruel imperialist, a racist pirate, and a slave trader; a man who did not discover America—because many explorers had been there before him; that is, before one even counts the 10 million people already living there—but instead, began the process of genocide of its indigenous peoples. His myth had curdled.

Christopher Columbus was born in Genoa, Italy, the son of a weaver who went to sea at 14. After marrying a Portuguese woman, he settled in Portugal, working as a mapmaker. Believing the world was round, he wanted to sail west, but the king of Portugal wouldn't finance him. Isabella of Spain financed three ships with 87 men, the first of four voyages to the New World. Columbus never realized that he had discovered the New World and died impoverished.

✳ Conversation with The Gatekeeper ✳

Help me to understand this man who now wallows in derision!

Columbus's mother Anna was Jewish. He concealed his heredity from the Holy Office. Anna wanted her eldest son to go to university to become a good lawyer, but the family couldn't afford this; instead, his father, Gilberto, organized for him to go to sea as an apprentice at 15, hoping to rebuild a trading empire through him. Christopher proved a good navigator, and within eight years, he was the first mate on the ship of a sizeable trader.

Did he have any chance at education?

Only a rudimentary form, with a tutor who wasn't very good. He was good at maths but didn't shine. He was small and bullied, and his father's view was to put him in a practical trade. By the time Columbus was 25, he'd made several voyages to West Africa, sailing down the coast of North Africa, trading to Benin and the Ivory Coast. There, he had a bad experience. Rough weather meant he had to stay off the coast and sail westward into the Atlantic with no navigational markers. An Arab slave who knew something of star navigation saved them, and Christopher was instantly excited by his skill. His excitement took him away from sailing while he went to Tyre to attend a special school. The Arabs had a reservoir of knowledge about map-making and navigation because they sailed around Africa to India, and had been doing so for centuries. Columbus traveled overland from Tyre along the caravan routes, across Saudi Arabia to Yemen to old Muscat. Here he learned that it was unremarkable to sail in the right seasons to India or China. Looking for a short cut, he figured if you sailed west across the Atlantic, you could reach China even quicker.

Why was he convinced of it?

He had two maps: one sold to him in Tyre, written in Arabic, which he got translated; another that he bought in Alexandria, written in Greek. They depicted India and China west of Europe and across a sea, rather than an ocean—a sea far smaller than the Atlantic Ocean actually was.

Why was he so convinced the world was round?

From the simple expedient of watching ships. If the world was flat, you should see a ship forever; instead, when a ship came over the horizon it showed its topsails before gradually revealing itself. It was only logical. The Arab sailors laughed at the silly idea that the earth was flat, but the very idea that the world was round could lead to the Holy Office questioning him, and scared that they would discover his Jewishness, he kept quiet.

How did he go about getting sponsorship for his voyage?

He worked his passage to England and went to the Tower of London to see Henry VIII, who wouldn't see him. He went to Portugal, where King John II was preoccupied, and then tried to reach the Pope, but couldn't get an audience. Columbus, aged around 30, was unkempt, his clothes stained, boots scuffed, hair greasy; a man who stammered and presented poorly. Isabella was sympathetic—she saw his sincerity and sense of destiny. Isabella and Ferdinand had a sparkling court; they were legends. They were both known to be imaginative, bold, looking for new ideas and attractive prospects.

How did the first meeting take place?

Isabella trusted him instantly. This is the moment when Beatrice and Dante meet again. Isabella's first feeling was of immense trustworthiness, while Ferdinand thought, "bloody adventurer." She grew to like him over the years, admiring his persistence and conviction. Ferdinand would develop a set against him, always intensely jealous of Isabella's regard. Columbus inspired her in the way Beatrice inspired Dante.

When Isabella saw him without Ferdinand, they talked about the logistics of financing the voyage. "You are going in search of an idea," she said. "What do you need?" Columbus had his list. Upon reading it, Isabella proposed appealing to the Pope, because if Columbus's claims about reaching India and China by sailing west were true, there was a whole new world to convert. The papal legate said that if the king and queen were prepared to supplicate to the Pope, there might be a chance of finance, but Ferdinand refused. He didn't want to risk his reputation for a penniless Italian seaman with a strange dream.

Why did it take seven years to get approval for Columbus's American voyage?

Isabella's inclination was to believe Columbus, but he was not her priority; she was still having babies. She couldn't go to the Pope without Ferdinand, and had limited access to the struggling treasury. She was trying to decrease the power of the aristocracy and build educational institutions. So time dragged on, and Columbus's request sat with an advisory council of priests.

How did Columbus maintain his dream during all this time?

Chiefly, his first reaction was hope. Isabella was the first person who displayed enthusiasm, and he frequently reappealed to her. He wrote her letters. He met her again after four years. She put up her crown jewels as surety and received enough money to outfit three ships. At last Columbus had a start. And some luck even though the three caravels he sailed were each smaller than James Cook's Endeavour.

What was her motive for support of Columbus?

To gain territory with a first-class chance of monopolizing major trade routes, leading to her second motive of gaining extra wealth. Her third motive was spreading Christianity, an attractive idea that assumed importance only when she spoke to Church representatives.

Was mounting his first voyage Columbus's greatest achievement?

It was essential, because he achieved everything from a non-existent power base. He would make four voyages to the Americas and was an impressive sailor. Columbus was a great visionary, an excellent navigator and a lousy leader. He proved himself to be unsympathetic and incompetent at government. He was autocratic, remote, and cruel in his leadership of his crew. As an explorer, he doesn't even rate. He was like Marco Polo: an entrepreneur, a merchant, motivated by future riches and trading routes.

Columbus has a low standing today. He rationalized looting, raping, murdering, and enslaving the Indian population. Is our view accurate?

That is a little harsh, but still close to the truth. What made Columbus a great visionary didn't make him a great leader. Power would corrupt him, until he bordered on megalomania. He tried hard to eliminate those tendencies, and by the time he returned as Sir Walter Raleigh, he had succeeded and married his soulmate immediately.

Did he go mad? He returned to Spain in chains.

Columbus had a mental breakdown that led to a profound depression but eventually came out of it.

Why did St. Germain incarnate as Christopher Columbus?

The idea of exploring and changing the world is irresistible to him. His mission changed European economies, the balance of power in Western Europe, and, ultimately, the world. Columbus's voyage was the most important event of its type in world history. The effect of his rediscovery of the Americas was immediate, concentrated, and powerful. To date, it is more important than the moon landing in terms of world evolution. It is one of St. Germain's most important lives, up there with Lao Tzu, Krishna, Homer, Gutenberg, and Edward de Vere.

Why did St. Germain use the Dante line to incarnate as Columbus and not the Imhotep line of Henry the Navigator?

The Dante line nurtures a dream. The Imhotep line is practical, sensible, modest, and ordered men. You need a poet to make a dream come alive.

What St. Germain qualities did he bring in?

He was given his persuasive visionary qualities, great determination, and the capacity to be selective about the truth, bordering on deceit. If there was a problem, the possibility of him being in error did not exist. But I must emphasize his dogged, sheer, stubborn persistence, vision, ability to dream, organizational ability, and excitement of discovery. Columbus is from the same reincarnational line as Marco Polo and, of course, Dante, and different from the line of explorers from Imhotep's line. After his lives as poets Homer and Dante, St. Germain was desperate for fame and fortune, so desperate that he was prepared to sail off the edge of the world to achieve it. Despite all his shortcomings, he was a man who changed the world. For heaven's sake, let's celebrate him on Columbus Day for that!

Katherine Parr (1512–1548), Last Queen of Henry VIII

Katherine Parr was the sixth and last wife of aged and ill Henry VIII of England. Having survived two previous arranged marriages to men twice her age, Katherine knew how to nurse and soothe invalid men. Her prior marriages provided her with a legitimate lack of virginity, removing the problem of some of Henry's other wives. Katherine married the king, not by choice but his command. She had fallen in love with the dashing Thomas Seymour, the brother of Henry's third wife, and was looking forward to, at last, marrying a man of her own choosing. He was the reincarnation of her former husband, Ferdinand, and Ulysses, an aspect of Kuthumi. It was at that moment that the king intervened and demanded her hand. Torn between love and duty, duty won, so she married Henry at Hampton Court in 1544, taking on one of England's most dangerous roles, that of wife to Henry VIII. But remember, she is the same aspect of Mary, Hephaestion, who loved her as Alexander the Great. This will be interesting.

Henry, in his fifties, was a broken man, suffering from syphilis and an ulcerated leg. He was a cruel, obese tyrant, crippled, and given to explosive rages, and he had already executed two wives and divorced two others, leaving his three children—Mary, Elizabeth, and Edward—motherless.

His court was split into warring theological camps: Bishop Stephen Gardiner for the Catholics and Archbishop Thomas Cranmer for the new Protestants. Katherine Parr, a profoundly religious, cultured, and tactful woman, was outwardly orthodox but inwardly radical. An informed

Protestant, she would move into the frenzied sights of Bishop Gardiner, the heretic-burning avenger of the Catholics, and her life, too, would be at risk.

By 1544, Henry was so confident in Katherine's abilities and her loyalty, he would trust her as regent while he campaigned in France. When, in 1545, Katherine's book, *Prayers and Meditations*, was published, the young Elizabeth would translate it into three languages, and it became a bestseller.

By January 1547, Henry was dead, the regency of Edward had begun, and she, at 36, was the queen dowager of England. Her eyes returned to Thomas Seymour, and they married. During her widowhood, Katherine published her spiritual autobiography, *The Lamentation or Complaint of a Sinner*. At Sudeley Castle, Katherine gave birth to a daughter, Mary, on September 1, 1548, and four days later, she died of puerperal fever.

❋ Conversation with The Gatekeeper ❋

Historically, Katherine was the after-thought, the sixth wife, and seems fairly colorless. I never thought of her as "great."

On the contrary, this is one remarkable woman. Her background: England was in the iron grip of the Roman Church, and the ordinary people opposed it. Bishops and clergy were bound by decisions made in Rome, when England was moving to greater independence and the injustice of the Church's mushrooming wealth grated on the poor. The monasteries were oppressive, exploitive, and hypocritical. Katherine Parr and Thomas Cranmer, the archbishop of Canterbury, unified against Rome.

Katherine was educated at the court's school until she was removed to strict Catholic instruction under Catherine of Aragon, Isabella's eldest daughter. This, however, did not have the desired effect on her; instead, she questioned it, and her independent spirit was frustrated by the replies she received. She was a good scholar, with a little Greek and fluent French, and she wrote very well. Later, she taught herself Latin and German, the *lingua franca* of commercial trading, so that she could read the commentaries of Martin Luther. Cranmer filled in the gaps in her knowledge of Latin poets and improved her Greek.

In our history books, Katherine is a shadowy figure. Sometimes she is out of the picture, literally, like when she is omitted from a Hampton Court family portrait, even though she was both Henry's wife and queen. She is seen as a dull sixth wife, who nursed Henry until he died. History is not kind to these retiring figures. It loves those who strut the stage, elbowing others away, like Anne Boleyn. Katherine was not the least concerned with her enduring fame. She was a fascinating conversationalist, essential at any dinner party, unless you were having a dance party, then you'd invite Anne Boleyn.

Cranmer had written *The Book of Common Prayer* in English as the first Protestant prayer book around the English Mass. Katherine wrote two books of prayer. John Whitcliff was the father of English Protestantism, Cranmer its midwife, and Katherine Parr its mother in her understated way. Some of the court found her influence on the king and archbishop radically dangerous. They believed that cutting loose from Rome would bring the wrath of the wealthy and powerful Spain, Portugal, and France—in fact, all Western Europe—onto English shores.

Meanwhile, Henry—an aspect of Hilarion, as you know—was mixing it up with the Dark, a dangerous game! He was obsessed with self-gratification, nourished by the gifts of his nature and the meanness of his father's parenting. Henry was a human being with vast conflicts, enormous gifts limited by his severe flaws, a complex man who used evil people to "dissolve" the monasteries.

Are you saying Henry himself was evil?

All is not what it seems. Evil is an addiction to power, and violence, greed, and cruelty all stem from that. Those addicted to power deceive the self and others. Power can promote real evil, but evil does not always promote evil; good sometimes works with evil to make something happen. In the case of Henry and Katherine, a major portal couldn't be opened just by the Light alone.

What is Katherine's life purpose?

Hers was a dual role. First, she was to be the mother of Protestantism by supporting Cranmer and, secondly, she was to minister, soothe, and save Henry. Who better than a soulmate!

Was Henry worth saving?

He was a great being of Light working with the Dark. When a soul is trapped in darkness, who do you send to the rescue? You'd send Demeter to rescue Persephone, Isis to rescue Osiris, Hephaestion the High Priestess, as Katherine Parr, to rescue Alexander!

To be confident in Katherine's ability to "save" him, they must have had prior experience.

And they did. Thousands of years earlier, Katherine was Henry's chief of staff and scribe, in his life as Sun Tzu, the Chinese military philosopher. He dictated to her his treatise on The Art of War. As queen, Katherine would read to Henry for hours. He could barely see, and after reading him inspiring works, she would engage him in long and deep conversations.

What qualities of Mary did Katherine bring in?

Katherine possessed compassion and practicality, good in emergencies. She had Marian's sensibleness, along with her piety and love of theology. Katherine demonstrated wit, intellect, and was a skilful advisor, similar to that seen later in Jane Austen's incarnation of the Mary Magdalene line. Katherine possessed Marian ability to examine a problem and reach sound conclusions based on the facts.

Katherine was good looking, charming, kind, loved animals and, like Isabella of Spain, operated with a sense of ethical values without being moralistic. Katherine's was a liberal in outlook, with Mary's scrupulous honesty. She was courageous. While she hated confrontations, she never shrank from one. Katherine was a peacemaker and a conciliator, who would have made a superb diplomat!

Why did Mary select this life?

Her life purpose was to develop Mary's human virtues.

What did she look like? By the way, her coffin was five feet ten inches long, which suggests a tall woman.

She was quite tall and slim, and inclined to asceticism, a handsome woman. She resembled in face and figure Katherine Hepburn, with that slight awkwardness you see in some tall girls.

Yes, she was exhumed in 1782, and her body was found uncorrupted, like a saint's, and her hair was chestnut. I saw a lock of it at Sudeley Castle, but it was corn-colored in her portrait.

It had a hint of bronze through it, which she lightened with camomile. Her eyes were gray-blue. She had strong hands, almost mannish, with a good grip and large feet, size 10½ shoes. She looked most men straight in the eye.

Katherine married two older men and was widowed twice. Was that on-the-job training for Henry?

Yes, exercises in loveless unions; her life was the assumption of responsibility. Both had poor health. Katherine, who was inclined to be a healer, treated them with herbs, expressing her compassion in practical ways. Throughout her second marriage, to Lord Latimer, she became an expert in herbalism and studied in monastery hospitals.

What did she think of King Henry?

Katherine thought the king was a lout, and he was, but she was one of those rare creatures who looked for redeeming features even in the worst people. While everybody else saw Henry as a self-indulgent man—raucous, bawdy, an overweight lecher— Katherine saw a lost boy who confused love with lust.

By now, Henry had stopped looking for romance and was captured by Katherine's intelligence and her kindness; plus, she dressed his festering leg wound with freshly macerated, crushed comfrey leaves and wrapped it in bandages soaked in a saline solution, giving him enormous pain relief. Henry suffered diabetes and genetic gout, and the ulcer was syphilitic, eating into his bone and causing secondary damage to his nervous system and eyesight. He also suffered hallucinations and periods of insanity.

Did Henry love her?

No, but he liked her and felt a parity with her. She was the first woman that Henry, who was paranoid, trusted. His impotence meant their marriage was unconsummated, and that saved Katherine from his syphilis.

How did Katherine feel about getting a proposal from the king?

There was no proposal. Henry commanded her, as he did all his wives. She was pragmatic, knowing that if she refused, she'd spend her life in the tower.

Katherine then embraced radical Protestantism, befriended Cranmer, and almost got herself beheaded. Can you tell me what happened behind the scenes? Who was plotting against her, and why?

Bishop Stephen Gardiner was an arch-conservative and wanted the English Church returned to Rome. He was jealous of Cranmer, lusting for his job as Archbishop of Canterbury. Gardiner tried to have Cranmer and Katherine prosecuted for an improper relationship, but that did not work as most people knew he was homosexual, so he tried heresy charges against Katherine. He got them endorsed by the Privy Council.

A copy of the council's heresy indictment, the list of charges, was dropped in the passage outside her room. Who did that?

I'd love to say God! But Cranmer's lover, who was secretary to the Privy Council, dropped it where Katherine would pick it up. Although fearful, she calmly realized all the accusations could be defended and rushed to the king. Henry's reaction reassured her. He wanted all the Privy Council arrested, and called for the execution of Wroisthley and Gardiner, in particular.

Katherine calmly advised Henry: "Don't make any more enemies, dearest one! Let it die." And knowing he did not have enough evidence, he let it die.

Was Katherine prevented from seeing the king on his deathbed?

The king had descended into delirium, and his advisors tried to keep her away, not wanting her to see him that way. However, with the help of Cranmer, Katherine visited him one last time. Using her advanced knowledge of simples, they drugged the king's chaplain, and Katherine, wearing clerical garb, entered the king's chambers disguised as one of a party of clerics. When they left, she remained, revealing herself to Henry and telling him: "I've come to save you, Henry, from the demons ready to carry you away." Katherine extracted more remorse from Henry in ten minutes than anyone else could in ten years. The king, standing on his dignity, couldn't admit doing wrong to any of his clerics, but with Katherine he could. She left him ready for absolution, completing her Marian role in soul rescue of her soulmate.

Is there any historical verification of this account?

The official account mentions last rites, but there is no mention of his confession. Only Katherine could hear his confession; in Katherine, the king had absolute trust.

You told me that sometimes a major portal can't be opened up by the Light. You need both the Light and the Dark. In Henry's case, he worked with the Dark. Can you explain what you meant?

Sometimes, it is necessary to work with evil people. If Henry had left the monasteries alone, as I know you would have preferred, they would have formed a power base for a Counter-Reformation. As it was, Henry's physical greed played a great part in the dissolution of the monasteries. He thought it was foolish to leave England's largest industry, the wool industry, in the hands of its biggest enemy. It was his most brutal act, and apart from that, Henry allowed the Reformation to take its course. Henry went so close to losing his soul. Once you allow one sin to take control, like greed or lust, the others come in quickly, and he gave himself over to self-indulgence. But with Katherine's help he gained insight and remorse.

Between lives, he would be rewired to exorcise his tyrannical behavior, so that by the time he has another prominent life, he will be a model of probity. And who is that you ask? Another tall, red-haired man who loved his best friend's wife, Sally Fairfax, a reincarnation of Katherine Parr, and his name was . . . George Washington. I know he is one of your most admired men: the upright, I-can't-tell-a-lie George!

It's hard to accept that Washington was Henry VIII reincarnated.

But you can be sure of one thing. George may have loved Sally, but it was as remotely as Dante loved his Beatrice, and definitely not as lustily as Henry loved his Anne Boleyn!

After Henry's death, Katherine can marry Seymour and find happiness. What happened?

Katherine married Seymour after a year of mourning Henry and became pregnant but died from puerperal fever at 36. Her purpose was over. She escaped disillusionment with Seymour, which would have happened quickly, died in love, happy, after a life well lived.

What was her greatest achievement?

In a temporal sense, helping the birth of English Protestantism. In her spiritual context, it was her consistent, practical morality. She inspired all those around her. In Queen Elizabeth's regard, she was an icon. She was sanctity, with sleeves rolled up, the Mother Theresa of her day. English Protestantism caused a significant shift in Europe's balance of power to create an equal balance of power in the New World. Her life is a perfect example of the Mary energy at work behind the scenes, where getting credit is not important. Katherine's life is a modest exhibition of impeccable behavior, which you can see now from scholarly examination. Marian energy is reticent, my friend. Join the dots, and follow the trails of breadcrumbs, rather than have Mary do it for you! These are no accidents. She saved her soulmate.

Thinking about These Lives

The lives of Beatrice, Queen Isabella, and Katherine Parr connect through the devotional line of Mary's energy, the one that seeks partnership. Each of them had a prior life agreement with St. Germain, Kuthumi, or Hilarion. They formed a union that would inspire them to be the best they could be, whether in poetry, creating a language, uniting Spain, discovering America, or assisting in soul rescue.

Beatrice's role was a walk-on part. Ravaged throughout her life by tuberculosis, she probably spent a total of three hours in Dante's company. Still, she spent a lifetime in his memory and became, as the poet Dante says, "the glorious lady of my mind." Dante idealized her. In doing so, St. Germain created a mystical tribute to his divine love, Mary.

Two hundred years later, we can observe Beatrice's direct descendant as a partner working with an aspect of Kuthumi, Ferdinand of Aragon. Isabella, the complex queen of Castile, reunited with Dante as Columbus. All that they could remember was their mutual feeling of trust. Whatever it was, it was enough. Although seven years elapsed from their first meeting to her granting Columbus funds for his project to sail west to China and India, Isabella pawned her crown jewels to fund his voyage.

Isabella's business partnership with Columbus had a significant effect on world events, instigating Spain's golden age of exploration and its development as the world's first superpower since Rome. Her unique partnership with her husband Ferdinand, where the two monarchs effectively shared a throne, created a union that continues to fascinate us.

Isabella's life showed such promise. Blessed with a sharp intellect, a commanding stature, a strong character, and a subtle understanding of diplomacy's nuances, she married the love of her life, the warrior-king Ferdinand. She reformed a profligate and licentious court, sponsored new schools, and deftly managed the complexities of dual rulership while also giving birth to a royal family of five surviving children. Isabella's Catholicism would be as strong as Katherine Parr's Protestantism, their dedicated faiths a function of their historical and cultural context, together with this line of Marian's love of theology.

Modern biographers see Isabella in black and white. They see her as devoted to the will of her male spiritual advisors, who convince her to implement the Spanish Inquisition, and they see Isabella's Catholicism as driving her need for national religious conformity, which the Inquisition would enforce. The economic arguments she advanced to Torquemada (1420–1498) in favor of the retention of the skills, knowledge, and business acumen of the Jews are well known; she is nevertheless depicted as being easily persuaded by her Dominican confessor, not only to establish the Inquisition but also allow the expulsion of the Jews in 1492. Hence, Isabella gains the reputation as the anti-Semitic bigot who also endorsed the removal of the Moors.

But The Gatekeeper revealed a different Isabella—one who argued passionately against bigotry but was cornered by her Catholicism. Isabella sacrificed her reputation by her silence, dreading spiritual expulsion from the Church and the resulting lockout from heaven, while fearing the imposition of canonical law and the breakup of the newly united Spanish nation. She died of cancer full of regrets.

When she reemerged eight years later, as Katherine Parr, Isabella was the epitome of Mary's devotional line. Before incarnating, she agreed to partner and "save" the obese, vengeful tyrant Henry VIII. Is this one courageous being? Or, as The Gatekeeper questioned, did her own harsh judgment of her life as Isabella lead her to take on, as restitution, a mission impossible?

In two arranged marriages with much older men, Katherine demonstrated care, devotion, tact, and charm. She wrote spiritual books, learned natural medicine, and fell madly in love with her Galahad, Thomas Seymour.

After she was widowed a second time, at 31, the 51-year-old Henry commanded Katherine's hand, and she accepted one of the most dangerous roles in Britain: king's consort and regent. Katherine smoothed down his harsher measures, organized the royal succession on his death, re-established young Elizabeth's right to inherit, while she tended lovingly to his putrid, rodent ulcer, outmaneuvered her enemies in court, and helped birth Protestantism. She was also the first woman in Britain to publish a book using her own name. With Cranmer's support, she assisted in Henry's final confession by gently encouraging him to acknowledge his life of murder and debauchery.

Briefly, she married Seymour before dying in childbirth, her mission impossible achieved. Still happily in love, she exited before Seymour's unfaithfulness corroded her self-worth.

Both Isabella and Katherine married kings, lived in turbulent religious climates, and were pious and capable of complex theological argument. Both behaved with decorum and compassion and were kind, serene, and courageous; both had considerable intellects, learned Latin and Greek later on in their lives, and offered private advice to their spouses. But only one was destined to outlive her husband.

Why has Mary decided to reveal her role in these lives now? Her reasons include her desire to bring them out from the shadows, where her reticence has kept them, to show how her lives, devoid of self-promotion, achieved remarkable missions.

Mary told The Gatekeeper that she wants to inspire historical and feminist scholarship and encourage artists and writers to look in different places for the full story of women's lives. She wants to emphasize, in her lives of Beatrice, Isabella, and Katherine, the importance of spirituality and theology. With these revelations of her more modern lives, she shows how she is moving from her image of an icon of veneration, as Mary the Holy Mother of Jeshua, into more diverse and modern partnership and leadership roles.

And what about Dante and Columbus? At a time when women were considered titbits of the devil, Dante would exalt his Beatrice to the highest place in heaven and claim she was his salvation. Here was Mary, courteous, kind, and blessed, saving souls and providing the motivation for St. Germain, as Dante, to write one of the world's greatest love poems for her.

Dante captured three strong features of St. Germain: his creative exuberance, his intelligence, his sardonic wit. The contrast of Dante with Columbus, his future self, is interesting. Each man imagined a geographic universe—for Columbus, the focus was the earth; for Dante, it was the heavens.

Born a century later, Columbus had little in common with Dante, except for their Catholic faith and Italian nationalities. Columbus's path-finding voyage revealed a previously unknown populated continent and started a sequence of exploration, exploitation, conquest, and colonization without parallel in human history. While Columbus did not achieve the riches he hungered for, and his character was more flawed than most of St. Germain's creations, his courage and navigational skill created a path across an ocean that allowed the cross-fertilization of people and ideas between the Old World and the New, to create a new world order. All these love affairs and marriages demonstrate the way that soulmates make beautiful literature and breathtaking history.

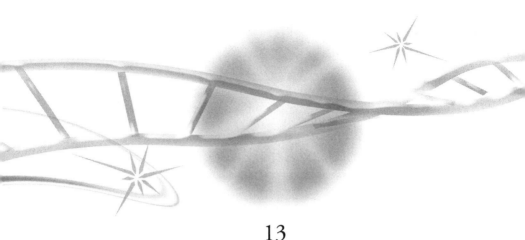

13

Pathfinders – Finding New Worlds

Pathfinders are leaders who discover a new way, mark out a different route, or explore an untrodden and often dangerous path. We've focused on some of St. Germain and Mary's prominent historical lives, and have briefly met some of their friends, rivals, lovers, and enemies. We left them in the 16th century, because the modern era begins with an explosion of opportunities for St. Germain and Mary in education, exploration, technological discoveries, and in the popularizing of music, opera, painting, sculpture, and drama. If newspapers had existed during that time, St. Germain's lives would have dominated the front pages.

We have already discovered that St. Germain is a vast masculine being that takes on myriad forms, including extraordinary lives on Earth. Surprisingly, the reticent Mary the Mother is his complementary energy. Together, they were two of the 12 Masters in the Mother/Father or God spectrum.

While this book has explored the spiritual DNA coming through 12 individual Masters, it has focused on just two of them: St. Germain and Mary. Why?

As a channeled book, the logistics of allowing 12 individual Masters (most of whom are prima donnas) to come through the channel are complex and challenging. There has to be an alignment between the energy of the person channeling and the entity coming in. Some prefer to speak in another language; some are not comfortable coming through male energy, while others are not comfortable coming through female energy. St. Germain prefers to talk French or Mandarin but can talk eloquently, standing underneath an Irish lake with a loaf of bread in his mouth, whereas the more discreet Mary happily steps aside waving him on saying, "Isn't he wonderful?"

All Masters have guides who are either other Masters or members of the angelic realm. Mary the Mother's main guide is her son, Jeshua ben Joseph (Jesus). St. Germain's guide is Mary the High Priestess. She serves as his steadying, compassionate force in order to balance his foolhardiness and encourage the breakthroughs needed to assist Earth.

When we first met St. Germain as Krishna, the Hindu deity of compassion, tenderness, and love, we could see how three Masters worked together with the angelic realm. St. Germain merged with Hilarion for his military expertise and to amplify his existing musical gifts to form Krishna. They created *The Bhagavad-Gita* ("The Song of the Blessed Lord"), the sacred book of the Hindu faith. It was recorded by Arjuna the High Priestess, who shared her life with Archangel of Earth, Sanat Kumara, bringing in his superb military skills.

In Elizabethan England, nearly 5,000 years later, St. Germain and Hilarion would again combine to create the inspiring genius Edward de Vere, Earl of Oxford, the actual author of William Shakespeare's plays, poems, and sonnets. At the same time, the High Priestess would return as DeVere's secretary, John Lyly. Lyly would methodically take dictation from De Vere and catch everything he created and tossed aside.

Their joint purpose was to ensure that every play, poem, and sonnet the Earl composed was published under the name of the semi-literate William Shakespeare. Why?

De Vere, fifth in line to Queen Elizabeth's throne, was the queen's most outstanding swordsman and her most nimble, multilingual spy. He had to protect both his identity and his treasonous creativity. Through his poetic voice, De Vere created the heroes and heroines that formed the touchpoints of the English-speaking world. The themes he chose to dramatize from the Elizabethan court included ambition, power, conflict, order, disorder, love and hate, ambition and evil, violence, guilt, anti-Semitism, tyranny, magic, fate, and free will.

Once you know that De Vere was a master of concealment and lived a double life, it should come as no surprise that the idea of disguise and the nature of appearance and reality dominated so many of his plots. His plays, however, had a universal appeal and traveled in the meager luggage of immigrants to English speaking countries, where they enriched speech and assisted in the acceptance of English as one of the world's dominant languages.

The stories of the Pathfinders involved in Krishna's and De Vere's stories reveal the secrets they keep, the courage they show, and how, despite a gap of 5,000 years, they continue to work with people they trust to reveal universal truths. Our opinions of them can change in the instant their own truth is revealed. Perhaps, now, you may know if you share their spiritual DNA.

The Pathfinders, as we have just explored, are the energies that take the story of humanity forward. St. Germain and his twin soul Mary, in all her three aspects, work together whenever possible, especially when St. Germain has a difficult life. Mother Mary is modest, loving, and always quietly delivers, just as she did as Leah, Jacob's wife. Although now she seldom incarnates, she has had some outstanding recent lives—as Impressionist artist Claude Monet; as recently canonized Mother Teresa; as Chancellor Angela Merkel of Germany, currently the most powerful woman in the world; and as Jacinda Ardern, prime minister of New Zealand, famous for her politics of kindness.

Mary the Magdalene chooses lives of intellectual brilliance that play to her strengths of social reform, governance, law, military leadership, and critical and creative writing. She loves painting. British artists John Constable and JMW Turner are outstanding lives of her talents, and there is more: she is the original drama queen—think of the musical performer Madonna. Mary was the social reformer Jane Addams, the first American woman to receive the Nobel Prize.

She often incarnates in law reform, and aspects of her currently sit on the supreme courts of most Western nations. Why? Because of her powerful intellect, her ease in assuming leadership, and her ability to tell hilarious and often bawdy jokes. The Magdalene was, for example, the former US Supreme Court Judge, Ruth Bader Ginsberg.

Whenever the Magdalene incarnates, she is under the guardianship of Jeshua ben Joseph. Their love is eternal, and Jeshua always holds her closely. He did this when she incarnated as the Russian-born Golda Meir. She had migrated to Wisconsin in 1906, and 15 years later, left the US to work with her husband on a kibbutz in Palestine. She helped found the state of Israel and was elected its fourth prime minister. Golda was a reincarnation of Deborah, first female judge of Israel, who died in 1067 BC. Finally, Deborah came home.

The Magdalene incarnated as the military hero Field Marshal Montgomery, the most decorated military leader of World War II. She also incarnates as novelists, playwrights, and poets. She was Lady Murasaki of Japan who, in AD 1000, wrote the world's first novel, and reincarnated in the 18th century as English novelist Jane Austen, writing with biting wit and challenging the social norms when women could not even sign a legal document. As the English novelist Virginia Woolf, she effectively invented the stream-of-consciousness method of expression; she was the unconventionally brilliant American poet Emily Dickinson; and as the prolific, bestselling English children's author Enid Blyton, she set new norms. The Magdalene loves the writer's life because it provides her with the sheltered lifestyle she needs in order to take on society. She did this as Rachel Carson, the American writer of 1962's ground-breaking *Silent Spring*, and she lives today as the Canadian novelist Margaret Attwood.

She loves fashion and chose to incarnate as the shy Yves St Laurent, the French designer of the pantsuit for the newly liberated woman. He/she made it exquisitely wearable.

I personally loved her in two very different lives.

Once, I was able to speak to her about her sorrowful life as beautiful Queen Guinevere. As a young bride-to-be, she fell in love at first sight with Sir Lancelot, a knight of her future husband's court who had been sent to escort her from Wales to her wedding to King Arthur. After more than 20 years of life as an abandoned queen to a king who was always fighting somewhere else, she lay once with her love, and Morgana, on hearing of their tryst, made sure Arthur would lose his two best friends. You know the rest. But was she a Pathbreaker? Guinevere, with Merlin's help, created the most famous court of Camelot, not only celebrated for its warm hospitality but also for its schooling of children of knights and soldiers and the military hospital for those injured in war.

When I spoke to Martha, she had married her second husband, George Washington, an aspect of Hilarion whom we met earlier as Alexander the Great. Theirs was a spectacularly happy marriage, despite George, when they first married, being in love with his best friend's wife, Sally Fairfax, a reincarnation of his great love, Hephaestion. Martha had two sides to her. First, there was the soldier's wife with strong laugh who privately told jokes that could make a sailor blush. Whenever she joined the general, whom she called "my old man," for the winter encampments during the Revolutionary War, they lived in large rented houses. Her public side was sweet tempered, devout, prayerful, compassionate, and hospitable. She was a woman who had already buried two of her four children from her first marriage. When George's best friend, Lord Fairfax, died in England, Washington invited Sally, his penniless widow to live with them, and Martha in her postscript invited her as well. Sally, by that stage very ill, graciously declined. Martha, whose heart was even larger than her laugh, was the perfect First Lady to the first US President— warm, generous, and loving. She was a Pathbreaker because she lived sometimes on summer campaigns with the Commander-in-Chief in a primitive tent, and assisted in field hospitals, and later was a gracious hostess to visiting dignitaries at their residence at Mount Vernon. Martha set the role model for future Presidential wives. Can you see yourself sharing the Magdalene DNA of these lives?

As we have learned, Mary the High Priestess, frequently incarnates as queens or national leaders focused on reform. We examined her pathbreaking lives as Isabella of Castile, where she bankrolled Columbus's voyage of discovery to America by hocking her crown jewels, or as Katherine Parr, where she became the founding mother of the Church of England. She also incarnated as Queen Anne of Austria, mother of Louis XIV, who we will discuss later, and Elizabeth, the long-lived, discreet, and much-loved Queen Mother of Britain, who as wife to George VI was called by Adolph Hitler "the most dangerous woman in Europe." So far, the reason for his declaration has not been revealed to us, but remember, she was the Isis energy and Churchill the Osiris energy as Serapis Bey. There are no accidents. Elizabeth refused to leave London during the Blitz, and was delighted when Buckingham House was bombed because now, she said, she could look East Enders in the face. Speaking of courage, the High Priestess comes in the male form as Nelson twice: once as the great Admiral Horatio Nelson, and later, as Nelson Mandela, president of South Africa. Both of these men are regarded as national heroes for their unique styles of leadership, bravery, and vision. The High Priestess was assassinated twice: as Prime Minister of India Indira Gandhi, and as Prime Minister of Pakistan Benazir Bhutto, but usually, her Pathfinder lives are much quieter and safer.

The High Priestess shares with the Magdalene a love of writing and painting and enjoys breaking down barriers for women or bringing to the world's attention issues they have been blind to. As Mary Shelley (1787–1862), she invented the new genre of science fiction with her novel *Frankenstein*. As Harper Lee (1928–2016), she explored issues of racial and gender prejudice in the international bestseller *To Kill A Mockingbird*, in which she imaginatively fashioned a coming-of-age novel combined with the Southern Gothic genre. As Henry Thoreau (1817–1862), she wrote of self-reliance in the beauty of nature in *On Walden Pond*, another best-seller, in which Thoreau reflects on the simple life, thereby combining a memoir with a spiritual quest. In these four instances, these Pathfinders have written their ideas and have either created a new genre or combined existing genres to create a new form of expression.

St. Germain, the great innovator, serves to improve life on Earth by experiencing millions of lives. He is a gracious, cultivated, charming Renaissance man. St. Germain does, however, have his limits. He doesn't do popes, he doesn't do chefs, and he doesn't do bodybuilders. Founding fathers? Think Benjamin Franklin. Presidents? Definitely. Think Theodore Roosevelt, Bill Clinton, Barack Obama. Dancers? Now that is his style—wowing audiences as he leaps higher and pirouettes faster . . . Nureyev on steroids! Pilots, astronauts, explorers, movie stars, racing car drivers—he is the child who hangs from the roof and yells "Look, Mom! No hands!" But there is yet another side, his Joseph side. Jesus himself chose Joseph to be his father. Why? Because he was firm and gentle, hard-working and compassionate, intelligent and industrious. Because he knew he would get up at night when Jesus was squawking and mewling and sing to him as he showed him the stars. Listen to him speak:

> My true service is to improve the world and humankind
> by selecting lives that reflect my ability as a growth catalyst.
> I trigger our impulse to the stars, driving you upwards.

Pathfinders from 15th to 20th Century

We are now going to look across five centuries, and I will select some exceptional lives of Masters carrying a range of spiritual DNA and assess their success as Pathfinders. When a soul incarnates on Earth, there is already a rough plan of the experience the soul will manifest. For example, let's look briefly at the life of President John F. Kennedy, an aspect of Hilarion. When he selected life as a president, Kennedy made it very difficult to align himself more closely with God. Choosing assassination, however, changed everything, and it always is a brave choice.

Each of us is a grain of sand in the great desert of the Universe. Sands shift and move, yet every grain, no matter how large, or small plays its part. Whether we are an Ascended Master like Kennedy or not, we are still part of that great flowing ocean of sand. Each grain has a connection to God, and that connection can be as broad, vast, and profound, as Jeshua ben Joseph's, or as slender as a filament, finer than a hair, and down through that connection comes energy. Looking across the last 500 years we see some outstanding souls who incarnated with strong connections to the God energy, and a few who did not. Let's highlight some of their lives.

Gandhi (1869–1948)

Mahatma Gandhi, my first choice, was an aspect of Hilarion. Through his use of prayer, meditation, nonjudgment, nonviolence, and humility, he did not try to temper the divine force within him, nor did he have a universal mission—he just saw injustice and wanted to remedy it. And he did, not through physical action nor through the kind of power that being a president could give him but by being in the flow of the moment. He was a grain of sand flowing in concert with the Universe. In that life, Hilarion kept his human body so ethereal and so insubstantial that if it were any finer, you would be able to see right through him. He had one foot in our dimension and another foot in the next. He was forever loving and attentive, and ascended at the moment of his assassination.

Michelangelo (1475–1564)

Michelangelo, my second choice, goes back to the beginning of the Renaissance, that energetic and explosive time of rebirth emerging from the shattered shell of the Middle Ages. Hilarion, the controling master of the Renaissance, limited himself to three significant lives: Henry VIII of England, who triggered the English Reformation: Louis XIV of France, who built his magnificent palace and gardens at Versailles; and Pope Julius II, who commissioned Michelangelo to paint his personal chapel at the Vatican. At the same time, El Morya, leader of the Ascended Masters, decided to become the conduit for the head of the angels, Archangel Michael. Together, they chose the name Michelangelo after agreeing to incarnate together in the same body. We see this rarely: for example, when the High Priestess incarnated with Archangel Sanat Kumara to record as Arjuna the teachings of Krishna; however, this time, the role of the human and the archangel were to illustrate God's creation of humanity. El Morya and the Archangel's connection to the God energy was so strong, they celebrated it. Just one look at the ceiling of the Sistine Chapel in Rome and the *Creation of Adam* illustrates Michelangelo's concept of our divine connection to God. You will notice that Adam's sex organ is particularly small. This was deliberate, because the Divine reaches us through our higher energy centers: those that deal with prayer, meditation, and inspiration and not those that deal with our physical desire. And then, of course, there was the sublime art to show us that truth.

Leonardo da Vinci (1452–1519)

My third choice is a life of Kuthumi, that of Leonardo da Vinci. In this life, da Vinci experienced no demarcation between art, mathematics, or science; to him, everything was one. That was his message—all is one—but where does the message driven through an unparalleled intellect come from? It is drawn in from elsewhere, carried on light through a spiritual helix, a vibrational frequency that seeks to find expression in earthly creation. The life of da Vinci was not a comfortable one. There was no archangel to help ground this energetic force, because the energy coursing through him was never still. Today, we would diagnose him as autistic with obsessive-compulsive personality. At times, the energy moved so strongly it was painful, and other times, it drove him to work for days on end. He would keep creating until he collapsed from exhaustion. His self-portraits seem to hint at a man strung out almost like an addict, but he accomplished so much, allowing his energy to resonate and permeate our world

Isaac Newton (1642–1726)

Each grain of sand that incarnates finds a physical form in its quest for creative expression; for some, the energy will be abundant, as it was for da Vinci. Another such life is that of my fourth choice: Isaac Newton, an incarnation of Serapis Bey. In previous lives, he had been Confucius, King Solomon, and Thomas Aquinas; this time, from birth, Newton came prepared to drive a scientific revolution in a world on the cusp of growth. Britain and other conquering nations, such as Spain, France, Holland, and Portugal, reached across the world to enforce dominion over other countries. People believed that the earth was the center of the universe; that it was flat, men superior to women, and the white man superior to all other races. Newton incarnated to transform those beliefs and develop a new global pool of thought and ideas. An astronomer, mathematician, physicist, and author, he made humanity smarter by answering the question "Why does an apple fall to the earth and not take off into the sky?"

A more intelligent race looks to the stars and strives for a higher purpose beyond base desire. While this may have been the intention during Newton's time, positive developments also gave rise to the negative, as a result of the duality of the world; thus, alongside this golden age of thought, lay conquest, exploitation, and genocide that led to subjugation of indigenous people all over the world and exploitation of the East Indies. Such is the nature of duality. We could ask the question "If Newton had never come along, if he had never existed, would the converse have happened?" And the answer must be, "Who knows?"

James I (1566–1625)

King James I of England (James VI of Scotland) is my fifth choice. He consolidated what Queen Elizabeth I had started by nurturing a new consciousness for humanity and, from the literary art of Edward de Vere and other Elizabethan poets, inspired the creation of a beautiful language, one that could unite the Old World and the New World. James, an aspect of Mary the High Priestess, was fiercely Protestant. He masterminded a group of poets and priests and literati, led by the Dean of St. Paul's Cathedral, the poet John Donne, to create a new translation of the Bible: the King James's Version of the Bible. A classic of English literature and a work of remarkable beauty was thus written, like Shakespeare, to be read aloud. It became an important unifying principle among England, the US, and the Commonwealth countries. King James I was the unsung hero of the English language, now spoken daily by over two billion people.

Christopher Wren (1632–1723)

My sixth choice, a contemporary of Newton, born ten years apart, is Christopher Wren, an aspect of St. Germain. He was a polymath, astronomer, scientist, mathematician, inventor, and architect. He attended Oxford University as a prodigy and became friends with the men who would form the core members of the Royal Society. By the age of 28, he was a professor of astronomy at Oxford. Wren, left-brained, and part of the Imhotep line of inventors and architects, was also a master mason. St. Paul's Cathedral in London was his masterpiece.

It did not come easily. He had to fight the dean of St. Paul's to design it in the way Hilarion, the invisible Master who oversaw London, desired. In the 17th century, Hilarion wanted him to build a dome capable of withstanding the bombs of the Luftwaffe in the 20th century. Wren became captivated by the dome's mathematics. He studied Brunelleschi's *Duomo* in Firenze, Italy, and St. Peter's in Rome. Church leaders scoffed at Wren's design, calling it too Roman, too Catholic, too Byzantine.

He persevered, and his mastery of mathematics made the dome of St. Paul's the most stable in the world. He followed the sephiroth, or the Tree of Life of Cabbalistic design. If you look at St. Paul's through the eyes of a freemason, you can examine the degree of its angles, rectangles, numbers of right angles, squares, and one great circle, which are the required numbers in sacred geometry to raise a masonic lodge. The dome creates a protective cone of power over the cathedral. Even though it was hit during the Blitzkrieg, it withstood the three attacks.

The Great Fire of London in 1666 offered Wren the opportunity to rebuild the cramped, plague-stricken, mostly wooden, medieval city of London, but its aristocratic landowners prevented him from carrying out this project, and instead, he designed Kensington Place, Chelsea Hospital, Downing Street, and 51 superb churches. His buildings were symbolic of Britain's resilience against enemies, both natural and abroad.

Louis XIV (1638–1715)

Louis XIV, my seventh choice, became king of France as a four-year-old and his mother, Queen Anne of Austria, an aspect of Mary the High Priestess, became France's regent. Doted on by his mother, the young Louis survived thanks to her swift action in two violent uprisings of the nobles. Cardinal Mazarin, the Italian-born protégé of Cardinal Richelieu, became secretary of state on Richelieu's death.

Earlier, Jules Mazarin had insisted that the queen's family move into the safety of the Louvre apartments to protect her sons from their father, King Louis XIII, a predatory paedophile. Now, on assuming Richelieu's power, Cardinal Mazarin played a critical role in the future king's upbringing. Why?

Louis's father was actually Cardinal Jules Mazarin, an aspect of St. Germain. He was formerly Jacob, founder of Israel, but clearly any acknowledgment of Louis's paternity would deny his son's kingship. An elaborate ruse had been performed early in Queen Anne's secret pregnancy, whereby the king and queen had intercourse in front of an inner circle of courtiers to clearly establish his paternity.

Mazarin supervised all of Louis's education, devising ingenious games to teach him statecraft and diplomacy similar to our game of Risk. He insisted that Louis learn the language of each of France's enemies to understand their mindset as the basis of an aggressive foreign policy. Every treasury briefing that crossed Mazarin's desk would be shared with Louis to ensure that he understood France's financial position before it engaged on any military exploits. Mazarin prepared Louis to be absolute ruler of France and impose his will on nobles, allies, and enemies alike. Like Jeshua, connected to the Divine, Louis's greatest joy would be the garden at his Versailles palace, there he felt closest to heaven.

Was there ever a king of any nation like King Louis XIV of France? The answer lies in his unique backstory. About 6,000 years before that, Louis had been Horus, son of Isis and Osiris, and recognized by the Egyptians as Divine. For the Greeks, Louis had also been a god… Hermes. As the martyred cousin of Jesus, Louis, then John the Baptist, was canonized.

When one is so connected to the Divine, its expression knows no bounds. Louis understood that heaven was in the here and now, on Earth, at Versailles. He did not create his palace and gardens out of vanity and ego; rather, Versailles rose from his deep love of the Divine, and in prayer, he learned how to create a new heaven, a utopia.

But beneath its canopy of Light, Versailles harbored debauchery and subterfuge, and the king was not perfect. While the intention of his creation was pure, there were dark corners where rats built their homes. Following Mazarin's instructions, the king moved all his enemies into Versailles, but then gave them little attention. He focused instead on what interested him, the sun, which burst from him in his quest to build heaven on earth in homage to his great love for God. Look to the horizon, Mazarin taught him, love the Divine, pay attention—this was the requirement of an earthly life. Louis had obviously mastered that lesson when he later reincarnated as Gandhi, and ascended the moment he was assassinated.

Johann Sebastian Bach (1685–1750)

Kuthumi incarnated as Johann Sebastian Bach, my eighth choice, to be part of a musical family in Germany. He was the most celebrated composer and musician of the Baroque period, creating over a thousand instrumental and church pieces, including the St. Matthew Passion, Mass in B Minor, and the Brandenburg Concertos. His purpose was to activate humanity's souls by using the mathematical code of music.

At some level, Bach understood that music was a mathematical code, and his purpose was to inspire as many souls as possible of God's love for them, but he eventually realized that he could not express such love in words; he could only express it in musical code. He was a man born into a world where there was very little opportunity to communicate God's love on a wide scale, but he managed it by creating the message in music. He wanted hundreds to hear it, and before he died, thousands had heard it. Now, in our world, centuries later, it has reached more than a billion ears. Bach succeeded beyond his imagination!

Peter the Great (1672–1725)

Peter the Great brought Russia into the modern age and is my ninth choice. As an aspect of El Morya, Peter took on and expanded the cultural revolution of Russia. His skills of persuasion and a strategic and diplomatic mind meant that he only went to war to achieve his ends. Peter had a mesmerizing voice, typical of the line of El Morya, known as "God on the Voice." The great orators and singers, such as Mark Antony, Abraham Lincoln, Elvis Presley, and Bob Dylan, have had it, too.

Peter was a giant of a man, just like Lincoln, measuring six foot eight tall. Peter incarnated to modernize Russia and did that in a methodical and often brutal way by reforming its alphabet, creating a navy, secularizing schools, insisting that men at his court shave their large bushy beards, and applying his art of diplomacy with great skill. He built St. Petersburg to be the seat of his global power and reach. The old families of St. Petersburg still call him "The Great Papa."

James Madison (1751–1836)
and Dolly Madison (1768–1849)

James Madison, my 10th choice, followed Thomas Jefferson as the third President of the United States of America. He was tiny in stature—a simple, sober, loyal man, who saw life in black-and-white terms, had deep and consistent beliefs, and was a faithful follower of George Washington, the first US President. A first-class administrator, Madison was neither as inspired nor as inspirational as Jefferson, but was, instead, practical, detailed, and consistent. This is St. Germain as a methodical, sober, shy lawmaker, careful in preparation but revolutionary in his thinking, happy to borrow ideas from others and synthesize them into something new. I am a Madison fan. He's in my top five US Presidents, second only to Abraham Lincoln. I rank them as Lincoln, Madison, Washington, Franklin D. Roosevelt, and Jefferson.

His life purposes were to stabilize the new republic, draft the Bill of Rights, flesh out the Constitution, create proper public administration, and peacefully purchase new land. He fulfilled his purposes better than anyone else could. Madison was both imaginative and pragmatic and a technocrat—this is, remember, the Imhotep line. His attention to detail during his administration was a critical part of his perfectionism. He had a desperate need to explain and express his reasons to make sure he got everything right. You see that in his contribution to the Federalist Papers, the notes or minutes he took at the Constitutional conventions. Obsessive-compulsive around neatness, he dotted every "i," and kept his ruler at exactly 90 degrees to his blotter beside his left hand so he could rule off something easily and completely.

Madison's method of governance was different from George Washington's. Washington was always a general who had staff he commanded; Madison had colleagues and governed by consensus. Madison was not a showman. He hated the limelight and didn't make patriotic speeches of a stirring nature, but made a greater contribution than those who did. As secretary of state he made much of Jefferson's presidency efficient and effective. Before Jefferson and Madison incarnated, they carefully thought out their differences. They were a balance of genius and judgment, hot and cold, passionate and dispassionate, idealistic and practical, risky and safe, but never ever was Madison weak or indecisive.

Let us begin with his innovation as a result of his Renaissance Man combination of arts and science. His art was in his persuasive manipulation of people, similar to President Bill Clinton but without his sexual charm. Madison had a nonsexual, masonic, men's club charm. For example, he would say to a reluctant colleague, "I cannot think of anyone else whom I can trust this to but you, Walter." Madison had St. Germain's nimble mind, which cuts through quickly to the nub of the matter. He had an intellect like a laser and was an excellent committee man.

The light of his life was his wife Dolly (1768–1849), who was so warm, vivacious, and gay that she is still talked about in Washington DC as a model First Lady, 200 years later; a Pathfinder in her own right. Dolly was the White

House hostess for two Presidents: Jefferson and Madison. She was Madison's mirror opposite: an extrovert to his introvert; she loved balls, while he hated them; she was juicy and plump, while he was dry and wizened. It was simply a great love match, and they depended on one another completely and loved one another deeply. How is it possible to find a better Founding Father or Mother? Can you see yourself in them?

John Constable (1736–1837), J.M.W. Turner (1775–1851), and Claude Monet (1840–1926)

Mary the Magdalene reincarnated as two outstanding artists in 19th-century Britain, John Constable and JMW Turner, who together make up my 11th choice. This was not the first time Mary the Magdalene had incarnated as a famous artist—she had already been the Italian painter Titian (1487–1576), a contemporary of Michelangelo.

Together, Constable and Turner helped launch the British Romantic tradition of painting, and later inspired French Impressionist painter Claude Monet (1840–1926), who was experimenting with light on canvas. Monet enjoyed one of those rare incarnations of Mary the Mother, so he is my 12th choice, and one of my most important selections. As a devout Christian, Monet would ask God to work through him, saying, "I am your instrument, Lord. Be that through me!" Monet's work would create a paradigm shift in the art world from his radical use of light and brush strokes. His paintings created something beautiful and otherworldly.

An artist's connection to the creative force is often a strong one. As painters, Turner, Constable, and Monet caught the shimmering light. Each one, God-like and child-like, created Eden on their canvases and became part of the divine understanding of nature as a sanctified place, but Monet was the first to actually paint light on canvas. This was a paradigm shift, a glory of light. And when we look at Monet's sky or Monet's raft of lilies, we ask ourselves, how did he do it? Because his capture of light shows such perfection it cannot be from mere personality. It must have come from somewhere else. Probably heaven!

These three artists' lives of Mary the Magdalene and Mary the Mother were necessary after the countryside's desecration during the Industrial Revolution and the turmoil of the European wars. Their work allowed peace to grow again in the hearts of the people and encourage future generations to fight the wreckers of forests and bush and the ravages of pollution, logging, and mining.

Nikola Tesla (1856-1943)

Nikola Tesla (1856–1943) was one of St. Germain's most extraordinary lives, and he is my 13th choice. Tesla was different from everyone else, a genius who didn't appear to be from this planet. Of course, he was a brilliant scientist, inventor, and a mechanical and electrical engineer with a photographic memory. Tesla studied in Europe and then emigrated to the US, where he worked with Thomas Edison and George Westinghouse. Tesla spoke multiple languages fluently. He was eccentric, possibly suffering from Asperger's syndrome, a showman who suffered obsessive-compulsive disorders. Those disorders, though, were a part of his brilliance. When he saw light, it was often fractured, creating hallucinations that Tesla could theorize with an almost three-dimensional clarity. His disability was part of his genius. Despite his brilliance, Tesla's life was miserable, because he needed someone to care for him.

His purpose is clear now, but not so much back then. Tesla revolutionized technological progress, discovering the rotating magnetic field and creating the foundation for remote-controled radio, power transmission, robotics, and missile sciences. He made nanotechnology possible. Once, in the grip of a scientific problem, he could not rest. On his death, the FBI cleared out his hotel room, fearing (correctly) that America's hero, Thomas Edison, had stolen some of Tesla's patents and it would cause trouble if the public found out.

Albert Einstein (1879–1955)

One hundred and fifty years after his life as Isaac Newton, Serapis Bey reincarnated in Germany as the theoretical physicist Albert Einstein with the purpose of creating relativity theory. He is my 14th choice. Einstein is one of those rare people in the story of the world who was given a superb intellect. How different his and Newton's lives were: one a person of privilege, educated, and superbly creative, who changed the world; the other an Ashkenazi Jew, who eventually had to leave not only his homeland but all of Europe and emigrate to America to ensure his safety from the Nazis. Einstein's theoretical discoveries eventually led to both nuclear and solar power, theories of the creation of the universe, parallel universes, worm holes and black holes. His description of space and time—$E=mc2$—leads you to ask yourself, Where did that come from? It was as if a profound revelation had just been made, one that would change the world.

Joseph Stalin (1878–1953)

Stalin was a Soviet politician, and an aspect of El Morya, who ruled the Soviet Union as a dictator from the mid-1920s until he died in 1953. He used terror and murder to destroy his enemies and galvanize a nation and lead it to the brink of oblivion. He is not one of my choices at all, but he is included here for his devastating impact on the Russian people. Although he was not a teacher, he could move mountains with the force of his voice. Sound familiar? But what was his purpose? To save Russia from the onslaught of the Nazis, which he accomplished. To protect Russia from the rest of the world, which he also accomplished, by creating the Cold War. In another world, there would have been no Berlin if Russia had fallen, and that has to be one of his indirect achievements. But our world was left with Stalin's paranoic fear of the West's imperialism. He would isolate Russia so that it would eventually allow the rise of its economic power and its technology to occur. Meanwhile, Stalin oversaw, among other carnages, a famine that killed over seven million Russians and the gulags, or prison camps, which killed at least a million more. After his death, in the review of his life, when the balance between the good he had done was weighed up against the evil, a decision was taken that Stalin would not be permitted to reincarnate, and his soul was destroyed. Pure evil is never allowed to triumph, as we saw when Pol Pot, Adolph Hitler, and Heinrichs Himmler incarnated. Evil must exist so that we can hone our moral philosophy and choose not to follow it.

Now, as Russia's technology escalates, it manifests in an evil way in totalitarianism, and we see the rise of its oligarchs, espionage, counterespionage, and global penetration of other nations, keeping other nations fearful of it.

Gabrielle "Coco" Chanel (1883—1971)

Coco Chanel was a source of wonder, a French fashion designer who founded her own brand. While she was not a striking beauty, Coco created striking beauty in simple but elegant clothes like her "little black dress" and in her perfumes. Chanel's purpose was to give women the Divine in a practical expression. In creating her perfume Chanel No. 5, she asked herself, What does the Divine smell like? What would heaven itself smell like? And after long experimentation, she created Chanel No. 5 to give us a hint of heaven, a touch of the Divine. When Chanel entered the masculine world, she introduced the beauty and power of the feminine. The feminine can rebalance ideas through desire, not lust, and demonstrate the qualities of Mary, not through conquest but an indefinable quality of beauty. She fulfilled her purpose in that life, and her perfume still carries the qualities she instilled in it.

You will notice that I did not select Washington, Napoleon, Nelson, Lincoln, or Churchill, all of whom were outstanding, charismatic, wartime leaders with strong lines to God. But you know their stories already, whereas the ones Kuthumi and I selected could have had just as profound an effect on you through the sheer brilliance of their breakthroughs, the radical beauty of their art, their sheer attention to detail, or the great comfort they took in working with the Mother/Father. Our people above were chosen based on a number of criteria. First, they had consciously and spectacularly worked with the Divine as they achieved their life's purpose; and, secondly, they made a disparate impact in their field of expertise and this impact continued for centuries after their death.

Contemporary Pathfinders – 21st Century

Now for something different—some thumbnail sketches of contemporary Pathfinders who have the capacity to make a profound difference. Will they?

Contemporary Pathfinders are harder to determine because we haven't yet seen the end of their story, but here are some of today's most notable names with some thoughts and insights. Some are world leaders, and some have chosen a different route or an untrodden or even dangerous path.

Below are reviews of Joseph Biden, Kamala Harris, Barack Obama, Donald Trump, Vladimir Putin, Xi Jing Ping, Emmanuel Macron, Justin Trudeau, Queen Elizabeth, and Elon Musk.

President Joseph Biden is an aspect of St. Germain from the same empathetic line as St. Joseph, the father of Jeshua. Biden is a compassionate, loving, thoughtful man, who can heal the US after the pandemic of the coronavirus and the presidency of Donald Trump. He will attempt to re-establish the network of America's allies across the world.

Vice President Kamala Harris is an aspect of Lady Portia, the female expression of Kuthumi. She shares her first name with Nehru's wife, and they are both named after the sacred lotus of India. Her youth, vigor, and intellect will complement Biden's maturity. There is a temporary shield over her past lives. Of course, she should be regarded as a potential US President.

Former President Barack Obama is an aspect of St. Germain from one of the world's most distinguished lines of lawmakers and orators. His past lives include the ancient Greek philosopher Plato, the Roman playwright Seneca, the Roman statesman Cicero, and one of the founding fathers of the United States and drafters of the US Constitution, James Madison. He needed a new challenge, and his carefully chosen genetic mix, which included both American Indian and AfricanAmerican to help create the persona of a cool, multiracial intellectual. His contribution to the world continues.

Former President Donald Trump is from the line of Djwhal Khul, whose purpose as US President was to "fester the rot." Unconsciously, he showed us a detailed list of everything that needed to be reformed to make America great again. However, Djwhal Khul has often been a monarch (most recently as the much-loved wartime King George VI of Britain) and a US President (as Ronald Reagan). Trump himself most enjoyed his time as pharaoh when he had absolute power. Two of Trump's other remarkable lives were Hercules and Martin Luther.

President Vladimir Putin, current president of Russia, is an aspect of Lady Leto, the soulmate of Djwhal Khul. He is a ruthlessly charming man, determined to make Russia great again by doing whatever is necessary to achieve that aim. Putin and Trump got on well for obvious reasons, including that they are twin souls.

Great Masters often incarnate and reincarnate in the same place. President Emmanuel Macron, an aspect of El Morya, was the first Mark Antony, Julius Caesar's colleague, in conquering Gaul. Both of them deeply loved Cleopatra. When Antony returned as Napoleon, he loved Cleopatra again, this time as Josephine. Now he is back as Macron, with challenges just as complex, but this time without Cleopatra—his wife now is an aspect of Mary the Mother because Macron faces prodigious challenges. Peter the Great of Russia was a former life of Macron.

Xi Jing Ping is a reincarnation of Emperor Qin Shi Huang, who created the Entombed Warriors and gave China his name. He does not think of what China will be like tomorrow; he thinks of what China will be like in a thousand years. He has the energy of the brilliant St. Germain, but what on earth is he doing here? Expect more surprises; no guarantee they'll be pleasant.

Prime Minister Justin Trudeau is prime minister of Canada and an aspect of Hilarion. He is a handsome man of charm and intellect. Like Hilarion's many other heroic lives of leadership, such as Alexander the Great and George Washington, it seems his Master energy is well suited for this role. Watch this space.

Queen Elizabeth II is an aspect of Lady Portia, the feminine of Master Kuthumi. Often a queen or a member of royalty, and the same energy line as Princess Grace of Monaco but from a different Lady Portia line to that of Princess Diana.

Elon Musk, a gifted man with a strong intellect and a vivid, space-cadet imagination, is an aspect of Serapis Bey. Like Jeff Bezos, he came from nowhere and is an innovator. Working in alchemic ways, Serapis Bey thinks differently. Einstein and Isaac Newton were his predecessors, while Nikola Tesla, the true inventor of electricity, and Benjamin Franklin, both aspects of St. Germain, are Musk's only competitors in scientific invention.

CONCLUSION

This book tells the truth, the hidden story, of St. Germain and Mary. Unfortunately, it does not have room to honor, in depth, the stories of the other 10 Masters. Why?

Because after two long decades of me persuading them to reveal their Lines to God, they relaxed and poured out far more than they originally intended, and when DNA testing became commonplace, they also shared their most important secret: that everyone, on this planet, no matter who they were, ordinary or extraordinary, whatever their social standing or their race or whether they believed in God or not, everyone, without exception, has a direct Line to God through their spiritual DNA. When I inquired as to whether we can trace our spiritual DNA, they told me and permitted me to reveal this bombshell.

So why stop the Masters' stories in Tudor England, when lives were getting interesting? Time and energy were limited, and the vault of knowledge was huge and expanding. It was a pragmatic choice, enough to get you started and whet your appetite.

I asked Kuthumi who he thought had made some of the most significant contributions since the Renaissance across all the Master energies. He came up with a list, and I came up with some names. I thought he focused too much on the evil humans do; he thought I found it hard to go past Edward de Vere, Earl of Oxford. Finally, we came up with the people you read about in the last chapter.

The story of St. Germain and Mary and the other ten masters will always be unfinished. There is so much more to these beings, which are ceaseless in their pursuit of truth. St. Germain, for example, was often a brilliant king, inventor, Renaissance artist, invented opera and ballet, and as St. George the Dragon Slayer later had to be that Beatle called George. He added that he was enjoying lives on other planets! All I could say was: "Lordy, Lordy, please approach NASA. Do not ask me!"

Now you are starting to know this amazing man. He was, in an earlier life, the mathematician, astronomer, classical scholar, and physician who lived as Nicolaus Copernicus, but who, like De Vere, could not reveal his great work, either. When Copernicus discovered that the earth rotated around the sun, he was not living in a time, like today, when he could safely reveal the truth, so who better than another aspect of St Germain, Neil Armstrong, to be the first human to walk on the moon and watch the rotation of the earth?

My purpose in writing this book is to reveal that everyone on Earth has a pathway to return to God. It lives in our genetic code. I have sought to reveal that our spiritual universe is just as elegant as our physical one. I have found that every person on Earth, no matter who they are, is an aspect of one of these 12 Masters, who exist in loving and matching pairs of feminine and masculine. Everyone on Earth has a spiritual name and a physical name in their current life, but no matter who they are, they will be an aspect of one of those 12 Masters. Once you discover which Master you are an aspect of, this will never change. This is who you have been since your moment of creation; it is simply who you are forever. Regardless of your current race, nationality, intelligence, beauty, or disabilities, those attributes may not reflect your true self; they are simply choices of your current life. Although I am a female in this life, at least 30 percent of my lives have been as a male.

When I spoke to Jeshua ben Joseph, I asked: "Why didn't you select a woman as an apostle?" Jesus emphatically said that he had included a female apostle: Mary the Magdalene, an apostle of equal status to Simon Peter who led 11 other women disciples, and among the male apostles were three that were feminine entities having a male life, one of them being St. Philip. Mary the Magdalene's demonization by the Catholic Church in the third century all but extinguished her role in Church history.

The gifts and impairments of your personality will change with every life, but the gifts of your spiritual DNA are constant. They reflect your master code and carry that name. I will forever be an aspect of Mary the High Priestess, and one of my roles will be to chronicle the lives of the Great Ones.

The ultimate purpose of this book is to help you know the unknowable, the Mother/Father or God, and to understand that you have both spiritual and physical connections to All That Is and to the billions of others in your soul group.

I hope that this book will help you discover your spiritual DNA and your lineage and begin the journey of discovering where you fit into God's universal plan.

God bless!

Appendix

DECIPHERING YOUR LINE TO GOD

The Gatekeeper, a Tibetan lama, selected hundreds of outstanding individuals. Some of them had lived thousands of years ago, and through persuasive arm-twisting from St. Germain, agreed to share with us their deepest secrets. Of the 12 energies that populate our planet, we could only explore two energies in depth, and St. Germain selected them: Mary and himself.

Why them? St. Germain is a brilliant show-off and a superb storyteller, and Jesus himself selected him to be his father every time he incarnated on Earth. Mary, mother of Jesus and St. Germain's reticent twin soul, agreed to help him.

My role as the researcher, writer, and interviewer of the hundreds of lives they selected took 25 years. Now you have met the main characters of St. Germain and Mary. You have also glimpsed some of the other players, such as the brilliant man-of-twists-and-turns Kuthumi, the dashing conqueror Hilarion, the beautiful and highly accomplished Lady Portia, and the take-no-prisoners Pallas Athene. Perhaps you can recognize yourself in one of them.

Everyone reading this book is on a quest. You want to know who you are, what line of energy you are, what spiritual DNA you hold that connects you to the Mother/Father, that connects you to God. Like all quests, this journey will take you up blind alleys and have you making wrong turns. I have learned that while there are no easy ways to find out who you are, it is possible, using the knowledge of the Masters that I have built up over the years, to figure out your particular line to God.

Finding Your Master Energy

The first way in is your name. On the following pages you find some charts with alphabetically listed names, each associated with a Master name respectively spiritual energy. Following this are Master charts which tabulate groups of names associated with each of the spiritual energies. These will give you an overview of the energy field connected with each master. Here's how you decipher which energy you are.

Step 1

Have a look at the name tables starting on page 253 for your first name and find the Ascended Master that your name is associated with.

Identify your second or third names from the same list to discover whether you resonate with the names of the Ascended Master associated with either of them. There is a good chance you may come up with two different Master energies. Which one do you choose?

Ask yourself: how did I come to receive those names? Were they family or baptismal names, or the names of popular idols? Were they to honor an important person in your family's life like a sporting, political, film star, or military hero? Or was it your Mother's favourite name? Or did your father insist on you being called after his father? There is a very good chance that whatever the reason they gave you they were guided to that name by none other than you, their incarnating bundle of joy, a Master returning to the Earth and giving them very helpful clues.

Step 2

If you find you do not resonate with any of those potentially three Master names, or if you do not find your name in the tables to start with, how do you proceed?

Look into the reasons for your parent's choice of naming you, then sit quietly, or go for a walk, a jog, a swim, or a sleep and command your Master energy to reveal their name to you. In response you might hear it spoken or sung, see it written on the cover of a book or jump out at you in some way. It might also reveal itself as an inner knowing; something you notice and resonate with.

For another approach, you could explore the charts of the Master names (p. 261 ff.) that detail a group of names associated with them and see if you find resonance with any of their energies, colors, or name groupings, even if your own name is not mentioned. Or ask yourself seriously if it was your choice, what name would you choose?

If you still feel unsure, the Being who is the official representative of your Master energy is there to help. Give him or her a call saying: "I need your help whoever you are!" Promise me to believe what you hear them answer!

Step 3

Read up further on the biographies of those personalities embodying the Master whose energy you feel drawn to in order to familiarize yourself with their spiritual energy. The channelled and researched material in this book provides a good basis for exploring reincarnations of the Master with their facets and challenges. You might already find some resonance with your own life in these pages, recognize character traits or connections

Here is an example:

I will analyze for you a case study of the spiritual DNA of the founding fathers of the United States, and where possible, those of their wives. We are fortunate that, except for George Washington, their incarnating selves were able to influence their parents' selection of their names to reflect their spiritual energy. George Washington is a special case. He required a heroic name to lead a revolutionary army to success. He selected George, after St. George the Dragon Slayer, a St. Germain name. An inspirational choice!

President/Wife	Spiritual Energy
George Washington	Hilarion
Martha Washington	Mary the Magdalene
John Adams	El Morya
Abigail Adams	Mary the High Priestess
Alexander Hamilton	Hilarion
James Madison	St. Germain
Dolly Madison	Lady Portia
Thomas Jefferson	Serapis Bey
Benjamin Franklin	St. Germain
Deborah Read Franklin	Mary the Magdalene
John Jay	Kuthumi
Sarah Jay	Mary the High Priestess

Once you notice the repetition of male and female energies, you will see that this approach is not infallible, because while the first and second President's names, George and John Adams, do not match their energetic names all the other founding fathers do. And most of their identified spouses are Mary energies. These issues beg three questions.

How will I know if their names match? I have been privileged to talk to the higher selves of all the founding fathers and mothers, and they have identified each of their spiritual energies. When they did not match, they offered two reasons. First, the family choosing their baby's name often felt they needed to honor a relative or an influential patron. Second, sometimes parents want their offspring to have the particular qualities of a saint or another person they admired who held that name, so they chose it in the hopes that the qualities of that person would transfer to their child. These name choices happen when mothers decide to call their child after a film star or other celebrity, military hero, or famous fictional character, or in George Washington's case, a Christian military hero, St. George. Fortunately, the incarnating child can usually influence their parents and persuade them to avoid names like Boobie, Thor, or Lady Gaga.

How will you know if their names do not match? You won't, but you can look for other clues. In our times, we can rely on their second or third names to provide a clue. Let's take the two assassinated Kennedy brothers: President John Fitzgerald Kennedy and Attorney General Robert Francis Kennedy. Sometimes, you have to dig for an answer. John or Jack Kennedy was definitely not a Kuthumi energy, who seldom incarnates as someone who will be assassinated or crucified. He prefers to die, if possible, in his bed (there are exceptions in John Lennon and Yitzhak Rabin). Hilarion, on the other hand, specializes in them. Hilarion's lives as Martin Luther King Jr., Gandhi, Alexander Litvinenko, and Malcolm X are four examples, and John Kennedy's second name includes the Hilarion name Gerald.

John Kennedy's brother's first name was Robert, one of the most common El Morya names, and he was the same energy as three other men famously assassinated: Abraham Lincoln, Leon Trotsky, and Lee Harvey Oswald. El Morya, too, clearly does dramatic deaths.

From this analysis, we can conclude that John Kennedy was most probably an aspect of Hilarion, and Robert Kennedy was most probably an aspect of El Morya. How can you be sure? Short of asking them directly in a channeled session, you can only build up a store of knowledge of Hilarion's or El Morya's lives. Only through the recognition of consistent similarities can you say with authority from which line of God they are descended, whose spiritual DNA they each share with millions of others. Fortunately, having spent many years learning about the Ascended Masters and their lives, I am in a position to do that.

Finally, did you notice the preponderance of Mary energy in the founding fathers' wives? The Bible makes clear that God selected Eve, an aspect of Mary, as the founding energy for the human race. Why? Mary the Mother excels in start-ups. She is calm, efficient, witty and warm, a loving partner, a friendly hostess, a sound critic, and a shrewd politician. Read their biographies. Any of them could easily run for President today. I had the pleasure of talking to Martha Washington once (she was an aspect of Mary the Magdalene), and she had all those qualities and the wisecracking wit of Bette Midler. Dinners at her table would never be dull! There is also a preponderance of Mary energies in female national leaders who have been assassinated: Indira Gandhi and Benazir Bhutto, both leaders of Asian nations and aspects of Mary the High Priestess. Assassination brings the reward of their spiritual progression, as well as their place in the history books.

Are there any other clues that can help in defining your energy line? Yes, by colors. By recognizing the predominant color in your auric field, you will get an idea which Master energy you possess. In the Master charts (p. 261 ff.), the colors associated with each Master energy are noted in parenthesis. The colors represent the shades that people with sight can see around the Ascended Masters. Hilarion is a vibrant emerald green, Kuthumi, dark blue; Lady Nada, both white and gold; St. Germain, violet; Lady Portia, purple and ruby. El Morya changes: in leadership roles he is red, when you're a dad or teacher his aura is royal blue.

Decoding your name is the first step, **identifying your Master color** is the next one, and **reading biographies** is the third. Recognizing character traits you share with prominent people, particularly quirky ones, helps build the profile of your spiritual DNA.

The Delphic Oracle had one message to all of humankind. "Know Thyself." Do you have the courage to begin?

Names and Spiritual Energies/Masters

Female Name	Spiritual Energy
Abigail	Lady Portia
Adelaide	Kwan Yin
Adeline	Kwan Yin
Alexis	Lady Nada
Alice	Lady Nada
Allison	Lady Nada
Amanda	Pallas Athene
Amber	Pallas Athene
Amelia	Pallas Athene
Amy	Pallas Athene
Andrea	Lady Nada
Angela	Mary the Mother
Ann	Mary the Mother
Anna	Mary the Mother
Aria	Mary the Mother
Ariana	Mary the Mother
Ashley	Lady Leto
Astrid	Pallas Athene
Audrey	Mary the Magdalene
Aurora	The Magdalene as the Cosmic Daughter
Avery	Mary the Mother
Barbara	Lady Leto
Betty	Pallas Athene
Beverly	Lady Leto
Brenda	Mary the High Priestess
Brie	Mary the Magdalene
Brittany	Mary the Magdalene
Camilla	Mary the High Priestess
Carmel	Mary the High Priestess
Carol	Mary the High Priestess

Carolyn	Mary the High Priestess
Catherine	Pallas Athene
Charlotte	Mary the High Priestess
Cheryl	Lady Portia
Chloe	Lady Portia
Christine	Mary the Magdalene
Claire	Lady Portia
Clara	Lady Portia
Cora	Mary the Mother
Cynthia	Pallas Athene
Daisy	Lady Nada
Danielle	Lady Nada
Deborah	Mary the Magdalene
Debra	Mary the Magdalene
Delilah	Mary the Magdalene
Denise	St. Germain
Diana	Mary the High Priestess
Diane	Mary the High Priestess
Dolly	Lady Leto
Donna	Mary the Mother
Doris	Mary the Magdalene
Dorothy	Mary the Magdalene
Eleanor	Pallas Athene
Elizabeth	Pallas Athene
Ella	Pallas Athene
Ellie	Pallas Athene
Eloise	Mary the Mother
Emily	Mary the High Priestess
Emma	Mary the Mother
Evelyn	Mary the Mother
Frances	Lady Portia
Freya	Pallas Athene
Genevieve	Mary the Magdalene
Gloria	Lady Portia

Grace	Lady Portia
Hailey	Pallas Athene
Hannah	Mary the Mother
Harper	Mary the Mother
Hazel	Lady Nada
Heather	Mary the Mother
Helen	Pallas Athene
Iris	Mary the High Priestess
Isabella	Mary the High Priestess
Isla	Mary the High Priestess
Ivy	Mary the Mother
Jacqueline	Lady Portia
Jane	Mary the Magdalene
Janet	Mary the Magdalene
Janice	Mary the Magdalene
Jean	Lady Portia
Jennifer	Mary the Magdalene
Jessica	Mary the Magdalene
Joan	Pallas Athene
Josephine	Mary the High Priestess
Joyce	Mary the High Priestess
Judith	Mary the Magdalene
Judy	Mary the Magdalene
Julia	Lady Portia
Julie	Lady Portia
Kaia	Pallas Athene
Karen	Lady Nada
Katharine	Pallas Athene
Kathleen	Pallas Athene
Kayla	Pallas Athene
Kaylee	Pallas Athene
Kelly	Pallas Athene
Kimberly	Lady Nada
Laura	Mary the Mother
Layla	Mary the Mother

Leah	Mary the Mother
Lillian	Mary the High Priestess
Lily	Mary the High Priestess
Linda	Lady Nada
Lisa	Pallas Athene
Lorelei	Mary the Mother
Lucy	Mary the Magdalene
Luna	Mary the High Priestess
Lydia	Lady Portia
Lyla	Mary the Magdalene
Madeline	Mary the Magdalene
Madison	Mary the Magdalene
Maeve	Mary the Magdalene
Maggie	Mary the Magdalene
Margaret	Mary the Magdalene
Maria	Mary the Mother
Marie	Mary the Mother
Marilyn	Lady Leto
Martha	Mary the Mother
Meghan	Lady Portia
Melanie	Lady Portia
Melissa	Lady Portia
Mia	Mary the Mother
Michaela	Pallas Athene
Michele	Pallas Athene
Mila	Lady Portia
Molly	Mary the Mother
Nancy	Mary the Mother
Naomi	Lady Nada
Natalie	Mary the High Priestess
Nicole	Lady Nada
Nina	Pallas Athene
Nora	Mary the Mother
Olivia	Lady Nada

Ophelia	Mary the Magdalene
Paisley	Lady Leto
Pamela	Mary the High Priestess
Patricia	Mary the High Priestess
Penelope	Mary the High Priestess
Poppy	Mary the High Priestess
Quinn	Mary the Mother
Rachel	Mary the Magdalene
Rebecca	Mary the High Priestess
Rihanna	Lady Portia
Rose	Mary the High Priestess
Ruby	Lady Nada
Ruth	Mary the High Priestess
Samantha	Lady Nada
Sandra	Lady Nada
Sarah	Mary the Mother
Scarlett	Lady Leto
Sharon	Mary the Mother
Shirley	Lady Portia
Sofia / Sophia	Pallas Athene
Stella	Mary the Mother
Stephanie	Mary the High Priestess
Susan	Kwan Yin
Teresa	Lady Portia
Zoe	Mary the High Priestess

Male Name	Master Name
Donald	Djwhal Khul (DK)
Douglas	Hilarion
Duke	Hilarion
Dylan	Kuthumi
Edward	St. Germain
Elias	Jeshua
Elijah	Mary the Magdalene
Elliot	Jeshua

Emmett	Serapis Bey
Eric	El Morya
Ethan	St. Germain
Eugene	Jeshua
Everett	St. Germain
Felix	Hilarion
Finn	Kuthumi
Frank	Kuthumi
Frankie	Kuthumi
Gabriel	Hilarion
Gary	DK
Gavin	El Morya
George	St. Germain
Gerald	Sanat Kumara
Grayson	Kuthumi
Gregory	El Morya
Harold	Hilarion
Harrison	Hilarion
Hayes	El Morya
Henry	Hilarion
Hudson	DK
Ian	Kuthumi
Isaac	Kuthumi
Jack	Kuthumi
Jackson	Kuthumi
Jacob	St. Germain
James	St. Germain
Jason	Hilarion
Jasper	Kuthumi
Jayden	El Morya
Jeffrey	Kuthumi
Jerry	El Morya
Jeremy	Sanat Kumara
Jeremy / Gerald	Sanat Kumara

Jesse	Jeshua
Joe	St. Germain
John	Kuthumi
Jonathan	Kuthumi
Jordan	Serapis Bey
José	St. Germain
Joshua	St. Germain
Josiah	Jeshua
Joseph	St. Germain
Juan	Kuthumi
Julian	St. Germain
Justin	Hilarion
Keith	Hilarion
Kelsey	El Morya
Kenneth	Mary the High Priestess
Kevin	Kuthumi
Kyle	DK
Landon	Sanat Kumara
Larry	El Morya
Lawrence	El Morya
Leo	El Morya
Levi	DK
Liam	Kuthumi
Lincoln	El Morya
Logan	Kuthumi
Louis	Kuthumi
Lucas	Mary the High Priestess
Luke	Mary the High Priestess
Mark	El Morya
Mason	St. Germain
Mateo	Sanat Kumara
Matthew	Sanat Kumara
Michael	El Morya
Miles	Hilarion

Mohammad	El Morya
Nathan	St. Germain
Nicholas	Hilarion
Noah	St. Germain
Oliver	Kuthumi
Oscar	St. Germain
Owen	El Morya
Paul	Hilarion
Patrick	St. Germain
Peter	El Morya
Phillip	St. Germain
Randolph	Serapis Bey
Raymond	Kuthumi
Richard	St. Germain
Robert	El Morya
Roger	Kuthumi
Roman	Hilarion
Ronald	Kuthumi
Roy	El Morya
Russell	St. Germain
Ryan	St. Germain
Samuel	St. Germain
Sawyer	El Morya
Scott	St. Germain
Sean	Kuthumi
Sebastian	Sanat Kumara
Shawn	Kuthumi
Steven	St. Germain
Terry	Kuthumi
Theo	Jeshua
Theodore	Hilarion
Thomas	Serapis Bey
Timothy	Serapis Bey
Tony	St. Germain

Travis	DK
Tyler	Serapis Bey
Vincent	DK
Walter	St. Germain
Wayne	Kuthumi
William	Kuthumi
Wyatt	St. Germain
Zachary	Hilarion

The following Master charts tabulate names associated with each of the energies. There are numerous names for Mary and St. Germain and, as you will see, few names for Djwhal Khul (DK). There are several reasons for this. In Western civilization Mary and St. Germain incarnate more frequently, DK prefers Asian or Eastern civilizations. Apart from this preference, as a whole, DK incarnates less frequently and Ladies Fortunata and Leto have fewer opportunities to incarnate in climates unsuitable for their talents.

Mary **(Mother Mary [blue, white, and gold], the Magdalene [dark blue], and the** **High Priestess [purple and ruby])**
Abigail, Gail
Anne
Antonia
Brigid, Bridie, Beatrice
Camilla, Carmel, Carmen, Chanel, Camille
Cleopatra, Cleo
Deborah
Diana, Dian, Diane
Emily, Emilia, Amelia
Eve, Evie, Evelyn
Guinevere, Gwendolyn, Jennifer, Gwen
Indira, Benazir
Isabelle, Isabella, Bella, Belle
Jane
Josephine, Josie, Jose
Leah

Margaret, Margot, Molly
Mary, Maria, Maree, Marian, Marion
Moira, Maya, Mia
Patricia, Patsy
Phillipa
Rose
Ruth
Sara, Sarah, Sally
Virginia
Zoe
Mary in Masculine Form (blue, white, and gold; dark blue; purple and ruby)
Hephaestion
Horatio
James
Luke, Lucas, Lucan
Nelson
Philip
Stuart

St. Germain (purple or violet) **(Magician, Soldier, Philosopher, Musician, Dancer, and Inventor)**
Aaron
Anthony, Tony
Apollo
Barak
Bart, Bartholomew
Benjamin, Jamin
Brendon
Charles, Carl, Claude
Christopher, Chris
Colum, Columba
Dante
Dennis
Edward, Eddie
George, Giorgio

Germain
Hiram
Homer
Jacob, Jake
James
Joseph, Joe
Jude
Julian, Julius, Jules
Kai, Kay
Lucas
Merlin
Nathan
Neil
Noah
Pa**trick**, **Pa**t, Paddy
Raphael
Richard, Dick
Samuel
Stephen, Steven, Steve
Walter

El Morya (red and royal blue)
Abraham
Archibald, Archie
Arthur
Borholt, Bors, Bernard
Bruce
Hector
Leon, Leonardo, Lenard, Lee
Mark, Marco
Michael, Mike, Mick, Misha
Muhammad
Peter, Simon
Robert, Rob, Roberto,
Victor

Pallas Athene (gold)
Athena
Elizabeth, Beth, Betty, Eliza
Helen, Helena, Eleanor, Ella
Joan, Joanna, Joannie
Katherine, Catherine, Kate, Cate
Lee, Leigh
Michelle
Roberta
Sienna
Simone
Sophia
Victoria
Virginia

Kuthumi (dark blue)
Francis, Frank
Gilead, Galahad, Gideon
Hugh
Jahan
John, Jonathan, Jack, Jackson
Jude
Kevin, Isaac, Yitzhak
Louis
Oliver, Olivier
Rodger, Roger
Ronald
Theodore, Theo
Tristan, Tristram
Ulysses, Odysseus
William, Liam, Bill, Billy, Wilhelm

Lady Portia (purple and ruby)
Anne
Christine

Clare, Clarissa, Clarice
Florence, Flo
Grace
Jacqueline
Jean
Lakshmi
Louise, Louisa
Marilyn
Mumtaz
Olivia
Thea, Theo
Therese, Terry, Tess
Veronica

Hilarion (green)
Alexander
Andrew
Bedivere
Gerald
Hadrian
Henry, Hank, Harry
Jeremy
Malcolm
Martin
Nicholas
Paul
Uther, Luther

Lady Nada (white and gold)
Andrea
Barbara
Hannah
Henrietta, Harriet
Hillary
Martina

| Paula |
| Virginia |

| **Serapis Bey (spirals of gold and white)** |
| Albert |
| Ignatius |
| Isaac |
| Leonard, Leonidas |
| Osiris |
| Thomas – after the Apostle – his favourite name (as in Thomas Stearns [T.S.] Eliot, St. Thomas, St. Thomas Aquinas, Thomas Cromwell, St. Thomas More, Thomas Jefferson, Thomas Paine, Thomas Hobbs, Thomas Mann, Tom Woolf, and Thomas the Tank Engine, because Serapis Bey has a wicked wit.) |
| Winston |

| **Lady Leto (emerald green)** |
| Eleanor |
| Helena |
| Marion |

| **Djwhal Khul (emerald green)** |
| Albert, Bertie |
| Caspar, one of the three wise men |
| Donald |
| Edgar |
| Martin |
| Ronald |
| Shiva |

| **Lady Fortunata (yellow)** |
| Gina |
| Heddy |
| Lola |
| Marilyn |

INDEX

ABOUT THE AUTHOR

Photo by Patrick Moran

Carmel Niland is the former CEO and leader of various government agencies on gender, racial equality, human rights, and child protection in New South Wales, Australia. She became well-known for fighting against sexual harassment and discrimination and advocating for women's and Aboriginal rights.

Raised in a Catholic family, Carmel has always felt a deep connection to spirit. Her lifelong quest for spiritual meaning led her to become the messenger, the one chosen to reveal the secrets behind our line to God. She has nurtured a long-held interest in history, myth, legend, and religion. The author of *A Darker Magic This Way Comes*, her first novel in the Merlin Secret's series, lay historian Carmel has a profound fascination for the life of King Arthur. She lives with her husband in Sydney, Australia.

For more information see her websites:
www.ourspiritualdna.com and **www.carmelniland.com**

FINDHORN PRESS

Life-Changing Books

Learn more about us and our books at
www.findhornpress.com

For information on the Findhorn Foundation:
www.findhorn.org